SRÌ-KRSNĀVATĀRA LÌLĀ

THE BIRTH OF KRISHNA

KASHMIRI TEXT WITH ENGLISH TRANSLATION.

SRÌ-KṚṢṆĀVATĀRA LÌLĀ

THE BIRTH OF KRISHNA

COMPOSED IN KASHMIRI

BY

DÌNA-NATHA.

TEXT

EDITED, TRANSLATED, AND TRANSCRIBED IN ROMAN CHARACTER

BY

SIR GEORGE A. GRIERSON,

K.C.I.E., PH.D., D.LITT., LL.D., F.B.A.

HONORARY FELLOW OF THE ASIATIC SOCIETY OF BENGAL

COSMO PUBLICATIONS

1999 INDIA

THE BIRTH OF KRISHNA

First Published 1999

ISBN 81-7020-893-9 (set)

Published by
MRS. RANI KAPOOR
for COSMO PUBLICATIONS Div. of
GENESIS PUBLISHING PVT. LTD.
24-B, Ansari Road,
Darya Ganj,
New Delhi-110002, INDIA

Typeset at
Cosmo Publications

Printed at
Mehra Offset Press

INTRODUCTION.

THE following edition of the *Śrī-Kṛṣṇâvatāra-līlā* is based on a single manuscript procured by me some thirty years ago in Kashmīr. The poem is a great favourite with the Hindūs of the Happy Valley, who often may be heard quoting stray verses from it, but the manuscript that then came into my possession is the only complete copy that I have seen. What is published therefore in no way pretends to be a critical edition of the text, but is offered merely as a good specimen of the comparatively little-known Kāshmīrī language, and, as such, I hope it will find acceptance.

It is well known that till, at the end of the last century, Īśvara Kaula laid down in his *Kaśmīra-śabdâmṛta* a fixed norm for spelling Kāshmīrī words, the spelling of Kāshmīrī manuscripts written in the Nāgarī or Śāradā character was totally without system. This was the case with my original MS. of the poem, and I therefore employed the late Mahāmahôpâdhyāya Mukunda-rāma Śāstrī to copy it out for me in Īśvara Kaula's system of spelling, and, at the same time to prepare in Sanskrit a *Chāyā*, or word for word commentary, of the whole. This *Chāyā*, besides enabling me to check the text, and to see that, at least, it contains no blunders and is a good specimen of correct Kāshmīrī, has been of great help to me in translating the poem into English. I have transliterated the text into the Roman character, and for this I have followed the system employed by me in my Kāshmīrī Dictionary, in my *Manual* of the same language, and in Sir Aurel Stein's and my edition of *Hātim's Tales*. In the translation, in quoting Sanskrit names, such as "Dēvakī" or "Kṛṣṇa," I have followed the system of the Royal Asiatic Society.

The work is a life of Kṛṣṇa, based, like the *Prēma-sāgara* of India, on the tenth *Skandha* of the *Bhāgavata Purāṇa*. It closely follows that work both in the general order of the events narrated and in details, and, indeed, some passages are almost translations. In order to aid reference to the older work, in giving the headings to each chapter of the English version, I have added references to the corresponding passages in the Purāṇa.

It is a curious fact that I have never been able to satisfy myself as to the identity of the author of this poem. The colophon of my MS.

gives his name as "Dīnanātha," and this is borne out by the author's reference to himself in verse 1172. It is, however, admittedly a pen-name, and his real name is not anywhere disclosed. At the time of purchasing the MS. I was told that he was one Paramânanda of Mārtaṇḍa, who was said to have died in 1822 A.D. at the age of 68 years. On the other hand, I have since been assured that Paramânanda was not the author of this work, and that he died some thirty years ago [or just when I was purchasing the MS.] at the age of about 80, his pen-name being Nanda-rāma. It is possible that there may have been two Paramânandas, for it is manifest that if both the above accounts are correct, they cannot refer to the same person. Another Kāshmīrī friend has lately written to me that the author was Prakāśa-rāma of Kurēgām, in Anantnāg Taḥṣīl of Kashmīr. He is said to have died about the year 1870, at the age approximately of 65, and to have been the same person as Divâkara-prakāśa Bhaṭṭa, the author of the *Śrī-rāmâvatāra-carita*. On the other hand, I have been assured that this very Divākara-prakāśa Bhaṭṭa was alive during the eight years of the reign of the Hindū king Sukhajīvana Siṁha, who came to the throne in 1786 A.D. According to this account, Divākara lived in the Gōjawōr (Sanskrit *Gulikāvāṭika*) quarter of Śrīnagar. In the face of all these mutually inconsistent traditions, it is impossible to make any definite statement regarding the author of the poem, save that his pen-name was Dīna-nātha. His identification must be left as a task to future enquirers. On the other hand, there can be no doubt as to the high esteem in which the poem is held, or as to its great popularity among the Hindūs of Kashmīr.

Save for a few irregularities, chiefly due to metrical exigencies, the language of the poem is the ordinary Kāshmīrī of the present day.

The author, for the sake of metre, not uncommonly makes use of an archaism often found in Kāshmīrī poetry. This is the substitution of an ancient *ē* for the final *i* of the modern language. This is here specially common in the case of *ni*, the oblique form of the termination *nᵘ*, but it is also found in the termination *zi* of the future imperative. Thus, for *-ni*, we have *wuchanē* (160), *kansāsŏranē* (468), *dapanē* (581), *shĕranē* (585), *tsalanē* (628), *karanē* (633), *vĕthanē* (659, 682), *tŏtanē* (681), *khĕnē* (1144), and many others. For the future imperative, we have such forms as *hövizē* (1121), for *höv'zi*, and *mäng'zē* (1122), for *mäng'zi*.

It will be remembered that in modern Kāshmīrī, as in Ṣiṇā and the

Ghalcah languages, the old present is ordinarily used in the sense of the future. Thus *asi* (< *hasati*), means 'he will laugh,' not 'he laughs.' In poetry, the force of the present is sometimes still retained. A number of such cases will be found in verses 968ff., where Kṛṣṇa's actions are described in a series of historical presents.

The past conditional is used as a past habitual in *kati bōzihēs* (141), how would he hear her? that is to say, he kept disobeying her. I mention this sporadic instance on account of the parallel use of the present participle in India proper, where (as, e.g., in Hindī) it is used both as a past conditional and a past habitual. The same tense is used as an optative in *mŏrdlī wāyüñ*^{ü} *bōzahös*, would that I might hear him playing the flute (260); *thaph karahas*, I would grasp him (596); *yimahö*, may I come! (704).

Hindūs generally form this tense by adding *hö* or *hē* to the old present, while Musalmāns prefer to add *ha*. Thus, a Hindū says *karahö*, while a Musalmān says *karaha*, for "(if) I had done." The author of the poem was of course a Hindū, and therefore generally used *hö* or *hē* but in one or two instances, for metrical reasons, we find *ha*. Thus, he has *wuchahas* (372), for *wuchahös*, *karahas* (596), for *karahös*, and *āsihas*, for *āsihēs*, in 777.

In Kāshmīrī, the conjunctive participle is used as in Hindī. Thus, *hĕth drāv*, having taken he issued forth, i.e. he took and issued forth, is equivalent to the Hindī *lē-kar niklā*. Our author is rather fond of inserting a pleonastic *ta*, meaning "thereupon," between the participle and the main verb. Thus (553) he has *hĕth ta drāv*, as if we were to say in Hindī *lē-kar tō niklā*. So we have (581) *phīrith ta dapanē log*^{u}, having returned he began to say, i.e. he began to say in reply; *wonukh yith ta* (838), having come they said, i.e. they came and said, and many others.

A more directly irregular verbal form is *wuch*^{i}*ta* (201), for *wuchta*, please to see, in which *i-mātrā* has apparently been inserted by contamination with the other persons of the tense (*wuch*^{i}*tav*, *wuch*^{i}*tan*). Another form not provided for by the grammars is *wötiha* (903), have they arrived? The regular interrogative suffix is *ā*, so that we should expect *wötyā* (*wöt*^{i} + *ā*), but here *ha* is employed instead of *ā*. Another is *bŏyi*, it will become (1156) instead of the more usual *bŏvi*. The grammars give a parallel form, *bŏyin*, for the 3rd singular of the Imperative of the same verb.

In ordinary Kāshmīrī, the conjunctive participle is not unoften used with the sense of a past participle passive. Thus, the Rāmāyaṇa, 1253, tells us about a house *karith burzuk*ᵘ, "made of birch bark." With some words the passive signification is the one in most general use. Thus, *barith*, literally "having filled," is commonly used to mean "filled" or "full." This participle, even when used in its ordinary active sense, occasionally takes the additional suffix *-an*, which is not mentioned in the grammars. Thus, in the village speech of *Hātim's Tales* (xi, 10), we have *rasad kärⁱthan*, for *rasad karith*, having made proportional division. In our present poem (223), we find a conjunctive participle, used in the sense of the past participle passive, given a similar suffix in *wanāh chuh phala-bärⁱthⁱⁱn* (for *phala-barith*), there is a grove filled with fruit.

In syntax a couple of minor points may be noticed. The post-position *pĕṭh*, on, usually governs the dative, as in *baṭhis-pĕṭh*, on the river-bank. In 702, we have, however, *boṭh*ᵘ*-pĕṭh*, in which it governs the accusative, (which has the same form as the nominative). This has evidently been so written for the sake of the metre.

The subject of an intransitive verb in a tense formed from one of the past participles is, of course, in the nominative case, while, if the verb is transitive, it is put into the case of the agent. Nevertheless, quite exceptionally, in 745 we have *Shĕmbärⁱ būzith drās*, Śambara, having heard, came forth to him. Here, although *drās* is an intransitive verb, the subject, *Shĕmbärⁱ*, is in the case of the agent,—an irregularity for which I am unable to account. We cannot explain *Shĕmbärⁱ* as merely an emphatic form of the nominative *Shĕmbor*ᵘ, for firstly, such a form would make no sense in the passage in which it occurs, and secondly, if an emphatic form, it would not be **Shĕmbärⁱ*, but *Shĕmboruy*. Moreover a Sanskrit commentary on the passage translates it "*Śambarēṇa śrutvā nirgataḥ.*" It looks as if we should take *būzith* as passive, and translate "having been heard by Śambara, he (Śambara) came forth to him," but such a construction would be very awkward, and, so far as my reading goes, without a parallel in Kāshmīrī.

A more important irregularity pervades the whole poem. A cursory examination will show that the first and third lines of each verse throughout end in the syllables *as ta*, and that in the great majority of cases [1] the *as* is preceded by a short syllable. The *ta* is generally a mere

[1] Not in every case. In some verses, especially in the earlier part of the poem, the *as* is preceded by a long vowel, as in *nāwas* (2).

pleonasm, so that it turns out that in two lines of nearly every verse of the poem this *ta* must be preceded by a word ending in an iambus (⏑ –), of which the last syllable must be *as*. The number of words in the language (such as *wanas*, *tsarĕtas*, and others), which comply with this requirement would be very few, were it not that the dative singular of every infinitive, or verbal noun in *un*, ends in *-anas*. Thus, from *karun*, we have a dative singular *karanas*; from *bōzun*, *bozanas*; and from *wanun*, *wananas*. This convenient fact gave the author a practically unlimited number of words of the required measure, for such a dative could be formed from any verb in the language. The meaning of the case, however, presented a difficulty, for these dative forms are infinitives of purpose. *Karanas* means "for doing"; *bōzanas*, "for hearing"; and *wananas*, "for saying." It is manifest that a poet could not employ such a dative twice in every verse of four lines. At the same time, with the verb *lagun*, this dative may be employed to form an inceptive compound, as in *log^u bōzanas* (11), he began to hear. The poet has taken advantage of this fact, but usually omits the verb *lagun*, leaving it to be understood; so that, under these circumstances, by *karanas*, we must understand *log^u karanas*, he began to do, and, by *wananas*, *log^u wananas*, he began to say. It will be found that nearly all these infinitive datives can be translated in this way,—*log^u*, or some other form of the verb *lagun*, being understood. But, in practice, "he began to hear" may be used as equivalent to "he heard"; "he began to do," as equivalent to "he did"; and "he began to say"; as equivalent to "he said." In this way,—as any tense of the verb *lagun*, past, present, or future, may be looked upon as omitted,—throughout the poem, these infinitive datives may be taken as standing for almost any finite tense of the verb, and translated as relating to any subject in any person and any number, whether acting in past, in present, or in future time.

As in the case of other Kāshmīrī poems, the metre of this work presents difficulties to the student familiar only with Persian or Indian prosody. As pointed out on pp. 144ff. of Dr. Barnett's and my edition of the *Lallā-vākyāni*,[1] Kāshmīrī metre is usually based on stress rather than on quantity. Apparently in ancient times Indian metres, such as the *dōhā*, *caupāī*, and so on, and, in later times, Persian metres, such as the *ramal* or *hazaj*, were employed for the composition of Kāshmīrī poetry. But, in Kāshmīrī mouths, these quickly became

---

[1] London, Royal Asiatic Society, 1920.

so distorted, that it is often impossible from their present form to say what was the original metrical foundation. At the present day all attention to quantity, or even to the number of syllables, is abandoned, and stress, and stress only, has become the basis of metre. The quantity of the syllables between each stressed syllable is a matter of small importance, so long as the metrical swing is not disturbed, and for a similar reason, within moderation, the number of syllables allowed between each stress is a variable quantity.

The present poem consists of verses of four lines each, the fourth line of each verse being the same throughout the entire work. As I have heard the verses read, they struck my ear as containing four stresses in each line. Thus, in verse 5, we have:—

rấzā Paríkshith ő's^u^ samayễs ta
tsákrawart sấriy prúthiviyĕ pĕṭh
pútur^u^ rṻd^u^-mot^u^ páta Arzŏnás ta
lấgas bŏh dásta dásta pampŏ́sh.

Possibly other Europeans may hear a different fall of the stress-accent, for it is never very strong, and varies from verse to verse. The most important stresses are those at the end of each line, which, in fact govern the whole verse. The first and third lines of each verse have throughout feminine endings, i.e. an accented syllable followed by an unaccented, as in *(sama)yễs ta*, *(Arzŏ)nás ta*, above. If we were using the language of quantitive prosody, we should say that each of these lines ended in a trochee (— ◡). On the other hand, the second and fourth lines of each verse have masculine endings. Each terminates in a single accented syllable, such as *pĕṭh* or *(pam)pŏ́sh*.

I propose to deal further with the question of Kāshmīrī metre in my forthcoming edition of the Rāmâvatāra-carita.

CONTENTS.

ERRATA.

Page 44, Verse 204, *read* " **sŏmb^{a}rith.**"

,, 48, Verse 221, *read* " **pöliki.**"

,, 55, Footnote, *read* " Probably."

,, 69, Verse 312, *insert* comma *after* " wives."

,, 74, Verses 338, 339, and 341, *read* " **Waikunṭhas,**" etc., *for* " **Vaikunṭhas,**" etc.

,, 81, *Substitute* the following translation of Verse 369 :—To them the command he gave his Death to destroy. " Why should my Death, that lieth in Kṛṣṇa's form, not die ? " Then all together did they hearten him.

,, 87, Verse 398, *read* " Kṛṣṇa."

,, 88, Verse 415, *read* " **sŏmb^{a}rith.**"

,, 91, Verse 423, *for* " flowers," *read* " flower-garlands."

,, 100, Verse 465, *read* " **dits^{ü}nas.**"

,, 104, Verse 491, *read* " **sọdras.**"

,, 105, Verse 493, *for* " Thereafter," *read* " Thence."

,, 112, Verse 527, *read* " **baktis ta.**"

,, 128, Verse 606, *read* " **nẹnd^{a}r^{ü}y.**"

,, 132, Verse 623, *read* " **push^{ü}r^{ü}n.**"

,, 140, Verse 660, *read* " **tat-kshĕna.**"

,, 149, Verse 700, *insert* " hurriedly " *after* " depart."

,, 164, Verse 769, *read* " **sŏmb^{a}rith.**"

,, 180, Verse 842, *read* " **Waikunṭhas.**"

,, 186, Verse 870, *read* " **tat-kshĕna.**"

,, 191, Verse 895, *insert* " Therefore " *before* " Sāmba."

अथ श्रीकृष्णावतारलीला प्रारभ्यते ॥

1–8

ATHA ŚRĪ-KṚṢṆÂVATĀRA-LĪLĀ.

Wasudēwa-rāzanis Krushna-zīwas ta
  lāgas bŏh dasta dasta pampōsh.

yus lagi Krushna-jyuwanis nāwas ta
  tas kari Krushna-jyuv sarŏ wŏpakār.
yiti yĕsh nith ta wāti Vishnu-bawanas ta. lāgas etc. 2.

pŏr^{i} pŏr^{i} Krushna-jyuwanis nāwas ta
  pŏr^{i} pŏr^{i} tasandis autāras
pŏr^{i} pŏr^{i} tasandis shŏba tsarĕtas ta. lāgas etc. 3.

tana mana lagith Vishnu-dyānas ta
  bōz Krushna-autāruk^{u} kāran
Vishnu-bawana kĕtha āv Krushn zanmas ta. lāgas etc.
4.

rāzā Parīkshith ôs^{u} samayĕs ta
  tsakrawart sāriy pruthivīyĕ pĕṭh
putur^{u} rūd^{u}-mot^{u} pata Arzŏnas ta. lāgas etc. 5.

yot^{u}-tāñ suh rāza ôs^{u} tĕli zanmas ta
  sāriy zagi ôs^{u} sārikuy sŏkh
tĕli tsāv kali-yŏg ta kĕh na bal tas ta. lāgas etc. 6.

darm ta karm ôs^{u} tsor^{u} sapananas ta
  kali-yŏg ôs^{u} tshĕpi rūzith-kĕth
pratāph rāza-sond^{u} ôs^{u} tsaranas ta. lāgas etc. 7.

anta-kāl yĕli wôt^{u} tas rāzas ta
  Bhāgawata-pŏrāna bōzani log^{u}
Shukadēv^{i} anugraha pārān kor^{u}nas ta. lāgas etc. 8.

---

[1] The words 'To him posy and posy,' etc., are repeated at the end of every verse. Henceforth I shall not translate them unless they are necessary to complete the sense, as, for instance, in verse 3.

[2] As a rule, verses 2 and 3 are repeated at the end of each chapter.

THE LAY OF THE INCARNATE KṚṢṆA.

I. THE PROMISE OF NĀRĀYAṆA. (Bhāgavata Purāṇa, X, i.)

1. To King Vasudēva and to Kṛṣṇa posy on posy do I offer lotuses.

2. He who beareth in his heart the name of Kṛṣṇa, to him will Kṛṣṇa every favour render. In this world glory will he win, and thereafter the abode of Viṣṇu will he reach. To him posy and posy do I offer lotuses.[1]

3. Ever dedicating myself to Kṛṣṇa's name, ever dedicating myself to his incarnation, ever dedicating myself to his auspicious deeds, to him posy on posy do I offer lotuses.[2]

4. Body and heart devote thou to meditation on Viṣṇu ; hear thou the cause of Viṣṇu's incarnation, and how from the abode of Viṣṇu Kṛṣṇa came to birth.

5. Once on a time King Parīkṣit was Emperor over all the world. Grandson was he of Arjuna.[3]

6. All his life, so long as he was King, in the entire world happiness was of all the lot, for though the Kali Yuga had then made its entrance, no power had it yet.

7. Plenteous were virtue and holy acts, and so the Kali Yuga remained concealed, while the glory of the King was ever on the increase.

8. When to that King there came the time of his end, he began to hear the Bhāgavata Purāṇa, which Śukadēva, in his graciousness recited to him.

---

[3] He was son of Abhimanyu, the son of Arjuna, the famous hero of the Mahābhārata. He succeeded to the throne of Hastināpura after Yudhiṣṭhira. The Kali Yuga, or Iron age, is said to have begun with his reign, in B.C. 3102. See the following verses. It is an age full of evil and tyranny.

Parīkshit^{i} prashn kor^{u} Shukadēwas ta
'wantam zi Krushna-jyuv kĕtha-pöṭh^{i} bǫw^{u}
ka'wa-putshy āyāv autāras ta
lāgas bŏh dasta dasta pampōsh. 9

Shukadēwan dop^{u} tas rāzas ta
'bāgĕn cyānĕn jai-jai-kār
yĕtshi patshi sastis Vishnu-baktis ta'. lāgas etc. 10.

wanun hyot^{u}nas, log^{u} bōzanas ta
tsĕth bŏdd lögith Vishnu-dyānas.
jai-kār Shukadēwanis wananas ta. lāgas etc. 11.

dwāpar-yŏg yĕli āv antas ta
ādĕ kali-yŏguk^{u} prakār tsāv.
kŏkarm ta pāph lag^{i} tsar^{i} sapananas ta. lāgas etc. 12.

rākhĕs bādēy bū-manḍalas ta
būtarāth bāri sũty ṭanga yini lüj^{u}
lögith kāma-dīn^{u} gayĕ Brahmas ta, lāgas etc. 13.

Brahmā-jyuv gav Nārāyĕnas ta
dēwatā sör^{i} hĕth khīra-sāgar
kāma-dīn^{u} sũty hĕth lag^{i} tŏtanas ta. lāgas etc. 14.

paurushĕ-sūkta sũty tŏth kür^{u}has ta
vinath wananas dôr^{u}nakh kan
vinath bōzanuk^{u} sŏbāv chuh tas ta. lāgas etc. 15.

Nārān tōṭhyōkh tath wananas ta
ākāshĕ-wöniyĕ dyut^{u}nakh war,
'bŏh zi yima pānay autāras ta. lāgas etc. 16.

'Wasudēwa rāzani yima zanmas ta
Māyā myöñ^{u} wāti Nandā-gōryun^{u},
dēwatā yiyin yim bū-manḍalas ta'. lāgas etc. 17.

Brahman ti āgyā dits^{u} zĕnas ta
dēwatā ta dēwa-māy āyĕ zanmas
kĕh Yādav kĕh gūr^{i} bāwas ta. lāgas etc. 18.

---

1 This is the name of the age immediately preceding the Kali Yuga.

2 The name of the 90th hymn of the 10th Maṇḍala of the Ṛg Vēda. It is

9. And Parîkṣit asked of Śukadēva, 'Tell me, prithee, how Kṛṣṇa into being came, and wherefore took he incarnation.'

10. Then to that King did Śukadēva make reply, 'Victory, Victory be to all thy fortunes,—of thee, devoted to Kṛṣṇa, who art rich in holy longing and in faith.'

11. So he began to tell, and he to hear, devoting heart and thought to meditation upon Kṛṣṇa. Victory be to the tale as told by Śukadēva.

12. When the Dvāpara[1] Yuga came to its end, and the manner of the incipient Kali Yuga took its entrance, wickedness and sin began to multiply.

13. Rākṣasas o'erran the circle of the world, and by their weight began the earth to be distressed. So took she the form of a milch-cow, and to Brahmā did she go.

14. To the Milky Sea, to Nārāyaṇa, did Brahmā go, with himself taking all the other gods and the milch-cow, and to Him he uttered praise.

15. With the *Puruṣa-sûkta*[2] did he praise Him. To his supplication did He lend His ear, for to hear such supplications is His wont.

16. Pleased was Nārāyaṇa at their words, and with a voice from the ether did he answer them. 'I, Myself, incarnate will become.

17. 'In the house of Vasudēva the King will I take birth, and Māyā, My illusive form, to the home of the Cowherd Nanda shall proceed. Likewise shall all these gods come to the earth.'

18. Brahmā gave forth the order to be born, and forthwith the gods and Māyā came to birth, some as Yādavas,[3] and as cowherds some.

---

regarded as peculiarly sacred.

[3] The Yādavas were the tribe to which Kṛṣṇa belonged.

kẽh gōv$^{\ddot{u}}$ gōpiyĕ āyĕ zanmas ta
    kẽh kul^{i} sapȧn^{i} yith kẽh wā̃dar
Krushna-jyuv zi ranzi-nā autāras ta
    lāgas bŏh dasta dasta pampōsh. 19.

būtarāth ti tōshān gayĕ pānas ta
    Krushna-autāras prārani lüj$^{\ddot{u}}$.
bāgĕwān ös^{i} yim tĕli zanmas ta. lāgas etc. 20.

yus lagi Krushna-jyuwanis nāwas ta
    tas kari Krushna-jyuv sarŏ wŏpakār
yiti yĕsh nith ta wāti Vishnu-bawanas ta. lāgas etc. 21.

II

Mathurāyĕ rājy ôs^{u} Wugrasēnas ta
    pŏtra-marun ôsus Kansāsŏr
Dēwakī ös$^{\ddot{u}}$s bāw^{a}za tas ta
    lāgas bŏh dasta dasta pampōsh. 22.

Wasudēwa rāza ôs^{u} tȧth^{i} nagaras ta
    Wugrasēn kĕkur^{u} Wasudēwun^{u}
Dēwakī nētri dits$^{\ddot{u}}$n rāzas ta. lāgas etc. 23.

Wasudēv rāza yĕli āv nētras ta
    rāza ta pradān sū̃ty hĕth-kĕth
pruthivī tsasith āyĕ tath wŏtsawas ta. lāgas etc. 24.

Brahmādĕkh āy maza wuchanas ta
    Wasudēv rāza yĕli lagnas khot^{u}
grünz$^{\ddot{u}}$-rost^{u} dana log^{u} dini dānas ta. lāgas etc. 25.

suh ti ôs^{u} Kashĕpa-ryush^{u} autāras ta
    Dēwakī ti Aditi ös$^{\ddot{u}}$ zanmas
mong^{u}-mot^{u} Bagawān pŏtra-bāwas ta. lāgas etc. 26.

dŏyi phiri ā-mȧt^{i} ös^{i} zanmas ta
    Wāman ta Rāma-jyuv pŏtra-băwas
trĕyimi Krushna-rūpa ākh zanmas ta. lāgas etc. 27.

---

1 Literally 'son-death,' equivalent to the Sanskrit *putra-hatakaḥ*.

2 She was daughter of Dēvaka, Ugrasēna's brother. She was therefore Kaṁsa's first cousin; but as terms of relationship are in such cases loosely applied, she is

19. Some came to birth as cows, and some as herd-maidens. Some became trees, and others took the form of monkeys; all that Kṛṣṇa might in his incarnation find delights.

20. Joyful to her home did the earth return, and there awaited she the time of Kṛṣṇa's incarnation. Blessed were they whose birth in those days happed.

21. He who beareth in his heart the name of Kṛṣṇa, to him will Kṛṣṇa every favour render. In this world glory will he win, and thereafter the abode of Viṣṇu will he reach.

II. THE CIRCUMSTANCES ATTENDING THE BIRTH OF KṚṢṆA. (Bhāgavata Purāṇa, X, i, 27; ii, iii.)

22. The kingdom of Mathurā was Ugrasēna's, and his vile[1] son was Kaṁsa the Asura, while Dēvakī was his brother's daughter.[2]

23. Of that land was Vasudēva the King, and Ugrasēna was his feudatory. It was to that King that Ugrasēna gave Dēvakī in wedlock.

24. When Vasudēva, accompanied by Kings and Chieftains, to the wedding came, the earth herself, full of joy, the festival attended.

25. Brahmā and other gods came down to see the happy spectacle, as King Vasudēva ascended to the marriage rite. Wealth beyond count did he give out in gifts.

26. He himself was the Saint Kaśyapa incarnate, and in Dēvakī did Aditi take birth, and to become their son did Bhagavān ask their leave.

27. Twice before had they taken birth, that the Dwarf and Rāma-candra[3] might be their sons. Now for the third time (were they incarnate) that Kṛṣṇa might be born of them.

---

commonly (*e.g.*, in verse 33) called his sister.

[3] The Dwarf and Rāma-candra were two famous previous incarnations of Viṣṇu, here called Bhagavān.

ĝara kun Wasudēv drāv prātas ta
Dēwakī mahārĕñ sūty hĕth-kĕth
sŏn mŏkta raṭ^{a}n kūt^{u} dəj dyut^{u}has ta
lāĝas bŏh dasta dasta pampōsh. 28.

sāsa-bȧd^{i} hȧst^{i} ĝur^{i} ratha dit^{i}has ta
sāsa-baza tsŏnza gah^{a}na pūrith-kĕth
Kansāsŏr drāv jilbi bēmas ta. lāĝas etc. 29.

ākāshĕ-wŏnī gayĕ Kansas ta
'yihonduy santān kāl cyôn^{u} chuy'
ūṭhimi-sandi tshĕn chuy āyĕs ta'. lāĝas etc. 30.

hīth ôs^{u} Kansāsŏr gālanas ta
tapa-boḍ^{u} ôs^{u} ta pōshĕhēs kus
aparād khŏr^{i} khŏr^{i} bal wôl^{u}has ta. lāĝas etc. 31.

wŏnī yĕli gayĕ tas asŏras ta
baḍi sŏkha manza pyōs boḍuy dŏkh
khōr ĝŏs rūzith pĕv pāyĕs ta. lāĝas etc. 32.

küḍ^{ü}n tarwār bĕñĕ māranas ta
raṭith kīshĕv bŏn wŏj^{ü}n
Wasudēv rāza log^{u} zāra-pāras ta. lāĝas etc. 33.

'balavīra na zi pazi bĕñĕ māranas ta
kyāh laĝi karun^{u} dayĕ-lŏnis
mata patshta asandis santānas ta'. lāĝas etc. 34.

bēma-sandi zāra-pāra ār āv tas ta
santān māranas āyĕs bŏd.
kĕh bŏd wāti na dayĕ tsarĕtas ta. lāĝas etc. 35.

tsŏnith ta bĕñĕ bēma bŏnd^{i}wānas ta
dŏshĕwȧn^{i} paikȧr^{i} wāra kȧr^{i}nakh
khabari rŏch^{i} ŏs^{i} prath samayĕs ta. lāĝas etc. 36.

---

1 *Jil^{a}b* is explained in the Comm. by the Sanskrit word *kaśya,* or 'flank.' Here it seems to mean 'bridle.' Cf. the Persian *jalav.* According to the Bhāg. Pu., Kaṁsa was actually driving the bridal chariot when he heard the voice.

28. At dawn did Vasudēva to his home set forth, with Dēvakī his bride. How great was the dowry of gold and pearls, and of precious stones given to him by them!

29. Thousands of elephants, of horse, and of chariots did they give him; thousands of slave-girls in jewelled array apparelled. Kaṁsa went forth to hold the horse's bridle.[1]

30. Then came there to Kaṁsa a voice from the sky, 'Of these two the son shall be thy death. Through the eighth child will be cut off thy life.'

31. This voice was but the agent[2] for his destruction, for great austerities had he performed, and who could prevail against him. Sin did he pile on sin, and by them was his might laid low.

32. When to the Asura came this voice, out of great happiness still greater grief befell him. Halting became his feet, and (to meditating) on some precaution did he fall.

33. To slay his sister his sword he drew, by her hair grasped he her and felled her from the chariot, as the while Vasudēva the King began him to implore.

34. 'O Mighty Hero, it becometh not to slay thy sister. What can be done to (ward off) Fate. Believe not thou that to her offspring will be born.'

35. At the entreaty of his sister's husband did he relent, and of slaying the children made he the resolve. But no wisdom is there that can reach the deeds of Fate.

36. Into a prison cast he his sister and her spouse, and both securely did he bind with gyves, and all the time, tidings to bring him, over them placed he guards.

---

[2] I.e., the first step towards his destruction. It started him on the road, and made him determine to kill Dēvakī's children. The eighth child was Kṛṣṇa, and, in attempting to kill him, Kaṁsa was destroyed.

gŏḍañuk^{u} shur^{u} zāv Wasudēwas ta
pānay Kansas nishĕ hĕth āv
mĕ zi pazi wönī püz$^{\ddot{u}}$ karanas ta
lāgas bŏh dasta dasta pampōsh. 37.

trāvyān Nārad^{i} yith won^{u}nas ta
'wulṭa zi yihuy mā āsi cyôn^{u} kāl,'
ṭ^{a}kān zi yuth^{u} bŏḍi aparādas ta. lāgas etc. 38.

asŏra-bŏz$^{\ddot{u}}$ sŏy tas bŏd āyĕs ta
Nāradun^{u} ʦhaḷ^{a}run^{u} zānihē kyāh
athi hĕth asŏran pāna môr^{u}nas ta. lāgas etc. 39.

Wugrasēn lajyās zāra-pāras ta
ʦakhi gōs lodun su-ti bönd^{i}wān
dop^{u}nas, 'söriy shur^{i} māras' ta. lāgas etc. 40.

shĕn garban tāñ yus zāv tas ta
suy suy santān mārani log^{u}
satimi Shēshĕnāg āv garbas ta. lāgas etc. 41.

Bagawön^{i} māyā tot^{u} sūz$^{\ddot{u}}$nas ta
Dēwakīyĕ garba nishĕ kaḍith nyūn
Rōhinīyĕ Haladar āv garbas ta. lāgas etc. 42.

su-ti ôs^{u} Shēshĕnāg autāras ta
nakha-ḍakha bôyāh goʦh^{u} Krushnas
Dēwakīyĕ ʦōri-māsi ôs^{u} garbas ta. lāgas etc. 43.

Rōhinī Nandani ös$^{\ddot{u}}$ chapanas ta
Wasudēwa rāzüñ^{u} āshĕñ pröñ$^{\ddot{u}}$,
Nanda-gūr^{u} mẹth^{a}r ôs^{u} Wasudēwas ta. lāgas etc. 44.

Dēwakī-mājĕ rūd^{u} na kēh garbas ta
Rōhiniyĕ garbuk^{u} prạkh^{a}cĕr ʦāv.
dayĕ-güʦ$^{\ddot{u}}$ pör^{i} lảg^{i}zi Bagawānas ta. lāgas etc. 45.

Rōhiniyĕ samay wôt^{u} yĕli prasanas ta
Haladar Rāma-jyuv zanmas āv
Shēshĕnāg pāna ôs^{u} autāras ta. lāgas etc. 46.

---

[1] Nārada, the minstrel of the gods, was often employed to set people at variance or to lead them into deadly sin.

[2] Śēṣanāga was a serpent with a thousand heads. He formed the couch of Viṣṇu, and is also said to bear the whole world on his head. He became incarnate

37. To Vasudēva was the first son born, and he himself to Kaṁsa carried it. Quoth he, 'It is becoming that I make my promise true.'

38. Nārada came and (to Kaṁsa) gave forth these words, 'Haply, to the oracle contrariwise, this child may be thy death.' This said he that Kaṁsa might be plunged more quickly into sin.[1]

39. To his Asura's mind did this thought commend itself, for how could he ken the guile of Nārada. So with his own hand the Asura killed the babe.

40. To him did Ugrasēna, his father, make entreaty, but with him too did he become wroth, and him too into prison cast, and thus said he to him, 'His children all and every will I kill.'

41. Six times was progeny to Vasudēva born, and each infant did Kaṁsa forthwith slay. Then at the seventh time did Śēṣanāga[2] enter Dēvakī's womb.

42. Bhagavān then sent forth His illusive power, and from Dēvakī's womb was Haladhara taken and lodged in Rōhiṇī's.

43. Verily was he thus incarnate Śēṣanāga, and as a brother and a helper of Kṛṣṇa was he needed. Four months had he lain in the womb of Dēvakī.

44. In Nanda's house had Rōhiṇī sought refuge; an earlier wife was she of Vasudēva; and Nanda, the Cowherd, was of him the friend.

45. In Dēvakī's womb no progeny remained, but in Rōhiṇī there became manifest the signs of pregnancy. Offer thou thyself as a sacrifice to Bhagavān before the ways of Fate!

46. When Rōhiṇī's full time was reached that she should bring forth a child, Haladhara (Bala-) Rāma came to birth, and of Śēṣanāga himself was he an incarnation.

---

as Kṛṣṇa's elder brother, Bala-rāma, also called Hala-dhara, or 'the plough-bearer.' As stated in the following verses he was first conceived by Dēvakī, but, during conception, was transferred to Rōhiṇī's womb. Vasudēva had several other wives besides Dēvakī, and of these Rōhiṇī was one.

kath ġayĕ kĕtha zāv māli-rost^{u} tas ta
Nārad mŏnīshŏr wanani ākh
'dayĕ-sünz^{ü} āġyā chĕh yiy bananas' ta
lāgas bŏh dasta dasta pampōsh. 47.

Māyā ti Yĕshōdāyĕ āyĕ ġarbas ta
Yĕshōdā triy ös^{ü} Nanda-gōrĕñ^{ü}
hīth ôs^{u} Nanda-gūr^{u} ti mŏkth karanas ta. lāgas etc.
48.

Baġawān ti tsāv pāna Wasudēwas ta
manas övish karith-kĕth
sūrĕ-sond^{u} cĕmakun^{u} tsāv rāzas ta. lāgas etc. 49.

Dēwakī-mājĕ āv yĕli ġarbas ta
Vishnu-rūp^{i} Krushna-jyuv pāna Baġawān.
sŏr^{i}tav zi kyāh wôt^{u} tas rāzas ta. lāgas etc. 50.

bönd^{i}wān rūpa sūty log^{u} ġŏhanas ta
Kansāsŏras vĕlarun^{u} tsāv
zônun zi 'kāl Krushn ām zanmas' ta. lāgas etc. 51.

biyĕ bŏd karyēyĕn bĕñĕ māranas ta
biyĕ ās mani 'kĕtha mör^{i}zĕn triy
santān zĕyĕs ta suy māranas' ta. lāgas etc. 52.

dēwatā wötith bönd^{i}wānas ta
tŏtā ta pūzā lag^{i} karanē
Dēwakī-mājĕ ta Wasudēwas ta. lāgas etc. 53.

'zaġi-hond^{u} ġarb āv tŏhĕ ġarbas ta
bāġĕn tuhandĕn jai-jai-kār
laġa pör^{i} zaġi-pālakas Krushnas' ta. lāgas etc. 54.

Krushna-jyuv yĕli āv shŏba-zanmas ta
ġwāh pĕv darthiyĕ s^{ü}-ĕn-hond^{u}
sŏth ös^{ü} rākhĕsan yitha maranas ta. lāgas etc. 55.

---

1 Māyā, the principle of illusion, became Yaśōdā's child, while Kṛṣṇa was simultaneously conceived by Dēvakī. As we shall see, the two children were interchanged immediately after birth, so that Kaṁsa killed Māyā under the erroneous impression that he was killing Dēvakī's eighth child. Yaśōdā herself was unaware at the time of the substitution, and at first considered Kṛṣṇa to be her own son.

47. A talk there was (and people doubted) how, without a father, a son could be born to her. But Nārada, that holiest of saints, came there to tell. Quoth he, 'Verily hath this come to pass by God's command.'

48. Then, into Yaśōdā's[1] womb did Māyā come. Now Yaśōdā of the Cowherd Nanda was the spouse, and this coming of Māyā was intended to bring salvation unto him.

49. And into Vasudēva's soul, by way of inspiration, entered Bhagavān Himself. The King did he enter shining like the sun.

50. And when through him Bhagavān came into the womb of Dēvakī, He Himself was Kṛṣṇa, a very form of Viṣṇu.[2] Bear ye in mind what (blessed lot) there came unto that king.

51. With his beauty was the prison filled with splendour; and trembling entered Kaṁsa's limbs, for this he knew, 'Kṛṣṇa, my Death, hath come to take his birth.'

52. Again did he determine to kill his sister, and again did he debate how a woman he could kill;[3] and thought he, 'The child that will be born, him will I kill.'

53. To the prison came the gods, and praise and worship did they begin to offer to Mother Dēvakī and to Vasudēva.

54. (And their song was this). 'The womb of the universe into your womb hath entered. Blessed be ye, and glory to your lot. To Kṛṣṇa, the protector of the universe, do we make ourselves an offering.'

55. When to his illustrious birth came he, a glory like that of suns upon the world did shine, and, like dead men, into a deep sleep fell the Rākṣasas.

---

2 The meaning is that, while other incarnations of Viṣṇu were only partial, on this occasion the entire Viṣṇu became incarnate as Kṛṣṇa.

3 According to the *Nārada-pañcarātra*, x, 76, the *mahāpāpīs*, or greatest sinners of all, are those who kill Brāhmaṇas, Bhikṣus, Yatīs, Brahmacārīs, women, or Vaiṣṇavas.

dēwatā sör^{i} låg^{i} pōshĕ-warshĕnas ta
manŏshy wŏtsav låg^{i} karanē
mīģ shĕbdas āy zan na zuv zanas ta
lāgas bŏh dasta dasta pampōsh. 56

Bādrapada ashṭamiyĕ aḍa-rātas ta
ģaṭa-pachĕ ṭsandrama log^{u} khasanē
Bŏd-wāri rōhiniyĕ vrushĕ-lạgnas ta. lāgas etc. 57

Krushna-jyuv yĕli āv autāras ta
tithay dyut^{u}nakh shŏba-darshun
Ṭsaturbŏz Nārān pĕṭh Garuḍas ta. lāgas etc. 58

mŏkạṭa shūbān shēri Vishnas ta
shĕnkh ṭsakr ģadā ta pampōsh hĕth
ramavüñ^{u} Lạkh^{i}mī wāma-bāgas ta. lāgas etc. 59

mŏkta-māla kaustŏb nöl^{i} kanṭhas ta
sŏna-kạr^{i} ta kana-wöl^{i} dörith-kĕth.
zuv pān wandahö tath darshĕnas ta. lāgas etc. 60

Dēwakī ta Wasudēv ṭsāv vĕṭhanas ta
bāģĕv sūty lob^{u} yuth^{u} darshun
yōgiyĕn ti dŏrlab chuh sŏranas ta. lāgas etc. 61

mŏd^{a}ri wöniyĕ tŏth kür^{u}has ta
kshĕna kshĕṇa pādan ḍĕka g^{o}h^{u}nas.
namaskār tihandis tath bāģĕs ta. lāgas etc. 62

Bagawān tọtukh ākh bōlanas ta
dop^{u}nakh zi ‘ trayĕ phiri tŏhĕ nishĕ zās
az pĕṭha biyĕ chum na yun^{u} zanmas ’ ta. lāgas etc. 63

Kansani bayĕ pĕy tim sŏranas ta
‘ kawa zön^{i} zi ƀōzi mā Kansāsŏr
mārawun^{u} yiyi mā asĕ māranas ’ ta. lāgas etc. 64

---

1 I.e., Everyone was wrapped in unconsciousness.

2 Garuḍa was a wondrous bird, chief of the feathered race, on which Viṣṇu rode.

3 These always accompanied Viṣṇu. Each has a mystic meaning. The conch indicates *sāttvika ahaṁkāra*, or pure self-consciousness; the discus, *manas*, or the

56. The gods poured forth a rain of flowers, and mankind to hold high festival began. The clouds gave forth a sound as of thunder, yet there was no life of men.[1]

57. Born was he on the eighth lunar day of the dark half of the month Bhādrapada (August-September), at the rising of the moon, on a Wednesday, the asterism of Rōhiṇī, and in the sign of Taurus.

58. When Kṛṣṇa thus became incarnate, in a glorious manifestation did he there and then show himself (to his parents), as the four-armed Nārāyaṇa, riding upon Garuḍa.[2]

59. Glorious, with the diadem of Viṣṇu on his head, holding the conch, the discus, the club, and the lotus, and on his left the lovely Lakṣmī.[3]

60. Necklaces of pearls and the Kaustubha jewel graced his neck, and bracelets of gold and earrings did he wear. Body and soul do I dedicate to that (wondrous) vision.

61. Then verily did Dēvakī and Vasudēva rejoice, for blessed indeed were they to gain so wondrous a vision,—a vision that even to the consciousness of Yōgīs is hard to gain.

62. With sweet voice did they extol him, moment after moment rubbing their foreheads on his feet. Reverence be to their predestined lot!

63. Bhagavān did they extol, and He began to speak to them. To them he said, 'Three times have I been born of ye. After to-day shall I not take birth again.'

64. Then remembered they, and into fear of Kaṁsa did they fall. 'How know we that perchance Kaṁsa may hear (of this). Perchance that murderer will come and murder us.'

---

thinking faculty; the club, *mahat*, or the intellect; the necklace, the elements, and so on. It was from the lotus that Brahmā, the creator, was born. Lakṣmī was Viṣṇu's energic force, typified as his spouse. The Kaustubha typifies the souls of the universe.

Bagawön^{i} dam dyut^{u} mājĕ babas ta
dop^{u}nakh zi 'tsintā bariv ma kĕ̃h
sŏth chĕ̃wa rāchĕ̃n yitha maranas' ta
lāgas bŏh dasta dasta pampōsh. 65.

dop^{u}nakh zi 'gatshun^{u} chum Gōkulas ta
Nanda-gūris chĕ̃h kūr^{ü} zāmüts^{ü}
Yĕshōdayĕ sŏr chuna wuñĕ pānas ta. lāgas etc. 66.

'tim ti ös^{i} låg^{i}-måt^{i} path tapas ta
mĕ nishĕ mongukh gindun^{u} myôn^{u}
timan-hond^{u} ti war pazi pālanas ta. lāgas etc. 67.

'rākhĕ̃s tåt^{i} yin tsår^{i} gālanas ta
yāñ wāti Kansāsŏras ti kāl
wötith pĕmas ta prān kaḍas ta. lāgas etc. 68.

'wŏthith kaḍith nim sŭ̃ty pānas ta
tör^{i} bar mutsarana pānay yin
rōzi na sŏr kuni kaīsi rākhĕ̃sas ta. lāgas etc. 69.

'Jamunāyĕ pād myön^{i} lög^{i}zi zalas ta
yĕli khasi hyor^{u} hyor^{u} pād namanas
wath diyi pānay tarith gatshahas ta. lāgas etc. 70.

'syod^{u} åts^{i}zi Nanda-gōrinis dwāras ta
tati ti āsi na kaīsi kĕ̃h sŏr
mĕ thåv^{i}zi tati ta kūr^{ü} ån^{i}zĕs ta. lāgas etc. 71.

'sa kūr^{ü} chĕ̃h Māyā tati zanmas ta
mĕ chum Nanda-gūr^{u} ti mŏk^{a}th karanī
Kansas ti yihuy chum hīth gālanas' ta. lāgas etc. 72.

dapith biyĕ gav bāla-bāwas ta
Wasudēwa rāzan tulith nyūn
tör^{i} bar mutsarana āy dwāras ta. lāgas etc. 73.

wati āv nyuk^{u} nyuk^{u} rūd pĕnas ta
Shēshĕnāg pĕṭha rūd^{u} karith tshāy
Jamunā hyor^{u} khüts^{ü} pādi namanas ta. lāgas etc. 74.

Wasudēv^{i} Krushna-pād lög^{i} zalas ta
wath lüj^{u} ta Jamunāyĕ tarith gav
hĕri bŏna zal rūd^{u} thāmi pānas ta. lāgas etc. 75.

65. Then his mother and his father did Bhagavān console, and to them He said, 'Have ye no care for this; a sleep like death hath come upon the guards.'

66. And further said He, 'To Gōkula must I go. There to Nanda the cowherd a daughter hath been born, and till now hath Yaśōdā no consciousness (of her birth).

67. 'Once on a day were they in austerities engaged, and from me did they ask the boon of my sporting (in their house). Now must I keep for them the promise of my boon.

68. 'Many will be the Rākṣasas that there to destruction will come, until the time of Kaṁsa's death be due. When that be due, upon him will I fall and his life-breath drag out.

69. 'Arise, and in thy company take me forth. The bolts and doors of themselves will open before thee, nor of aught will any Rākṣasa be ware.

70. 'When to the river Yamunā thou dost come, as its waters rise and rise to do homage to my feet, then let my feet touch them and they will make way for thee, and safely shalt thou pass over.

71. 'Enter thou straight at Nanda's door, nor aught will anyone be ware of it. There must thou leave me and take away the girl.

72. 'That girl is Māyā, my Illusive Power, who there hath taken birth. To Nanda the cowherd must I give eternal salvation. And in this my sole object is but Kaṁsa to destroy.'

73. He said these words, and again the form of a babe He took, and King Vasudēva took Him in his arms, and, lo, the bolts and doors of the gateway open flew.

74. On the way there fell a gentle rain, and (beneath his hoods) did Śēṣanāga, the Serpent of Eternity, shelter them. Up mounted the Yamunā to do homage to his feet.

75. Vasudēva touched the water with Kṛṣṇa's foot, and a way was opened to him, and safely across the Yamunā he passed. Above and below, of themselves, did the flowing waters halt.

Wasudēv rāza ti wôt^{u} Gōkulas ta
tsāv Nanda-gōryun^{u} Krishna-jyuv hĕth
kōrĕ-han hĕth drāv ta āv pānas ta
lāgas bŏh dasta dasta pampōsh. 76.

yithay gav tithay wôt^{u} biyĕ dwāras ta
tōr^{i} bar biyĕ āy dina pānay
sŏth ös^{ü} asŏran ti ḍīḍ^{i}wānas ta. lāgas etc. 77.

Vishnu-māyi rūdukh na kĕh ti tsĕtas ta
zan kūr^{ü} pānas^{ü}y nishĕ zāyĕkh
Dayĕ-gath yiyi na zi kaīsi zānanas ta. lāgas etc. 78.

Māyā-kūr^{ü} yĕli wöts^{ü} dwāras ta
prabāth phŏl^{u} ta tshüṭ^{ü}n bākh
sŏth tsüj^{ü} rāchĕn ta pĕy sŏras ta. lāgas etc. 79.

wŏthith ta lārān gay Kansas ta
būzun ta vĕlarun^{u} tatiy tsās
Kālañĕ shĕnkāyi tsāv naṭanas ta. lāgas etc. 80.

thörith ta nishĕ āv bĕñĕ bēmas ta
Dēwakī ör^{a}tsar lüj^{ü} karanē
'bāyĕ kōrĕ-han na zi pazi māranas' ta. lāgas etc. 81.

khåṭ^{i} khåṭ^{i} thawani lüj^{ü} nishĕ Kansas ta
rākhĕsas na zi kuni man kumalyōs
möj^{ü} kōrĕ-handi prīma tsāyĕ wadanas ta. lāgas etc.
82.

baḍi vĕha niyĕnas kūr^{ü} atha tas ta
khŏrav raṭith ta sŭty hĕth drāv
dits^{ü}n dörith pĕṭh brāndas ta. lāgas etc. 83.

atha pĕṭha kūr^{ü} gayĕ ākāshĕs ta
dīvī-darshun^{u} dörith rūz^{ü}
ashṭa-bŏz āyŏd athi sör^{i} tas ta. lāgas etc. 84.

shūbawun^{u} māla-trŏṭ^{u} nöl^{i} galas ta
söriy ābaran pūrith-kĕth
dēwatā sör^{i} āy tath darshĕnas ta. lāgas etc. 85.

76. In Gōkula did King Vasudēva arrive, and with Kṛṣṇa in his arms the homestead of Nanda the cowherd did he enter. Then took he up the girl-babe and home returned.

77. As he had departed, so through the gateway of his prison did he return, and, lo, the bolts and doors again did shut themselves. Deep was the sleep of the Asuras and of him who kept the gate.

78. For by Viṣṇu's Illusive Power naught to their consciousness came. It seemed to them as though a daughter of her own had been born to Dēvakī. The ways of God to no man's knowledge ever come.

79. When Illusion, as a girl-babe, had arrived within the prison gate, there blossomed forth the dawn, and then she uttered a cry of the weeping of a new-born child. The deep sleep fled from the guards, and to consciousness they woke.

80. Hastily they arose, and to Kaṁsa ran; when the news he heard withered in perturbation did he become, and, in the fear of death, to tremble he began.

81. Shaking did he approach his sister and her spouse, and to him began Dēvakī to make humble entreaty, 'Brother, it befitteth thee not to kill a little girl.'

82. Hiding it, hiding it, still did she lay it before Kaṁsa; but in no way softened she the heart of the Rākṣasa, as in love for the daughter a-wailing did the mother lift her voice.

83. In mighty poisonous hate took he the girl-babe from her hand. Holding it by its legs went he forth, and on the stone threshold dashed it down.

84. But forth from his hand sped the girl into the sky, and there in the aspect of a goddess did she stay. Eight armed was she, with every kind of weapon in her hand.

85. Round her neck was a necklace magnifical, and in all beauteous apparel was she arrayed. To view that spectacle came all the gods.

dĕkh-kāra-wönī gayĕ Kansas ta
'kāl cyôn^{u} brō̃ṭhuy zāmot^{u} chuy
tsĕ ti kē̃h wātihiy na myāni māranas ta
lāgas bŏh dasta dasta pampōsh. 86.

'khīd kawa putshy dikh bĕñĕ bēmas ta
kālas tsĕ-ti pāy sapaniy na kē̃h
tsĕ kē̃h-ti wôtuy na shur^{i} māranas' ta. lāgas etc. 87.

wönī yeli gayĕ tas Kansas ta
khūrith kyāh-tāñ sŏranē pĕv
khŏran pĕṭh pĕv bĕñĕ bēmas ta. lāgas etc. 88.

'köm^{u} ös^{ü} karüñ^{ü} pāna Pŏrashĕs ta
bål^{i} gōs aparād bŏvith-kĕth
tŏhĕ pazi khĕmā wŏñ karanas' ta. lāgas etc. 89.

kaḍith ta logukh mān karanas ta
mutsariṭh paikår^{i} atha trövith
Dēwakī bĕñĕ ta biyĕ bēmas ta. lāgas etc. 90.

mūri-hond^{u} kō̃pun^{u} tsāv Kansas ta
sŏth nĕh gölith wadanas tsāv
kālaki kō̃pa sū̃ty sôr^{u} moṭh^{u} tas ta. lāgas etc. 91.

yus lagi Krushna-jyuwanis nāwas ta
tas kari Krushna-jyuv sarŏ wŏpakār
yiti yĕsh nith ta wāti Vishnu-bawanas ta. lāgas etc. 92.

pör^{i} pör^{i} Krushna-jyuwanis nāwas ta
pör^{i} pör^{i} tasandis autāras
pör^{i} pör^{i} tasandis shŏba tsarĕtas ta. lāgas etc. 93.

III.

Yĕshōdāyĕ nĕnd^{a}r ös^{ü} tath samayĕs ta
yĕli wôt^{u} Krushna-jyuv kŏchi tal tas
wuchun ta man wŏnda ās phŏlanas ta
lāgas bŏh dasta dasta pampōsh. 94.

Nanda-gūr^{u} pŏtra-zāyi tsāv tōshĕnas ta
bāgĕn tasandĕn jai-jai-kār
yĕs āv Bagawān pŏtra-bāwas ta. lāgas etc. 95.

86. 'Shame on thee,' came her voice to Kaṁsa. 'Ere this already hath been born thy Death. From my murder can no profit come to thee.

87. 'Why dost thou oppress thy sister and her spouse? Against thy Death there is no possible resource for thee. No profit hast thou gained by murdering babes.'

88. When this voice to Kaṁsa came, in his terror did he somewhat come into his right mind, and at the feet of his sister and her spouse he fell.

89. 'My deeds were destined by the Supreme Himself. In vain have I sown the seeds of sin. Now it befitteth you to grant to me forgiveness.'

90. From the prison did he bring them forth and honour show them. From off their hands their gyves he loosed,—from the hands of Dēvakī his sister and her spouse.

91. Quivering, as of a tree-twig, of Kaṁsa possession took. Sleep and slumber put he far from him, and he to weep began. In his trembling before his Death all else did he forget.

92. He who beareth in his heart the name of Kṛṣṇa, to him will Kṛṣṇa every favour render. In this world glory will he win, and thereafter the abode of Viṣṇu will he reach. To him posy and posy do I offer lotuses.

93. Ever dedicating myself to Kṛṣṇa's name, ever dedicating myself to his incarnation, ever dedicating myself to his auspicious deeds, to him posy on posy do I offer lotuses.

III. THE REJOICINGS IN GŌKULA. (Bhāg. Pu. X, v.)

94. At that time, when she received Kṛṣṇa into her bosom, Yaśōdā lay asleep; and when she (awoke and) saw him, then blossomed forth her heart and soul.

95. At the birth of a son was Nanda the cowherd filled with joy,—to his blessed lot be victory proclaimed! he to whom in son's guise came Bhagavān.

ȧnin brāhman vēd paranas ta
yĕġañ ta hūm dān log^{u} karanē
vĕṭhān chuh wuch^{i} wuch^{i} bāla-Krushnas ta
lāġas bŏh dasta dasta pampōsh. 96.

dah sās kāmadīna ditsan dānas ta
sŏn mŏkta rạtna-māla pūrith-kĕth
an dana yiyi na zi kĕ̄h ti wananas ta. lāġas etc. 97.

gōpiyĕ sārĕy tsāyĕ natsanas ta
'Yĕshōdāyĕ Nārŏn^{i} bālukhāh dyut^{u}
kus zāni Nārān chuh pāna zạnmas ta.' lāġas etc. 98.

wadạvi gūr^{i} āy Nanda-gōpas ta
thȧñ^{i} ġĕv ta bȧḍ^{i} bȧḍ^{i} dŏda-tsȧḍ^{i} hĕth
sārĕn^{ü}y dana log^{u} dini dānas ta. lāġas etc. 99.

Gōkul sôr^{u} āv pushĕ phŏlanas ta
sŏris^{ü}y nagaras sōnth zan ôs^{u}
zan wŏt^{i} zinday Vishnu-buwanas ta. lāġas etc. 100.

pŏr^{i} pŏr^{i} lȧġ^{i}zi-nā Krushna-nāwas ta
pŏr^{i} pŏr^{i} tasandis autāras
pŏr^{i} pŏr^{i} tasandis shŏba tsarētas ta. lāġas etc. 101.

IV.

Nanda-gūr^{u} lāġ hĕth gav Kansas ta
Wasudēwa-rāzas ti mēlani āv
vüñ^{ü}n pŏtra-zāy tas mĕtras ta
lāġas bŏh dasta dasta pampōsh. 102.

dŏshĕway pānavüñ^{u} tsāy tōshĕnas ta
wadạvi ta ŏhiyĕ lȧġ^{i} karanē
'he Dayĕ, lȧs^{i}tan yith samayĕs' ta. lāġas etc. 103.

Wasudēwa-rāzan shĕch^{i} vüñ^{ü}nas ta
dop^{u}nas zi 'bālakan chĕh büḍ^{ü} pīḍā
rŏch^{i} karta Krushnas ta Balabadras' ta. lāġas etc. 104.

Kansan zi bŏd kür^{ü} shur^{i} māranas ta
'bāla-rūp^{i} Kāl myôn^{u} mari-nā-san.'
Pūtanā sūz^{ü}n prath bālakas ta. lāġas etc. 105.

96. Brāhmaṇas brought he to read the Vedic texts; sacrifices and burnt offerings did he begin to make; and full of joy is he as again and again he looketh on the baby Kṛṣṇa.

97. Ten thousand milch-cows did he give in gift, adorning them with gold and pearls and jewel-garlands. Nor can it e'er be told how much of food and goods he did distribute.

98. The cowherd wives began their dance, as they sang that Nārâyaṇa to Yaśōdā a son had given. 'Who knoweth,' sing they, 'perchance it be Nārâyaṇa Himself who hath taken birth.'

99. With gratulations came the herdsmen to Nanda, bringing butter and ghee and many huge churns of milk, and to all did he forthwith lavish wealth in gifts.

100. All Gōkula more and more began to blossom forth in joy. 'Twas as though the spring festival was being kept in all the country round, or as though all mankind in their lifetime Viṣṇu's heaven had reached.

101. Ever must thou dedicate thyself to Kṛṣṇa's name; ever must thou dedicate thyself to his incarnation; ever must thou dedicate thyself to his auspicious deeds. To him posy on posy do I offer lotuses.

IV. NANDA VISITS MATHURĀ. THE FATE OF PŪTANĀ. (Bhāg. Pu. X, v, vi.)

102. Nanda the cowherd went (to Mathurā) to pay his tribute unto Kaṁsa. There met he also King Vasudēva, and to his friend told he how a son had been born unto him.

103. With mutual content did both rejoice, and with gratulations and blessings each the other greeted, as they prayed that, this time, the babe's life might be saved.

104. To Nanda did King Vasudēva impart the truth of the case. 'Great woes did Kaṁsa wreak upon the children. Therefore, prithee, Kṛṣṇa and Baladēva safely guard.'

105. Now Kaṁsa had determined in his heart to slay (all) children, 'for,' quoth he, '(if this I do), how shall the infant that is my Death not die?' And so dispatched he Pūtanā against each child.

Pūtanā chĕh phērān prath garas ta
nikàṭ^{i} dŏda-shur^{i} mārān chĕh
'ts^{a}h gatsh ta ṭ^{a}kān röch^{i} kartas ta'
lāgas bŏh dasta dasta pampōsh. 106

Nanda-gūr^{u} būzith ta log^{u} kōpas ta
Wasudēwa-rāzas ti mīlith gav
lōla kin^{i} Krushnani log^{u} lāranas ta. lāgas etc. 107.

Pūtanā tsāyĕ Nandanis dwāras ta
atsharatsha vihāh dörith-kĕth
söriy màt^{i} gay tas wuchanas ta. lāgas etc. 108.

Yĕshōdāyĕ bālukh nyūn^{u} gindanas ta
Krushnas ḍiji-ḍiji lūj^{u} karanē
yĕtshi sān dit^{i}nas tan dāmas ta. lāgas etc. 109.

Krushna-jyuv^{i} tan ràṭ^{i}nas dāmas ta
zuv prān kàḍ^{i}nas khĩcith-kĕth
wasith ta traṭh zan pĕyĕ ãganas ta. lāgas etc. 110.

kruhan shĕn tāñ wôt^{u} pān tas ta
kul^{i} kàṭ^{i} bajĕ kañĕ sūr sõpàn^{i}
shĕbd gav ākösh^{i} ta būmi gav tsas ta. lāgas etc. 111.

Nanda-gūr^{i} būz^{u} wati gav āshtsaras ta
'Dayĕ, Dayĕ,' 'Krushna, Krushna,' log^{u} karanē
Pūtanā pyēmüts^{u} ös^{u} ãganas ta. lāgas etc. 112.

wadạvi gūr^{i} āy Nandạ-gūris ta
'az môn^{u} bālukh zi Narön^{i} roch^{u}
āpadā āyĕ ta ànd^{i} kür^{u}nas ṭa.' lāgas etc. 113.

zöj^{u}kh Pūtanā yi-na gānd yiyĕs ta
tasandi d^{u}ha nishĕ sŏgand drāv
mŏk^{u}ts^{u}-hond^{u} hīth ôs^{u} yihuy mā tas ta. lāgas etc.
114.

kàr^{i}tav jai-kār Nanda-gōpas ta
Yĕshōdā-mātāyĕ namaskār
yĕman ôs^{u} Bagawān athi gindanas ta. lāgas etc. 115.

106. From house to house doth Pūtanā wander, and little suckling babes doth she destroy. 'Therefore,' said he, 'speedily go thou forth and make me safe against him.'

107. This news heard Nanda the cowherd when he had visited King Vasudēva, and he was filled with trembling. Straightway, in his great love for Kṛṣṇa, set he forth running.

108. (But meanwhile) Pūtanā had entered Nanda's gateway arrayed in fairy guise, and as they looked upon her each and every wight was ravished by the lovely vision.

109. She took Yaśōdā's babe as though to toy with it, and Kṛṣṇa sought she to dandle in her arms, as full of (false) affection offered she him her breast to suck.

110. Kṛṣṇa grasped her breasts that he might drink, and at them sucked he with such might that through them he dragged forth her breath and life. Like a huge thunderbolt, in the courtyard fell she prostrate.

111. Over twelve long miles her body lay extended, while trees and shrubs and mighty rocks were crushed to powder as she fell. From the sky echoed a thunder-roar, and in the earth a chasm formed itselt.

112. On his way home, Nanda the cowherd heard the crash, and with astonied terror was he filled. 'O God! O God!,' 'Kṛṣṇa! Kṛṣṇa!' cried he, when he saw Pūtanā lying in the courtyard prone.

113. To Nanda came the cowherds with their gratulations. 'To-day, we wot that Nārāyaṇa Himself hath saved the child. A calamity came to him, and far away hath it been banished.'

114. Lest a stink should come from it, Pūtanā's body did they burn; but, lo, from the smoke of the pyre it was a fragrant scent that issued forth, for, I ween, death at the hands of Kṛṣṇa was a cause of even her salvation.

115. Cry ye victory to Nanda the cowherd! to Mother Yaśōdā pay ye reverence meet! For into their hands it was that Bhagavān came to sport.

yus laġi Krushna-jyuwanis nāwas ta
tas kari Krushna-jyuv sarŏ wŏpakār
yiti yĕsh nith ta wāti Vishnu-bawanas ta
lāgas bŏh dasta dasta pampōsh. 116.

pör^{i} pör^{i} Krushna-jyuwanis nāwas ta
pör^{i} pör^{i} tasandis autāras
pör^{i} pör^{i} tasandis shŏba tsarĕtas ta. lāgas etc. 117.

V.

boḍ^{u} hagurāh ôs^{u} manz āganas ta
māji thow^{u} manzul^{u} hagaras pĕṭh
Krushnas sövith ġayĕ pānas ta.
lāgas bŏh dasta dasta pampōsh. 118.

manzål^{i}-nĕṇd^{a}r ös^{ü} Krushna-jīwas ta
koḍun nĕṇd^{a}rē khōran kāḍ
hagaras khōr log^{u} ta chala sapañĕs ta. lāgas etc. 119.

yus laġi Krushna-jyuwanis nāwas ta
tas kari Krushna-jyuv sarŏ wŏpakār
yiti yĕsh nith ta wāti Vishnu-bawanas ta. lāgas etc. 120.

pör^{i} pör^{i} Krushna-jyuwanis nāwas ta
pör^{i} pör^{i} tasandis autāras
pör^{i} pör^{i} tasandis shŏba tsarĕtas ta. lāgas etc. 121.

VI.

Kansāsŏr pĕv wāra sŏranas ta
'kāl myôn^{u} zi prakh^{o}ṭ^{u} sapanun^{u} hyot^{u}'
rākhĕsan āgyā kür^{ü}n phēranas ta
lāgas bŏh dasta dasta pampōsh. 122.

āgyā sŏpün^{ü} Trunāwartas ta
yĕchĕs dyār zan röv^{i}måt^{i} ös^{i}
Krushnas nishĕ āv log^{u} phēranas ta. lāgas etc. 123.

āwalana tulith nyūn ākāshĕs ta
Krushna-jyuv^{i} dab dith ta trövith tshun^{u}
pāna pĕṭh bihith ta wach tsoṭ^{u}nas ta. lāgas etc. 124.

116. He who beareth in his heart the name of Kṛṣṇa, to him will Kṛṣṇa every favour render. In this world glory will he win, and thereafter the abode of Viṣṇu will he reach. To him posy and posy do I offer lotuses.

117. Ever dedicating myself to Kṛṣṇa's name, ever dedicating myself to his incarnation, ever dedicating myself to his auspicious deeds, to him posy and posy do I offer lotuses.

V. KṚṢṆA AND THE WAIN. (Bhāg. Pu. X, vii.)

118. In Nanda's courtyard there was a great large wain, and on it once his mother Kṛṣṇa's cradle set. Therein put she him to sleep, and went about her household works.

119. In the cradle lay Kṛṣṇa sleeping, and in his sleep he stretched out his (little baby) legs. Lo, when his foot reached the edge of the wain, the wain (by the mighty push) was broken into fragments.

120. He who beareth in his heart the name of Kṛṣṇa, to him will Kṛṣṇa every favour render. In this world glory will he win, and thereafter the abode of Viṣṇu will he reach. To him posy and posy do I offer lotuses.

121. Ever dedicating myself to Kṛṣṇa's name, ever dedicating myself to his incarnation, ever dedicating myself to his auspicious deeds, to him posy and posy do I offer lotuses.

VI. THE FATE OF TṚṆÂVARTA. (Bhāg. Pu. X, vii.)

122. Into deep thought fell Kaṁsa. 'My Death,' quoth he, 'hath manifest become.' So to the Rākṣasas he gave command in search of him to wander forth.

123. To Tṛṇâvarta, the whirlwind demon, was given the command. (He was to search) as though the wealth of the god of wealth had been lost. Forth wandered he, and Kṛṣṇa did he approach.

124. In a whirlwind took he him up, and off into the sky he carried him. But Kṛṣṇa gave him one blow, and felled him to the earth. Then seated he himself upon him and open tore his breast.

yus lagi nĕth 'Krushna, Krushna' karanas ta
tas kari Krushna-jyuv sarŏ wŏpakār
yiti yĕsh nith ta wāti Vishnu-bawanas ta
lāgas bŏh dasta dasta pampōsh. 125.

pör^{i} pör^{i} lȧg^{i}zi-nā Krushna-nāwas ta
pör^{i} pör^{i} tasandis Krushna-nāwas
pör^{i} pör^{i} Krushnanis tath tsarĕtas ta. lāgas etc. 126.

VII.

Garga-ryŏsh^{u} Wasudēv^{i} sūz^{u} Nandas ta
shurĕn zi nāma-karan karanē
Haladara-rāmas ta Krushna-zīwas ta
lāgas bŏh dasta dasta pampōsh. 127.

Garga-ryŏsh^{u} yeli āv tot^{u} Gōkulas ta
tas nishĕ sôruy pṛakh^{o}ṭuy ôs^{u}
Nanda-gūr^{u} brōṭh drāv tas brāhmanas ta. lāgas etc. 128.

Nanda-gūr^{i} pŏtra-zāy vüñ^{ü} brāhmanas ta
bālakas zātukh lēkhani log^{u}
Garga-rĕsh^{i} r^{a}t^{i} r^{a}t^{i} lakhĕn wȧn^{i} tas ta. lāgas etc. 129.

lạg^{a}n zanmuk^{u} yĕli gonḍ^{u}nas ta
gŏḍa byūṭh^{u} tsandrama Vrushĕ-lạg^{a}nas
dŏyum^{u} Mĕthuni Rāh ôs^{u} tas ta. lāgas etc. 130.

Karkaṭi Bruhaspath bŏy^{i}-bāwas ta
Simhi Shŏkr ta Öyith boḍ^{u} balawān
Kañi Bŏd santān wŏpadāwanas ta. lāgas etc. 131.

Tōli Saur shĕyum^{u} sh̄ĕth^{a}r gālanas ta
Vrushciki Baum satyum^{u} triyĕ karanas
Dani Kīth ashṭum^{u} phēranāwanas ta. lāgas etc. 132.

---

[1] Garga (cf. verse 484) was the tribal priest of the Yādavas. According to the Bhāgavata Purāṇa (X, viii, 5) he was the founder of the science of Astrology, so that Kṛṣṇa's horoscope could not be in better hands. He was a confirmed

125. He who ever crieth 'Kṛṣṇa, Kṛṣṇa,' to him will Kṛṣṇa every favour render. In this world glory will he win, and thereafter the abode of Viṣṇu will he reach. To him posy and posy do I offer lotuses.

126. Ever dedicate thyself to Kṛṣṇa's name, ever dedicate thyself to his incarnation, ever dedicate thyself to his auspicious deeds. To him posy and posy do I offer lotuses.

VII. THE NAMING RITE. (Bhāg. Pu. X, viii.)

127. To Nanda's home did Vasudēva send Garga the sage, that he might duly carry out the naming rite of the children Haladhara-Rāma and Kṛṣṇa.

128. When he came there to Gōkula, all was known to him, and to welcome the Brāhmaṇa came forth Nanda the cowherd.

129. To the Brāhmaṇa, (in formal wise) Nanda the cowherd made known the birth of a son. Then the sage Garga began to write the horoscope, and declared to him each sign to be propitious.[1]

130. When he had made due computation of the moment of the birth, in the first place found he the moon in Taurus, and in the second place the Ascending Node in Gemini.

131. (In the third place), like unto a brother (to the former two), was Jupiter in Cancer, Venus was in Leo, the sun was mighty in its influence, and, for the begetting of manifold progeny, was Mercury in Virgo.

132. As a sixth, for the destruction of enemies, Saturn was in Libra, as a seventh, for the marrying of (many) wives, was Mars in Scorpio, and, for long wanderings, in Sagittarius was the Descending Node.

---

bachelor, and appears subsequently in a much less favourable light in Chapter xxviii.

dop^{u}nas 'yih zi pazi boḍ^{u} sõpanas ta
dēwan ti tsor^{u} āsi asonduy tīz
rāja sör^{i} danḍawath ta mān karanas ta
lāgas bŏh dasta dasta pampōsh. 133.

'asond^{u} nāv baḍi tri-buwanas ta
zātakȧk^{i} lakhĕn yithiy chis'
Krushna-nāv kor^{u}nas Shyāma-sŏndaras ta. lāgas etc. 134.

tawa pata lyūkhun Balabadras ta
wuchuṅ yih zi āsi boḍ^{u} balawān
Balabadr-nāv pĕv Haladaras ta. lāgas etc. 135.

ryŏsh^{u} log^{u} tawa pata rasöy^{i} karanas ta
Krushna-jyuv doyĕ trayĕ tshĕṭ^{a}rith gōs
Yĕshōdā lüj^{ü}s zāra-pāras ta. lāgas etc. 136.

'hē gŏra, nĕcyuw^{u} myôn^{u} chuh cikacāwas ta
bŏh ti chēs pŏtra-bŏch^{ü} ta dayā cyöñ^{ü}
yina krūd khasiy ta shāph dihas' ta. lāgas etc. 137.

yitha titha rasöy^{i} karith byūṭh^{u} khĕnas ta
ȧch^{i} ṭuvith Vishnas arpani log^{u}
Krushṇa-jyuv ṭ^{a}kān yith ta khĕth tsolus ta. lāgas etc. 138.

Garga-ryosh^{u} chuh tōshān tath tsarĕtas ta
Yĕshōdā khōtsān tsakhi brāhmanas
dēwatā chih tsĕkhalān ākāshĕs ta. lāgas etc. 139.

möj^{ü} biyĕ biyĕ lüj^{ü} syod^{u} ananas ta
Krushnas phir^{i} phir^{i} path raṭavüñ^{ü}
yāñ sapanĕs tāñ biyĕ yiyĕs ta. lāgas etc. 140.

---

1 Another name of Haladhara (the Plough-bearer) or Bala-Rāma. See verses 42, 43, 46. He was elder brother of Kṛṣṇa, and his constant companion.

2 Garga was a Brāhmaṇa, and Kṛṣṇa ostensibly a cowherd, whose touch would defile a Brāhmaṇa's food. According to established precedent, it was to be expected that, when his food was thus defiled, Garga should utter a terrible Brāhmaṇa's curse against the defiler. Yaśōdā fully expects this, and begs for mercy on the ground that she has long been hungering for a son, that Kṛṣṇa is her only son, and that

133. And further quoth he to him, 'great, verily, is this child destined to become. His glory, and his alone, will be greater than the glory of the gods, and to him honour and reverence will all kings pay.

134. 'Throughout the three worlds will his name wax illustrious. Such were the indications of the horoscope,' and to the dark and comely babe he gave the name of 'Kṛṣṇa' (i.e. 'the Dark One').

135. Thereafter wrote he the horoscope of Bala-Bhadra [1], and saw that he would become a man of might; and so to Haladhara there became allotted the name of 'Bala-Bhadra' (i.e. 'Excellent in Might').

136. Thereafter the sage began to prepare his food. Twice or thrice did Kṛṣṇa render it defiled,[2] and fain was Yaśōdā to plead for the forgiveness of the holy man.

137. 'Ah, Reverend Sir, but frolicking is my child. I am one hungry for a son, and on thy mercy (do I throw myself), that anger arise not in thy heart and thou curse him not.'

138. In one way or another did he at last prepare his food and took his seat to eat. Then closed he his eyes, and with meet reverence to Viṣṇu did he dedicate it, and straightway Kṛṣṇa hurried up, ate of it, and ran away.

139. Right pleased is Garga the Sage at this deed. Yaśōdā is filled with fear of the Brāhmaṇa's wrath, and at the sight joyfully in the heavens sport the gods.

140. Time and again doth the mother correct him, again and again doth she hold Kṛṣṇa back and tell him that, once the saint hath finished (with his food), then and not till then may he approach him.

---

he is but a child. Garga, however, does not curse and at last manages to get his food in an eatable condition. Before eating, he says grace, the grace being a dedication of the food to Viṣṇu. Kṛṣṇa, being an incarnation of Viṣṇu, claims the food as his own and makes away with it. Garga, of course, knows the truth about Kṛṣṇa, and instead of becoming angry is highly pleased, as also the gods, at this revelation of his deity. Yaśōdā, on the contrary, being ignorant of the true facts, is terrified at what she fears will be the certain fate of her son.

möj^{u} path raṭĕs kati bōzihēs ta
'yih zi chum arpāṇ kōna khĕma bŏh
nonuy wanana ti kyāh tsēnihēs ta
lāgas bŏh dasta dasta pampōsh. 141.

purōhĕth rasöy^{i} khĕth gav pānas ta
an dana dakhĕnā kūt^{u} dyut^{u}has
Nanda-gūr^{u} öhiy log^{u} manganas ta. lāgas etc. 142.

namaskār Nanda-gōrĕnis bāgĕs ta
Yĕshōdāyĕ pŏtra-mājĕ namaskār
namaskār Krushna-jyuwanis nāwas ta. lāgas etc.
143.

yus lagi Krushna-jyuwanis nāwas ta
tas kari Krushna-jyuv sarŏ wŏpakār
yiti yĕsh nith ta wāti Vishnu-bawanas ta. lāgas etc.
144.

pör^{i} pör^{i} tasandis khēla-karanas ta
pör^{i} pör^{i} tasandis autāras
pör^{i} pör^{i} tasandis shŏba tsarētas ta. lāgas etc. 145.

VIII.

khŏkhaci nērihē Krushna-jyuv asta
phērān dŏda-tsāḍ^{i} phirān ôs^{u}
'Dŏda-gūr^{u}' nāv log^{u} bāla-Krushnas ta
lāgas bŏh dasta dasta pampōsh. 146.

zanga āyĕs ta log^{u} pakanas ta
shŏñdār ruñĕ tas pāda-kamalas
phīrith ta yiyihē prath garas ta. lāgas etc. 147.

thūñ^{u} khĕna maza log^{u} bāla-Krushnas
thañĕ-tsūri shikharĕn lad karihē
'Thañĕ-tsūr' nāv log^{u} thañĕ-tsūras ta. lāgas etc. 148.

thañĕ-tsūri phērihē prath garas ta
tsartsani rōzahön gūr^{i}-bāyĕ tas
shĕnkawun^{u} wuchihē pata brŏṭhas ta. lāgas etc. 149.

141. His mother held him back, but in no way did he heed her. 'To me this sage doth dedicate the food. Wherefore should I not eat of it?' But even though he thus spoke plainly, how should she understand him?

142. The priest, his meal consumed, set forth for home. How great was the gift of food and money that Nanda the cowherd gave him, as he asked for the parting blessing of the holy man!

143. Reverence be to Nanda the cowherd's lot. Reverence be to Yaśōdā the Mother of the Son. Reverence be to the Name of Kṛṣṇa, to whom posy and posy do I offer lotuses.

144. He who beareth in his heart the name of Kṛṣṇa, to him will Kṛṣṇa every favour render. In this world glory will he win, and thereafter the abode of Visṇu will he reach. To him posy and posy do I offer lotuses.

145. Ever dedicating myself to his playful frolics, ever dedicating myself to his incarnation, ever dedicating myself to his auspicious deeds, to him posy and posy do I offer lotuses.

VIII. THE BUTTER-THIEF, KṚṢṆA AND THE MORTAR, YAMALA AND ARJUNA.

(Bhāg. Pu. X, viii–xi.)

146. Kṛṣṇa (in due time) would slowly creep outside the house, and as he went along the jars of milk would he upset. Thus did the childKṛṣṇa gain the name of 'Dugdha-gōpa' (i.e. 'Milkman').

147. As his legs gained strength began he to walk with little bells tinkling on his lotus-feet, and thus would he go round from house to house.

148. The child Kṛṣṇa acquired a taste for eating butter, and to pilfer it would he climb up on to the swinging shelves on which they stored it. Thus did he gain the name of 'Butter-Thief.'

149. To pilfer butter would he wander from house to house. Watching for him would the wives of the cowherds stand, as he (would come along) looking fearfully behind him and before.

thañĕ-tsūri-hātsh lāğahŏn Krushnas ta
dyūn^{u} zan wuchihēkh ȧch^{i} phir^{i} phir^{i}
ȧch^{i} phirith wuchanas pān wandahas ta
lāğas bŏh dasta dasta pampōsh. 150.

thañĕ-tsūri phērihē prath shikharis ta
kañ^{i}-kājĕ wŏkhal tala thȧv^{i} thȧv^{i}
ḍēshākh yāñ tāñ laği tsalanas ta. lāğas etc. 151.

barith dŏda-ğol^{u} kuni āsi tas ta
nĕshŭ̃k^{u} gūr^{i}-bāyĕ yiyi athi zan
zöğith dŏda-phuk^{u} buth^{i} diyi tas ta. lāğas etc. 152.

dŏda-phuki achĕn on^{u} pĕyi tas ta
Krushna-jyuv atha tala ğatshi nīrith
shur^{i} hĕth lağēs nāla tulanas ta. lāğas etc. 153.

dŏda-thöj^{u} kuni āsi thadi shikharis ta
lōrĕ sŭ̃ty tȧl^{i} kin^{i} zȧd^{i} karihēs
ös^{u} dörith ta rōzi dŏda-cĕnas ta. lāğas etc. 154.

kĕ̃h cyāvi bālakan kĕ̃h pānas ta
kĕ̃h wȁdaran ta panzĕn kĕ̃h
kĕ̃h rāwari chĕki labi tālawas ta. lāğas etc. 155.

gūr^{i}-bāyĕ yihŏn lāri Krushnas ta
thŭ̃n^{u} dŏd rāwarun mājĕ wananas
Yĕshōdā lağĕkh zāra-pāras ta. lāğas etc. 156.

gūr^{i}-bāyĕn log^{u} srĕh baḍanas ta
dŏd sōrihēkh ta mŏl^{i} anahŏn
dĕwa ami hīta yiyi sôn^{u} khēlanas ta. lāğas etc. 157.

gūr^{i}-bāyĕ sārān dŏd tsūri tas ta
khŏtsān atsihēkh mājĕ kŏchi tal
mājĕ kŏchi atsanas pör^{i} lagahas ta. lāğas etc. 158.

150. A charge of butter-theft would they bring against Kṛṣṇa, and he, in sham humility, would let his eyes roam hither and thither as he watched them. Lo! to his watching and to the roaming of his eyes do I make myself a sacrifice.

151. To steal butter would he peregrinate from swinging shelf to swinging shelf, putting grinding-stones and mortars under them to stand upon, and so reach up; but the moment they caught sight of him, away he scampereth.

152. Sometimes doth he fill his mouth with milk, and unabashed let himself fall into the hand of some cowherd's wife. Then fixeth he his eyes upon her and spurteth a stream of milk right full into her face.

153. When her eyes thus become blinded with the spurted stream of milk, Kṛṣṇa slippeth away from 'neath her hand, and collecting a mob of boys a hubbub raiseth.

154. Sometimes there may be a milk bowl high up upon a swinging shelf, and with a stick would he poke holes in its bottom. Then setting his mouth below it standeth he drinking from the issuing stream.

155. At one time giveth he a drink to the other children, at another to himself, at another to the monkeys and the bears, and yet another time doth he waste it and scatter it upon the wall or ceiling.

156. The cowherds' wives would come in chase of Kṛṣṇa. To his mother would they tell the waste of butter and of milk, and for their forgiveness doth Yaśōdā pray.

157. Yet still the love of the cowherds' wives kept on increasing. If their store of milk ran short, they would buy more (for him to steal). 'For, perchance, by this stratagem,' thought they, 'he may be enticed into our house to play his tricks.'

158. The cowherds' wives privately set milk in his way, fearing that (he would leave them and) find his way into his mother's lap. And to his nestling in his mother's lap do I dedicate myself.

laṭi aki mŏma đyut^{u} māji Krushnas ta
    Krushna-jyuv ās ös^{ü} dörith-kĕth
vishŏ-rūph drēṭh āv biyĕ moṭh^{u} tas ta
    lāgas bŏh dasta dasta pampōsh. 159.

mĕts^{ü} khĕñ^{ü} bōzōn māji Krushnas ta
    mutsarith ös^{ü} tas wuchanē lüj^{ü}
vishŏ-rūph ḍyūṭhun ta biyĕ moṭh^{u} tas ta. lāgas etc.
160.

dŏha aki möj^{ü} bīṭh^{ü} dŏda-mandanas ta
    kŏchĕ kĕth Krushna-jyuv narĕ raṭihēs
dŏda-thöj^{ü} ti grakavüñ^{ü} pĕṭh dānas ta. lāgas etc. 161.

graki sūty thājĕ āv dŏda pĕnas ta
    Krushnas trövith wŏkowun tath
paṭ^{i} kin^{i} biyĕ dŏđ sôr^{u} trôw^{u}nas ta. lāgas etc. 162.

dŏda-pĕna tsakhi gayĕ möj^{ü} Krushnas ta
    lāryēyĕ pata tas zi dĕwa raṭihēs
rüṭ^{ü}-rost^{u} raṭanas kĕtha yiyihēs ta. lāgas etc. 163.

lārān lārān thüc^{ü} möj^{ü} tas ta
    mājĕ-handi thakana ör^{a}tsar ās
raṭanas pön^{i}-pān dyutun tas ta. lāgas etc. 164.

raṭith chĕh anān möj^{ü} Krushnas ta
    gudāmi sūty lüj^{ü} ganḍanē tas
ganḍa-rost^{u} kĕtha sana yiyi ganḍanas ta. lāgas etc.
165.

gudöm^{i} ganḍān chĕh möj^{ü} Krushnas ta
    ongul z^{a}h kåṭ^{i} gay prath ganḍa tas
gudöm^{i} sör^{i} ganḍith biyĕ push pĕyēs ta. lāgas etc.
166.

sāsa-badi gudāmi ganḍ kor^{u}has ta
    Krushna-jyuv na zi yiyi ganḍana tas
ār ās ta ganḍanas pān dyut^{u}nas ta. lāgas etc. 167.

---

1 Yaśōdā never recognized Kṛṣṇa as a divinity. To her he was her darling baby boy, and this was in accordance with his wishes. But every now and then he granted her visions of his real nature, as the Supreme Deity, of whom all creation is but a manifestation. But, necessarily, these acts of graciousness were but moment-

159. Once on a time did his mother give Kṛṣṇa her breast to suck, and to her, for the drink, did he open wide his mouth. She looked within it, and lo! therein was manifested unto her the whole creation. Then straightway was it by her forgotten.[1]

160. Another time did his mother hear that Kṛṣṇa had been eating earth. His mouth she opened and therein she looked, and therein again was shown to her the whole creation, and again straightway it, too, did she forget.

161. (Bhāg. Pu. X, ix.) One day his mother to churn milk took her seat, and Kṛṣṇa (came and nestled) in her bosom, and caught her arms to stop her at the work. Moreover, on the stove there was being heated a pan of milk.

162. Suddenly the pan of milk began to boil over, and she hastily put him down (and ran) to cool down the (foaming milk); but behind her back he upset all the other milk that was in the churn.[2]

163. On the upsetting of the milk at Kṛṣṇa waxed the mother wroth. After him did she run, that somehow she might catch him. But how could she seize Him who hath no bounds nor limits?

164. Pursuing him, pursuing him, became his mother weary, and when he saw her weariness sorrow came upon him, and by her he let himself be caught.

165. The mother caught him and brought him home. With a cow's halter she began to tie him up. But how can He who hath no bonds be bound?

166. With the cow's halter doth his mother Kṛṣṇa bind, but each time that she would tie it, the halter was two fingers short. Then together tied she all the halters, but still were they all too short.

167. Thousands of halters did she knot together round him, but still (they were too short and) Kṛṣṇa with them by her could not be tied. At the last compassion came to him, and he suffered his body to be bound by her.

---

ary, and she was not permitted to remember them afterwards.

[2] According to the Bhāgavata Purāṇa he upset the churn because he was angry at the sudden cessation of the suckling.

akiy gudāmi gonḍun wŏkhalas ta
prazi-hond^{u} swömī ganḍana āv
prāna-razi ganḍahön tsĕth-wŏkhalas ta
lāgas bŏh dasta dasta pampōsh. 168.

möj^{u} gayĕ kāmĕ zi ganḍ kor^{u}mas ta
Krushna-jyuv wŏkhol^{u} hĕth lŏti lŏti drāv
nishĕ wôt^{u} Yĕmalas ta biyĕ Arzŏnas ta. lāgas etc. 169.

kul^{i} z^{a}h zi tas ös^{i} nishĕ āganas ta
Yĕmal ta Arzŏn^{u} ôsukh nāv
sāsa-bad^{i} waharan-hand^{i} baḍanas ta. lāgas etc. 170.

kulĕv dŏyav manz^{i} drāyāv asta
wŏkhalaci zēri sūty mūla nishĕ pĕy
dēwa-rūph saponukh ta āy Krushnas ta. lāgas etc. 171.

Nāradani shāpa ös^{i} kul^{i}-bāwas ta
na-ta ös^{i} santān Vaishrawanan^{i}
Krushna-darshĕna gōkh shāph antas ta. lāgas etc. 172.

kul^{i}-pĕna söriy gay āshtsaras ta
wari ta waḍavi lag^{i} karanē
Krushn sôn^{u} rachun ôs^{u} Nārānas ta. lāgas etc. 173.

Nanda-gūr^{i} kar^{i} mīṭh^{i} Shrī-Krushnas ta
zônun na kāran ath zi kyāh ôs^{u}
kul^{i}-pĕnas ta shāph-tsalanas ta. lāgas etc. 174.

bālakh āyēy poz^{u} wananas ta
yim kul^{i} zi Krushnañi zēri sūty pĕy
yiyihē bāla-Krushnüñ^{u} patsh kas ta. lāgas etc. 175.

yus lagi Krushna-jyuwanis nāwas ta
tas kari Krushna-jyuv sarŏ wŏpakār
yiti yĕsh nith ta wāti Vishnu-bawanas ta. lāgas etc. 176.

pör^{i} pör^{i} Krushna-jyuwanis nāwas ta
pör^{i} pör^{i} tasandis autāras
pör^{i} pör^{i} tasandis shŏba tsarētas ta. lāgas etc. 177.

168. Then, by one single halter did she tie him to a rice-mortar. Behold, the Lord of all that liveth could be bound! By the halter of my life-breath may I also bind Him to the mortar of my thoughts.

169. Quoth his mother to herself, 'Now have I tied him up,' and to her household works she went; but Kṛṣṇa quietly went forth outside taking the mortar with him, and came up close to the two trees, Yamala and Arjuna.

170. (Bhāg. Pu. X, ix.) These were two trees close to the court-yard. Their names were Yamala and Arjuna, and for thousands of years had they been growing.

171. Between the two trees progressed he slowly, and by a single push of the mortar became they both uprooted from the ground. Then assumed they the forms of two gods, and Kṛṣṇa did they approach.

172. By a curse of Nārada's had they been changed to trees, for otherwise were they sons of the god Vaiśravana. But, when they looked upon Kṛṣṇa, ended became the curse.

173. (Bhāg. Pu. X, xi.) At the falling of the trees were all astonied. Rejoicing and gratulations began they to utter, 'Our Kṛṣṇa hath been protected by Nārāyaṇa Himself.'[1]

174. Kisses did Nanda the cowherd shower on Kṛṣṇa, for he knew not the cause of the happening, neither of the fall of the trees nor of the raising of the curse.

175. The children (who had seen it) came up to say the truth. 'It was at a mere push from Kṛṣṇa that the trees fell.' But of the child Kṛṣṇa who could this believe?

176. He who beareth in his heart the name of Kṛṣṇa, to him will Kṛṣṇa every favour render. In this world glory will he win, and thereafter the abode of Viṣṇu will he reach. To him posy and posy do I offer lotuses.

177. Ever dedicating myself to Kṛṣṇa's name, ever dedicating myself to his incarnation, ever dedicating myself to his auspicious deeds, to him posy and posy do I offer lotuses.

---

[1] Literally 'was an object of protection to Nārāyaṇa.'

IX.

phala-wājĕñ āyĕ phal k^{a}nanas ta
Krushna-jyuv dā̃-mŏchi phal hĕni drāv
dā̃-phali raṭ^{a}n drāv phala-mŏlas ta
lāgas bŏh dasta dasta pampōsh. 178.

dŏha aki Nanda-gūr^{u} ôs^{u} harshĕs ta
bāla-Krushnañĕ tsarĕ bāshĕ wuch^{i} wuch^{i}
gūr^{i}-shur^{i} ta gūr^{i}-bāyĕ āsa tsĕkhalanas ta. lāgas etc. 179.

āshtsar būzith pĕy sŏranas ta
Puti-hond^{u} ta hagaruk^{u} Trunāwartun^{u}
kul^{i}-pĕn^{i} ti sŏr^{i} sŏr^{i} pĕy ḍaranas ta. lāgas etc. 180.

samith sŏr^{i} pĕy nīth karanas ta
kyāh tāñ zi wŏtpāth chuh ath nagaras
yĕli tĕli röch^{ü} kür^{ü} Dáy^{i} Krushnas ta. lāgas etc. 181.

günḍ^{ü}kh kath ta khát^{i} wanas ta
söriy shur^{i} böts^{ü} ta khyol^{u} hĕth-kĕth
Gōwardana-parbuth ta Vrundāwanas ta. lāgas etc. 182.

gōpiyĕn ras log^{u} wan khasanas ta
sŏn mŏkta raṭna-māla āsa pūrith
khēlān chĕh gindān bāla-Krushnas ta. lāgas etc. 183.

bālakh chih khēlān bāla-Krushnas ta
shŏñdār ruñĕ ta gŏḍa-kár^{i} tas
muñĕ bŏh ti wandahas pāda-kamalas ta. lāgas etc. 184.

tsōra-pöntsa-wahur^{u} tsāv wátsh^{i} rachanas ta
prazi-hond^{u} pālakh chuh wátsh^{i}-rachawun^{u}
gūr^{i}-shur^{i} sŏr^{i} ös^{i} pata paṭą tas ta. lāgas etc. 185.

wátsh^{i} hĕth ta phērān ôs^{u} wanas ta
Watsāsŏr āv wotsh^{u} lögith
tsīnith ta Krushnan hôw^{u} Haladaras ta. lāgas etc. 186.

---

[1] The word *bāshĕ* properly means 'words,' especially 'childish babblings.' But here, as in verse 220, it is extended to mean 'baby pranks.'

IX. KṚṢṆA AND THE FRUIT-WIFE, THE MIGRATION TO VṚNDĀVANA, THE FATE OF VATSÂSURA. (Bhāg. Pu. X, xi.)

178. Once on a day a fruit-wife came to sell her fruit, and Kṛṣṇa went forth to buy of her fruit with a handful of paddy. But when he paid it as the price, instead of each grain there issued from his hand a jewel as the price.

179. Once on a day Nanda the cowherd was filled with joy, as he watched the many infant pranks [1] of Kṛṣṇa, the while romped together the cowherd boys and the cowherd wives.

180. Then fell they all sore amazed as they called to mind Pūtanā, the wain, and Tṛṇâvarta, and as they thought and thought upon the crashing of the trees they became filled with fear.

181. To hold counsel met they all together. 'What mean these portents that befall this land [2] ? Blessed be God who saved Kṛṣṇa each time that they occurred.'

182. So thus did they resolve and to the forest (*vana*) set they forth, all with their children, wives and flocks, and reached the mountain of Gōvardhana and Vṛndāvana.

183. Arrayed in gold and pearls and jewels, sporting and playing with the infant Kṛṣṇa, filled with happiness are the herd-maidens as to the forest they ascended.

184. The boys frolic with Kṛṣṇa, as sweetly tinkle the bells upon his anklets. Yea, to his lotus-feet do I dedicate the pupils of mine eyes.

185. When Kṛṣṇa became four or five years old, he began to watch the calves. The Protector of all that liveth hath become a watcher of calves, and (as their leader) all the cowherd lads did follow him.

186. He was used to take the calves to wander in the forest. There, as a calf disguised, came Vatsâsura (the calf-demon), and him did Kṛṣṇa recognize, and to Haladhara did he point him out.

---

[2] In Kāshmīrī, the word *nagar*, like *shĕhr*, is often used to signify 'a tract of land,' in addition to the usual meaning of 'city'

patim^{i} rạṭ^{i}nas khōr asŏras ta
gilavith kala pĕṭh^{i} zuv koḍ^{u}nas
mŏk^{a}th gav Krushnani atha maranas ta
lāgas bŏh dasta dasta pampōsh. 187.

yus lagi Krushna-jyuwanis nāwas ta
tas kari Krushna-jyuv sarŏ wŏpakār
yiti yĕsh nith ta wāti Vishnu-bawanas ta. lāgas etc. 188.

pör^{i} pör^{i} Krushna-jyuwanis nāwas ta
pör^{i} pör^{i} tasandis autāras
pör^{i} pör^{i} tasandis shŏba tsarĕtas ta. lāgas etc. 189.

X.

tawa pata Bakāsŏr āv Krushnas ta
braga-sond^{u} vihậh dörith-kĕth
Pūti-hond^{u} bôy^{u} ôs^{u} ta tsor^{u} vĕh tas ta
lāgas bŏh dasta dasta pampōsh. 190.

braga-mŏkha Krushna-jyuv nyūn nĕngalanas ta
gĕg ās tsaṭana ta kaḍith nyūn
Krushna-jyuv^{i} tōnth^{u}y tshĕna kür^{u}nas ta. lāgas etc. 191.

Agāsŏr ôs^{u} bôy^{u} Bakāsŏras ta
bĕñĕ bôy^{u} mārana yüts^{u} tsakhi gav
azagara-rūpa āv nishĕ Krushnas ta. lāgas etc. 192.

ös^{ü} wahörith ta rūd^{u} manz wanas ta
butarāth ta ākāsh zan drĕ̄ṭh āv
kruha-bạd^{i} wath zan zĕv ös^{ü} tas ta. lāgas etc. 193.

zĕvi pĕṭh^{i} shur^{i} sör^{i} lạg^{i} gindanas ta
āshtsarĕ shāyāh wuchanē lạg^{i}
rākhyus chuh tōshān grās karanas ta. lāgas etc. 194.

Krushna-jyuv chuh tsīnith mot^{u} lāganas ta
wati zan phērān ta gĕg roṭ^{u}nas
prān phoṭ^{u} asŏras brahmānḍas ta. lāgas etc. 195.

kaḍith shur^{i} nīn sūty pānas ta
anta-lāy chĕc^{u}nas tas zīv gay
dēwatā sör^{i} lạg^{i} pōsh warshĕnas ta. lāgas etc. 196.

---

1 A magic powder. When sprinkled upon anyone it kills him. Here the expression is metaphorical, and it simply means that when, as mentioned in the preceding

42

187. He caught the Asura by hind legs, and round and round above his head he whirled him till the demon's life he had torn out. Thus did Vatsâsura obtain salvation, for it was at Kṛṣṇa's hands that death he met.

188. He who beareth in his heart the name of Kṛṣṇa, to him will Kṛṣṇa every favour render. In this world glory will he win, and thereafter the abode of Viṣṇu will he reach. To him posy and posy do I offer lotuses.

189. Ever dedicating myself to Kṛṣṇa's name, ever dedicating myself to his incarnation, ever dedicating myself to his auspicious deeds, to him posy and posy do I offer lotuses.

X. THE FATES OF BAKÂSURA AND AGHÂSURA. (Bhāg. Pu. X, xi, xii.)

190. That after, to Kṛṣṇa came Bakâsura, as a crane disguised. Brother was he of Pūtanā, and with mighty hatred was he filled.

191. Into his crane's mouth took he Kṛṣṇa and swallowed him. But Kṛṣṇa, as he reached his throat, so tore it that the demon pulled him forth again. Then Kṛṣṇa merely tore his beak asunder (and so destroyed him).

192. (Bhāg. Pu. X, xii.) A brother of Bakâsura was Aghâsura, and at the slaughter of his sister and his brother him did rage consume. So, and as python huge disguised, came he to Kṛṣṇa.

193. Wide opened he his mouth and waited in the forest. Like the ground and like the sky appeared (his lower and his upper jaw), and as a miles-long road so seemed his tongue.

194. The children all began to frolic on his tongue, and looked around in marvel at the curious place. Well pleased, I wot, was the Rākṣasa as he swallowed them.

195. But Kṛṣṇa recognized him, and pretended to be mad. He wandered down the road and seized his throat. Then, through his suture cervical burst forth the Asura's breath.

196. Then led he forth the children with him. Upon the demon scattered he the death-dust,[1] and so died he his deaths. The gods the while rained flowers upon Kṛṣṇa.

verse, Kṛṣṇa seized his throat, the demon died.

namaskār asŏran tath bāgĕs ta
namaskār Krushnanĕn khēla-bājĕn
namaskār tĕlikis prath zanas ta
lāgas bŏh dasta dasta pampōsh. 197.

yus laġi Krushna-jyuwanis nāwas ta
tas kari Krushna-jyuv sarŏ wŏpakār
yiti yĕsh nith ta wāti Vishnu-bawanas ta. lāgas etc.
198.

pör^{i} pör^{i} Krushna-jyuwanis nāwas ta
pör^{i} pör^{i} tasandis autāras
pör^{i} pör^{i} tasandis shŏba tsarĕtas ta. lāgas etc. 199.

XI.

ġūr^{i}-shur^{i} āsahön sūty Krushnas ta
nānā prakör^{i} tim khēla karawån^{i}
z^{a}rawana yiyihē na kaīsi dēwas ta
lāgas bŏh dasta dasta pampōsh. 200.

aki laṭi Brahmāhas ġav manas ta
'wuch^{i}ta yim ġūr^{i}-shur^{i} båḍ^{i} bāgĕwān
prath brinzi āsān sūty Krushnas ta'. lāgas etc. 201.

'asĕ chuh dŏrlab dyāna sŏranas ta
yiman chuh āsān ġindanas sūty.'
hĕkun na z^{a}ravith ta pĕv tsalanas ta. lāgas etc. 202.

dŏha aki Krushna-jyuv drāv prātas ta
ġūr^{i}-shur^{i} ta khĕn cĕn sūty hĕth-kĕth
rachani wåtsh^{i} nīkh sūty pānas ta. lāgas etc. 203.

bata khĕni yĕli biṭh^{i} köj^{i}-samayĕs ta
prath kaīsi-hond^{u} nyūn pānas nish
sŏmbarith khĕni log^{u} pön^{i}-pānas ta. lāgas etc. 204.

kaīsi kun hövith khĕyi pānas ta
akh chus mĕnḍi mĕnḍi pāna āparān
akh chus niwān thapi Krushnas ta. lāgas etc. 205.

kaīsi diyi thaph kĕh thaph din tas ta
kaīsi kari åch^{i}-nŏṭh myonḍ^{u} hāwān
åch^{i}-nŏṭi warihē mĕ ti abalas ta. lāgas etc. 206.

197. Reverence be to the blessed lot of that Asura! Reverence be to Kṛṣṇa's playmates! Reverence be to each and all who in those days lived!

198. He who beareth in his heart the name of Kṛṣṇa, to him will Kṛṣṇa every favour render. In this world glory will he win, and thereafter the abode of Viṣṇu will he reach. To him posy and posy do I offer lotuses.

199. Ever dedicating myself to Kṛṣṇa's name, ever dedicating myself to his incarnation, ever dedicating myself to his auspicious deeds, to him posy and posy do I offer lotuses.

XI. THE RAPE OF THE COWHERD BOYS BY BRAHMĀ. (Bhāg. Pu. X, xiii.)

200. Ever near Kṛṣṇa would stay the cowherd boys, and in many varied ways did they frolic. (But out of jealousy) none of the gods could bear this sight.

201. One time came it into Brahmā's thought, 'Behold, how blessed are these cowherd lads, who every moment spend in Kṛṣṇa's company.

202. For us with difficulty is gained the power of calling him to mind by contemplation, and with these lads is he ever present in their frolics.' This could he not endure, and forthwith found he himself compelled to flee (the sight).

203. Once on a day at dawn set forth Kṛṣṇa, and with him to watch the calves took he the herd lads and for them meat and drink.

204. When, at the time of the midday meal, they all sat down to eat the food that each had brought with him, and after Kṛṣṇa had assembled them, he began to eat himself.

205. To one lad offereth he a piece of food and then eateth he it himself. Another lad himself putteth gobbet after gobbet into his mouth, and yet another is picking and stealing Kṛṣṇa's food.

206. From one doth he something snatch, and from him another snatcheth, at another he winketh as he showeth his gobbet. Would that he would deign one wink at me the feeble one!

bata-myonḍ^{u} athi ôs^{u} Krushna-zīwas ta
būzun zi wȧn^{i} khyol^{u} ȧch^{i}-tala gav
bata-myonḍ^{u} athi hĕth log^{u} lāranas ta
lāgas bŏh dasta dasta pampōsh. 207

nēb kuni lobun na ta phyūr^{u} wanas ta
Brahmāhan pȧt^{i} kin^{i} shur^{i} khȧṭ^{i}nas
khyol^{u} kuni ḍyūṭhun na phyūr^{u} pānas ta. lāgas etc. 208.

wôt^{u} yĕli khĕna-shāyi pĕv sŏranas ta
zônun zi Brahmā tshạl^{a}rani āv
tshalas tasandis muh tshun^{u}nas ta. lāgas etc. 209.

panañi güts^{ü} shur^{i} ta khyol^{u} now^{u} kor^{u}nas ta
nowuy wȧtsh^{i}-khyol^{u} tyuth^{u} yuth^{u} ôs^{u}
Dayĕ-güts^{ü} kaĩsi āv na kĕ̃h ti tsēnanas ta. lāgas etc. 210.

waharas tāñ nȧv^{i} shur^{i} gindanas ta
nȧv^{i} wȧtsh^{i} ti mājĕn sũty khēlān
wahara pata Brahmā pĕv sŏranas ta. lāgas etc. 211.

Brahmā mōha nishĕ āv tsēnanas ta
wasith Krushnas pādan pĕv
wȧtsh^{i}-khyol^{u} shur^{i}-khyol^{u} anith dyut^{u}nas ta. lāgas etc. 212.

shur^{i}-khyol^{u} yĕli wôt^{u} nishĕ Krushnas ta
bata-myonḍ^{u} suy ôs^{u} athi Krushnas
timan rost^{u} kĕtha sana myonḍ^{u} wasihēs ta. lāgas etc. 213.

māyā-khyol^{u} tsāv Krushna-pānas ta
Krushn^{ü}y ösith Krushn^{ü}y bọw^{u}
Vishnu-māyi pör^{i} pör^{i} Krushna-zīwas ta. lāgas etc. 214.

yus lagi Krushna-jyuwanis nāwas ta
tas kari Krushna-jyuv sarŏ wŏpakār
yiti yĕsh nith ta wāti Vishnu-bawanas ta. lāgas etc. 215.

pör^{i} pör^{i} Krushna-jyuwanis nāwas ta
pör^{i} pör^{i} tasandis autāras
pör^{i} pör^{i} tasandis shŏba tsarētas ta. lāgas etc. 216.

207. A gobbet of boiled rice was in Kṛṣṇa's hand, when he saw that from beneath his very eyes the herd had flitted far into the forest. So holding the gobbet still within his fingers after the herd he ran.

208. Long did he wander in the forest but no trace of the cattle did he find, and behind his back Brahmā hid the herd-lads away. When Kṛṣṇa nowhere saw the herd, returned he back to the place whence he had set forth.

209. When he had come back to the place where they had been eating, then did he understand, and knew that Brahmā had come to cozen him, and over that cozening cast he his Illusive Power.

210. By his own might created he anew a troop of lads and herd. The new herd of calves the former exactly did resemble, and by God's might no one discerned the change.

211. For a whole year the new lads were there a-frolicking, and the new calves were frisking round their mothers. Then, after the year, Brahmā understood.

212. Out of delusion came Brahmā to understanding. From heaven did he descend and fall at Kṛṣṇa's feet. He brought and rendered back the herd of calves and the whole troop of lads.

213. When the troop of lads came up to Kṛṣṇa, still held he within his fingers that very gobbet of rice. For, in their absence how could it have gone down his throat?

214. Into Kṛṣṇa's body was the illusory troop absorbed. As it had been but (an emanation of) Kṛṣṇa, so Kṛṣṇa, and nought but Kṛṣṇa, did it again become. To the Illusive Power of Viṣṇu ever do I dedicate myself.

215. He who beareth in his heart the name of Kṛṣṇa, to him will Kṛṣṇa every favour render. In this world glory will he win, and thereafter the abode of Viṣṇu will he reach. To him posy and posy do I offer lotuses.

216. Ever dedicating myself to Kṛṣṇa's name, ever dedicating myself to his incarnation, ever dedicating myself to his auspicious deeds, to him posy and posy do I offer lotuses.

XII.

badyōv ta Krushn tsāv gōv^{ü}-rachanas ta
wanan gōv^{ü} hĕth ta yiyi phīr^{i} phīr^{i}
tatiy dŏda-bata möj^{u} āparĕs ta
lāgas bŏh dasta dasta pampōsh. 217.

nērahön kāmadīna hĕth wanas ta
Jamunāyĕ bȧṭh^{i} bȧṭh^{i} khēla karawȧn^{i}
Haladar ta sör^{i} shur^{i} pata pata tas ta. lāgas etc. 218.

dŏha aki drāmȧt^{i} ȧnd^{i} wanas ta
shāyāh ḍīṭh^{u}kh amöb^{u} jān
sar kul^{i} kȧṭ^{i} phal tati shūbanas ta. lāgas etc. 219.

logukh boḍ^{u} maza tati gindanas ta
ranga ranga shur^{i}-bāshĕ lȧg^{i} karanē
lör^{i} lör^{i} tshĕp^{i} tshĕp^{i} lȧg^{i} gindanas ta. lāgas etc. 220.

kuni gur^{i} lāganas ta guri khāranas ta
kuni hast^{i}-ambārĕ gindanāvĕkh
kuni shukra-pāliki khös^{i} dinas ta. lāgas etc. 221.

gōv^{ü}n manz atsi Krushna-jyuv asta
s^{a}h zan lögith khōtsanāvĕkh
tsari-mŏnji-wāda yiyi tsĕkhalanas ta. lāgas etc. 222.

Shrīdām dōri āv Krushna-zīwas ta
won^{u}nas ‘wanāh chuh phala-bȧr^{i}th^{ü}n
kam maza banahön tati khēlanas’ ta. lāgas etc. 223.

‘kyāh kȧr^{i}zi rākhyusāh chuh tath wanas ta
khara-vih dörith khēlāh hĕth’
Krushna-jyuv^{i} būzun ta pĕv hōshĕs ta. lāgas etc. 224.

Dēnuka-nāv ôs^{u} tas rākhĕsas ta
gatshith pēs ta kor^{u}has ḍās
Haladara-rāman prān kȧḍ^{i}nas ta. lāgas etc. 225.

rākhyus gol^{u} ta lȧg^{i} khēlanas ta
nānā phal khĕth ta phīrith āy
pör^{i} pör^{i} Krushna-zīwanas khēlanas ta. lāgas etc. 226.

XII. THE FATE OF DHĒNUKA. (Bhāg. Pu. X, xv.)

217. Kṛṣṇa grew older, and began to watch cows (not calves). Into the forests taketh he the cows and then wandereth home. And when he cometh back his mother feedeth him with rice and milk.

218. With the milch-kine into the forest would they wend forth, frolicking along the bank of the Yamunā, he, followed by Haladhara and all the lads.

219. Once on a day they went out beyond the forest, and there of surpassing delight a place did they behold. Adorned was it with lakes and trees and shrubs and fruits.

220. There with fullest joy did they frolic, and with many and many a kind of childish game did they disport. Here did they run and there they ran, as hide-and-seek they played.

221. Here did some pretend to be horses and others riders, there others played at being elephants' howdahs, there others, riding on each other's shoulders, played at the game of 'Śukra's palankeen.'

222. Kṛṣṇa stealthily slippeth among the kine, and terrifieth them by pretending to be a lion. Then clapping his hands doth he return with bursts of laughter.

223. Śrīdāman[1] came running to Kṛṣṇa. Quoth he to him, 'here be a grove filled with fruit. Merry should we be when playing there.

224. 'But what are we to do? In that grove there is a Rākṣasa. The forms of asses have he and all his crew assumed.' So Kṛṣṇa heard, and then he understood.

225. That Rākṣasa was Dhēnuka hight. They went, they fell upon him, they utterly destroyed him, and Haladhara Rāma his vital breaths tore out.

226. Thus was the Rākṣasa destroyed, and they began their frolics; fruit of many kinds did they eat, and then returned they home. To Kṛṣṇa's frolics do I dedicate myself.

---

[1] See verse 253.

yus lagi Krushna-jyuwanis nāwas ta
tas kari Krushna-jyuv sarŏ wŏpakār
yiti yesh nith ta wāti Vishnu-bawanas ta
lāgas bŏh dasta dasta pampōsh. 227

pör^{i} pör^{i} Krushna-jyuwanis nāwas ta
pör^{i} pör^{i} tasandis autāras
pör^{i} pör^{i} tasandis shŏba tsarētas ta. lāgas etc. 228.

XIII.

dŏha aki nēth pöṭh^{i} drāy prātas ta
gūr^{i}-shur^{i} ta kāmadīna hēth khēlān
Jamunāyē bāṭh^{i} bāṭh^{i} lȧg^{i} phēranas ta
lāgas bŏh dasta dasta pampōsh. 229

akis shāyi ġara ôs^{u} Kāli-nāgas ta
tati sör^{i} trēsh cĕth ta bĕsŏr ġay
Krushnañi drēshṭi sũty pĕy sŏranas ta. lāgas etc. 230.

wuchun zi Kāli-nāġ chuh manz zalas ta
tawa kani zal tati bĕha-sost^{u} ôs^{u}
sŏbāwa sũty pĕv dushṭ gālanas ta. lāgas etc. 231.

khasith kuli pĕṭha krakh kür^{u}nas ta
tsari-mŏnji-wāda sũty tambalôwun
Kāli-nāġ khara ġav ta log^{u} wuchanas ta. lāgas etc.
232.

zalas tȧm^{i} pata khŏluw^{u} kor^{u}nas ta
Kāli-nāġ tsakhi ġav tala hyor^{u} khot^{u}
Krushnan zalas manz wŏṭh löy^{u}nas ta. lāgas etc. 233.

Kāli-nöġ^{i} bal hôw^{u} Krushna-zīwas ta
shur^{i} sör^{i} baṭhi pĕṭha kõpani lȧg^{i}
Haladar Rām wôt^{u} maṭha karanas ta. lāgas etc. 234.

Nanda-gōrin^{i} lȧg^{i} sör^{i} kõpanas ta
yĕch yĕch lakhĕn tati sõpȧnikh
söriy wŏthith āy pata Krushnas ta. lāgas etc. 235

ḍyūṭhukh Kāli-nāġ sās kala tas ta
Krushna-jyuv roṭ^{u}mot^{u} tal sarpan
Yĕshōdā ta söriy tsāy wadanas ta. lāgas etc. 236.

227. He who beareth in his heart the name of Kṛṣṇa, to him will Kṛṣṇa every favour render. In this world glory will he win, and thereafter the abode of Viṣṇu will he reach. To him posy and posy do I offer lotuses.

228. Ever dedicating myself to Kṛṣṇa's name, ever dedicating myself to his incarnation, ever dedicating myself to his auspicious deeds, to him posy and posy do I offer lotuses.

XIII. THE CONQUEST OF KĀLĪYA NĀGA. (Bhāg. Pu. X, xvi, xvii.)

229. Once on a day, as ever, went forth at dawn the herd lads with their kine a-frolicking, and all along the Yamunā bank did they begin to wander.

230. At a certain place was the home of Kālīya Nāga. There did they all drink, and straightway fell they all aswoon. But conscious became they again when Kṛṣṇa cast his glance upon them.

231. He saw that in the water was Kālīya Nāga, and through that cause was the water fraught with poison. So, as his nature ever was, to destroy that evil one he set himself.

232. Into a tree he climbed and from it sent he forth a challenge and loudly clapped his hands. Thus became Kālīya Nāga attent, and he began to gaze at him.

233. Next Kṛṣṇa stirred the water up and muddied it, till Kālīya Nāga wroth became, and to the surface ascended from below. Then into the water Kṛṣṇa leaped upon him.

234. Against Kṛṣṇa great might did Kālīya Nāga display, and on the bank began all the lads to tremble, till up Haladhara Rāma came to comfort them.

235. To tremble began all the household of Nanda the cowherd, and there, in the house, did many evil portents hap; so all arose, and in the search for Kṛṣṇa hurried forth.

236. There saw they Kālīya Nāga and his thousand heads, and by the serpent[1] Kṛṣṇa downward pressed; and as they looked, Yaśōdā and all began to wail.

---

[1] Kālīya Nāga was a serpent with a thousand heads

wuchān chih kĕh bal thow^{u}mot^{u} na tas ta
Krushna-jyuv kalav pĕṭh^{i} wŏṭa lāyān
Krushnañi lata-mŏnji rath phoṭ^{u} tas ta
lāgas bŏh dasta dasta pampōsh. 237.

anta-kāl wātani log^{u} sarpas ta
sarpiñĕ āyēyĕ shĕran sārĕy
sŏndari rūpa lajĕ zāra-pāras ta. lāgas etc. 238.

sŏbāw zār bōzanuk^{u} Shrī-Krushnas ta
tōṭhyōkh ta dop^{u}nas 'nīrith ṭsal.'
saruph ti mŏkalith log^{u} ṭsalanas ta. lāgas etc. 239.

path-kāli sarpa-wair ôs^{u} Garuḍas ta
yāñ saruph ḍēshihē tāñ khĕyihēs
saraph āy ṭanga ta ān mŏñ^{u}has ta. lāgas etc. 240.

rĕta pȧt^{i} saruphāh khyon^{u} gonḍ^{u}has ta
prath kaīsi anwār panüñ^{ü} ös^{ü}
Garuḍ anwāri prāri rĕtas ta. lāgas etc. 241.

anwār yĕli wöṭs^{ü} Kāli-nāgas ta
bala-sost^{u} Garuḍas laḍanas āv
pūsh^{u} na ta ṭsalanas wath āyĕs ta. lāgas etc. 242.

ati ôs^{u} ryoshwāh akh boḍ^{u} tapas ta
Kāli-nāg yith ta shĕran ās
ryosh^{u} Garuḍas athi kĕtha diyihēs ta. lāgas etc. 243.

tana pĕṭha Kāli-nāg ṭshĕpi zalas ta
basawun^{u} tati ôs^{u} shur^{i} ta böṭs^{ü} hĕth
kaḍith ṭshun^{u} Krushna-jyuv^{i} ta gav samudras ta.
lāgas etc. 244.

drāv yĕli Krushna-jyuv manza zalas ta
khōṭsān mājĕ log^{u} bĕbi aṭsanē
pör^{i} pör^{i} lagahös prath vihas ta. lāgas etc. 245.

---

1 Regarding Garuḍa, see note to verse 58.

2 That is to say, he had been appearing in the character of a mighty warrior.

237. Then see they that the serpent hath no power left. From head to head Kṛṣṇa on its heads was leaping; and at each kick of Kṛṣṇa forth spouted blood.

238. The serpent's last hour to approach began, and suppliants for mercy to Kṛṣṇa came all his wives, and in beauteous form began they to implore him.

239. Prone to hear supplication is Kṛṣṇa's quality. Gracious to them became he, and to the serpent said he 'Flee thou from hence.' And thus released the serpent fled away.

240. (Bhāg. Pu. X, xvii.) In olden time did Garuḍa [1] hold the snakes in hate, and every serpent that he saw him would he devour; till harassed so did they become that to obey his commands they did agree.

241. And thus were the terms of peace. Each month should Garuḍa one serpent devour, each as his turn came round, and he should wait a month for the appointed turn.

242. But when to Kālīya Nāga the turn came round, mighty in strength, at Garuḍa he came to fight. But he could not prevail, nor could he find a way to flee.

243. Now in that place there was a certain mighty saint plunged in austerities. To him did Kālīya flee, and with him refuge took. Then how could the saint deliver him into Garuḍa's hand?

244. From that day, with his wives and children, did Kālīya hidden in the water dwell; and when he by Kṛṣṇa thence was driven, to the Ocean did he take his way.

245. When Kṛṣṇa came forth from the water, he crept like a frightened child into his mother's bosom.[2] To each part he played may I dedicate myself.

---

and now he suddenly changed his appearance, and became the child again. The author dedicates himself to each of the many rôles assumed by Kṛṣṇa.

möj^{u} pör^{i} lagĕs pān wandanas ta
byon^{u} byon^{u} nālamat^{i} sör^{i} karanas
dapān zi 'röch^{u} Dáy^{i} kĕtha kür^{u}nas' ta
lāgas bŏh dasta dasta pampōsh. 246.

pör^{i} pör^{i} tasandis prath tsarĕtas ta
khēlanas laḍanas biyĕ khōtsanas
biyĕ Vishnu-māyĕ sūty mạsh^{e}rāwanas ta. lāgas etc. 247.

yus lagi Krushna-jyuwanis nāwas ta
tas kari Krushna-jyuv sarŏ wŏpakār
yiti yĕsh nith ta wāti Vishnu-bawanas ta. lāgas etc. 248.

pör^{i} pör^{i} Krushna-jyuwanis nāwas ta
pör^{i} pör^{i} tasandis autāras
pör^{i} pör^{i} tasandis shŏba tsarĕtas ta. lāgas etc. 249.

XIV.

grīshmani rĕta āy pōsh phŏlanas ta
Krushna-jyuv tsarĕ log^{u} khēla karanē
khēlanas tasandis pān wandahōs ta
lāgas bŏh dasta dasta pampōsh. 250.

dŏha aki ras log^{u} tas khēlanas ta
Pralamba rākhyus manz-bāg tsākh
shur^{i}-vih lögith log^{u} gindanas ta. lāgas etc. 251.

pānawöñ^{u} khāsĕn lág^{i} gindanas ta
yus hārihē tas khôs^{u} dyun^{u} ôs^{u}
Haladar hĕyihē na khôs^{u} Krushnas ta. lāgas etc. 252.

khôs^{u} khot^{u} Shrīdāmun^{u} Krushnas ta
Krushna-jyuv pāna moṭ^{u} dörith ta rūd^{u}
Shrīdām aṭa-bāri khot^{u} Krushnas ta. lāgas etc. 253

246. For him doth his mother offer herself as a sacrifice, and one by one do all embrace him as they cry, 'Wondrous was it how God protected him.'

247. To each deed of his do I dedicate myself, to his frolics, to his fighting, to his baby fear, and yet again to his making them forget (his godhead) by his Illusive Power.

248. He who beareth in his heart the name of Kṛṣṇa, to him will Kṛṣṇa every favour render. In this world glory will he win, and thereafter the abode of Viṣṇu will he reach. To him posy and posy do I offer lotuses.

249. Ever dedicating myself to Kṛṣṇa's name, ever dedicating myself to his incarnation, ever dedicating myself to his auspicious deeds, to him posy and posy do I offer lotuses.

XIV. THE FATE OF PRALAMBA. THE FOREST CONFLAGRATION.

(Bhāg. Pu. X, xviii, xix.)

250. In the season of summer the flowers began to bloom, and many were the frolics that Kṛṣṇa played. To his frolics would I dedicate myself.

251. Once on a day, when in his frolics he was full of joy, Pralamba, the Rākṣasa, entered their midst. The form of a lad did he take, and with them he began to play.

252. Among themselves began they to play the game 'Khāsĕn,' and this was the manner of it, that when one (party of boys) was defeated (in a game), the lads of that party should carry the lads of the other party on their shoulders. (Haladhara was the leader of one party and Kṛṣṇa of the other.) Haladhara had not to take Kṛṣṇa on his shoulders (because his party won).

253. Śrīdāman[1] (was of the winning party and had the right to) mount on Kṛṣṇa's shoulders, so Kṛṣṇa stood and offered his back, and Śrīdāman rode upon it.

[1] See verse 223. Probaby the Sudāman of verse 423 and of chapter xlvii.

Haladȧr^{i} khôs^{u} khôr^{u} shur^{i}-asŏras ta
aṭa-bāri khŏrith ta kaḍith nyūn
ṭam^{i} ti zôn^{u} mushtị aki prān koḍ^{u}nas ta
lāgas bŏh dasta dasta pampōsh. 254.

maza-mȧt^{i} shur^{i} sŏr^{i} tsāy vĕṭhanas ta
Haladar Rāmas lȧg^{i} tŏṭanē
ākŏsh^{i} dīv lȧg^{i} pōsh warshĕnas ta. lāgas etc. 255.

tawa pata yĕli lȧg^{i} garạ gatshanas ta
wanas manz dŏd^{i} ogun log^{u}mot^{u} ôs^{u}
ȧch^{i} ṭuwanŏvith ṭa wŏt^{i} pānas ta. lāgas etc. 256.

yus lagi Krushna-jyuwanis nāwas ta
tas kari Krushna-jyuv sarŏ wŏpakār
yiti yĕsh nith ta wāti Vishnu-bawanas ta. lāgas etc. 257.

pŏr^{i} pŏr^{i} Krushna-jyuwanis nāwas ta
pŏr^{i} pŏr^{i} tasandis autāras
pŏr^{i} pŏr^{i} tasandis shŏba tsarĕtas ta. lāgas etc. 258.

XV.

Krushna-jyuv nērihē yĕli khēlanas ta
shur^{i} hĕth shur^{i}-bāshĕ karān ôs^{u}
bŏh ti shur^{i}-bāshĕn pŏr^{i} lagahŏs ta
lāgas bŏh dasta dasta pampōsh. 259.

mŏrȧlī wāyĕnas pray gayĕ tas ta
mŏrȧlī wāyān Mŏrȧlīdar
mŏrȧlī wāyūñ^{u} bŏh ti bōzahŏs ta. lāgas etc. 260.

yāñ lagihē suh mŏrȧlī wāyĕnas ta
kāmadīna rōzahŏn gāsa-khĕna path
wȧtsh^{i} dŏd cĕna tath kan dāranas ta. lāgas etc. 261.

mŏrȧlī wāyān log^{u} nēranas ta
gōpiyĕn tāñ ôs^{u} man nērān
lagahŏn Krushnas pata lāranas ta. lāgas etc. 262.

254. Haladhara had the right to mount on the shoulders of (Pralamba) the Asura disguised as a lad. Pralamba took him up as a rider and at once carried he him off. But Haladhara knew what he would have done, and with a single fist-blow tore out his life-breath.

255. Joyfully did all the lads exult; Haladhara Rāma did they praise, while the gods rained flowers from the sky.

256. (Bhāg. Pu. X, xix.) Afterwards as they were about to return home, in the forest there blazed a mighty conflagration. But Kṛṣṇa made them close their eyes, and safely reached they their homes.

257. He who beareth in his heart the name of Kṛṣṇa, to him will Kṛṣṇa every favour render. In this world glory will he win, and thereafter the abode of Viṣṇu will he reach. To him posy and posy do I offer lotuses.

258. Ever dedicating myself to Kṛṣṇa's name, ever dedicating myself to his incarnation, ever dedicating myself to his auspicious deeds, posy and posy do I offer lotuses.

XV. THE ENCHANTING FLUTE, THE MOONLIGHT SPORTS, THE THEFT OF THE HERD-DAMSELS' GARMENTS, THE RĀSA DANCE. (Bhāg. Pu. X, xxi, xxii, xxix–xxxiv.)

259. When to frolic Kṛṣṇa would go forth, taking the lads with him, childish pranks did he play. I also would dedicate myself to those childish pranks.

260. In playing the flute did he take delight, and from his playing the flute (gained he the name of) Muralīdhara (the Fluteplayer). Would that I also the playing of his flute might hear.

261. As he would begin playing on the flute, the milch-kine standing still did cease their grazing, and the calves would cease from drinking (their mothers') milk to listen to the sound.

262. As he went forth playing on his flute, forth too went the hearts of the herdmaidens, and after him would they begin to run.

gōpiyĕ sārĕ tati lajĕ matanas ta
Kāmadēv wuch^{i} wuch^{i} rōzihēkh na sŏr
lagahŏn kāmanā tsūr^{u} baranas ta
lāgas ƀŏh dasta dasta pampōsh. 263.

wuñĕ ôs^{u} bāla-pān Krushna-zīwas ta
Kāmadēv pānay kyāh wȧn^{i}zĕs
kāminiyĕ kāmanā kō-na baranas ta. lāgas etc. 264.

nĕth prath gōpiyĕ pata lāranas ta
kōm^{u}-kŏṭ^{u} trŏvith āsa pata tas
nālamati raṭahŏn Kāmadĕwas ta. lāgas etc. 265.

gōpiyĕn man log^{u} Kāmadēwas ta
samith sārĕv^{u}y dôrukh vrath
'srĕh sôn^{u} wuzi-nā bāla-Krushnas' ta. lāgas etc.
266.

korukh Mọnj^{u}hōranis rĕtas ta
Jamunā baṭhis pĕṭh ārādan
Kātyāyĕniyĕ lajĕ pūz karanas ta. lāgas etc. 267.

dīviyĕ āyĕ sārĕ war manganas ta
'Kāmadēv Krushna-jyuv asĕ wȧr^{i}tan'
yihay kāmanā lajĕ baranas ta. lāgas etc. 268.

dīvī tōṭhēyĕkh tath pūzanas ta
gōpiyĕn kāmanā sĕd sŏpūñ^{u}
pānay mani āv Krushna-zīwas ta. lāgas etc. 269.

prabŏt^{i} watsha yĕli snān karanas ta
Krushn ākh pata pata phĕran hĕth gōkh
kulis pĕṭh mŏrȧlī log^{u} wāyĕnas ta. lāgas etc. 270.

gōpiyĕ boṭh^{u} khatsa lajĕ tshāḍanas ta
prath kăh panunuy tshāḍani lūj^{u}
nĕtha-nañĕ biyĕ watsha manz zalas ta. lāgas etc. 271.

263. There did all the herdmaidens begin to be maddened, and swooned they as they kept looking on his Cupid-form. Filled with great longing for him did they eke become.

264. By this time Kṛṣṇa had attained to youthhood, and why need we speak of him who was himself a very Cupid, and how should not the damsels have been filled with longing?

265. Ever after him ran the herd-damsels, abandoning their household duties all, and with embraces would they clasp his Cupid-form.

266. To this Cupid so devoted became the hearts of the herd-damsels, that all with one consent they took vows of fasting, prating 'May love for us in Kṛṣṇa be awakened.'

267. (Bhāg. Pu. X, xxii.) In the month Mọnjᵘhōr (November-December) on the bank of the Yamunā did they offer prayers and worship the goddess Kātyāyanī.[1]

268. Before the goddess came they all to ask a boon, 'May Cupid Kṛṣṇa choose us for himself!' for this alone was the longing that they felt.

269. By their worship was the goddess rendered gracious, and the longing of the herd-girls was fulfilled, and thus into the thought of Kṛṣṇa himself did they come.

270. At dawn, when they descended to bathe, Kṛṣṇa came along after them and carried off their garments. Then up in a tree began he his flute to sound.

271. The herd-damsels ascended the bank and began to search. Each for her own garments began to seek. Then, finding themselves naked, again into the water they descended.

---

[1] One of the forms of Durgā, the spouse of Śiva.

kulis pĕṭh ḍyūṭhukh phĕran athi tas ta
nĕtha-nañĕ kĕtha-kana hāwanas pān
zala manza lajĕ tas zāra-pāras ta
lāgas bŏh dasta dasta pampōsh. 272.

'triyĕn zi kĕtha pazi nanga rōzanas ta
phĕran dita asĕ lagōy pör^{i}'
dop^{u}nakh zi 'rūziv-ay nanga pānas' ta. lāgas etc.
273.

dop^{u}has zi 'asĕ gatshi bang vratas' ta
dop^{u}nakh zi 'tuhond^{u} vrath saphal gav
yihay kāmanā ös^{u} tŏhĕ manas' ta. lāgas etc. 274.

zāra-pāra kôtwāh lajĕ karanas ta
'yima kama shur^{i}-bāshĕ, yih kyāh gav'
būz^{u}nakh na, mŏrálī ôs^{u} wāyĕnas ta. lāgas etc. 275.

tūri-dādi nangay boṭh^{u} khatsas ta
dop^{u}nakh zi 'namaskār hĕth rūziv'
namaskār dôrukh ta gayĕ nanga-masta. lāgas etc.
276.

kuli pĕtha wast^{a}r log^{u} dinas ta
yŏssa yiyi nanga brōṭh tas diyi brōṭh
maza log^{u} tath khēli bāla-Krushnas ta. lāgas etc.
277.

kuli pĕtha yāñ woth^{u} ta pān wond^{u}has ta
war mong^{u}has zi 'asĕ kāmanā pūr.'
wātsa-band hyot^{u}has bāla-Krushnas ta. lāgas etc.
278.

gōpiyĕv yiy wātsa-band hyot^{u}has ta
'asĕ sūty zi rāthāh krīḍā kar'
gōpiyĕn kal rūz^{u} táth[1] wātsas ta. lāgas etc. 279.

röts^{u} aki pūrn ös^{u} zūn^{u} rātas ta
Krushna-jyuv mŏrálī wāyān drāv
wātsa-band pālun pĕv Krushnas ta. lāgas etc. 280.

---

[1] In the Bhāgavata Purāṇa, this and the four following chapters (*adhyāyas*)

272. On the tree, holding their garments in his hand, did they see him; but, naked as they were, how could they show to him their forms? So from the water began they to him to make entreaties.

273. 'How becometh it for women to stay naked? To thee do we dedicate ourselves; give us, pray, our garments.' Quoth he to them, 'Aye, if (before me) naked as ye are ye stand.'

274. Quoth they to him, 'Our vow and fast broken will become.' Quoth he to them, 'Your vow hath become fulfilled, for this be the very longing that was within your hearts.'

275. How many entreaties did they make to him! 'What are these childish pranks! what be this that unto us hath happed!' But he heeded them not, and his flute continued he to play.

276. Tormented by the cold, naked as they were, on to the bank they climbed. Quoth he to them, 'There stand ye, and reverence to me make.' There were they stark naked as they bowed to him.

277. From the tree made he ready the garments to hand to them. 'She who first cometh before me naked, to her will I give her clothes.' So, with this frolic did he thus divert himself.

278. No sooner had he from the tree descended than to him did they their bodies dedicate, and begged from him the boon that he their longings would fulfil. Thus from the young Kṛṣṇa took they his spoken promise.

279. And this was the spoken promise that they took from him. (To their) 'Sport with us for but a single night' (he answered 'yea'), and only with that promise was the herd-damsels' yearning stayed.

280. (Bhāg. Pu. X, xxix.[1]) By night, all through the night shone the full moon, and playing on the flute forth Kṛṣṇa went, for his uttered promise needs must he keep.

---

together form a very famous section known separately as the *Rāsa-pañcādhyāyī*.

matsa gayĕ gōpiyĕ lajĕ lāranas ta
kāmi-kŏcĕ gara bār trövith kĕth
Krushna-jyuv brõṭh brõṭh sārĕ pata tas ta
lāgas bŏh dasta dasta pampōsh. 281

phērān drāyĕ yĕli phērĕ wanas ta
Krushna-jyuv mŏrālī wāyān ôs^{u}
gōpiyĕn ras log^{u} tath wāyĕnas ta. lāgas etc. 282.

khēlān matsa yĕli gayĕ khēlanas ta
manz-bāga tshạl^{a}rith pān khoṭ^{u}nakh
akhāh niyĕn sũty pānas ta. lāgas etc. 283.

gōpiyĕn vĕh pyōkh ta lajĕ matanas ta
matsa zan kulĕn lajĕ pritshanē
'nēb kuni āsi-nā bāla-Krushnas' ta. lāgas etc. 284.

kuni tshāy gatshihēkh ta pata lāranas ta
kuni Krushna-pád^{i} vina nēb labahön
padi padi Krushna-pád^{i} mīṭh^{i} karanas ta. lāgas etc. 285.

pod^{u} pod^{u} Krushnun^{u} āsa wuchanas ta
zanāna-podwāh ti sũty wuch^{u}has
phyāh[1] lajĕ baranē pön^{i}-pānas ta. lāgas etc. 286.

'kŏssa sana gōpī sũty āsi tas ta
kŏssa sana bāgĕ-büd^{ü} priy gayĕ tas
kami sana asĕ manza man nyuv tas' ta. lāgas etc. 287.

wuchān chĕh triyĕ-pod^{u} na sũty biyĕ tas ta
akis shāyĕ Krushnun^{u} kunuy pod^{u}
zônukh zi khör^{ü}n bŏna nakhas ta. lāgas etc. 288.

akis shāyĕ gōpiyāh ös^{ü} wadanas ta
pryutsh^{u}has ta dop^{u}nakh 'tshạl^{a}rith gōm
ahankār gayām zi ṭöṭh^{ü} gayĕsas' ta. lāgas etc. 289.

'trövith gōm ta kyāh wana kas' ta
timan^{ü}y sũty sa ti lārani lüj^{ü}
matsar tihond^{u} yiyi na zi wananas ta. lāgas etc. 290.

---

[1] V. l. *batsh.*

281. Maddened did the herd-damsels pursuing him run forth abandoning their homes and household duties. Ahead ahead went Kṛṣṇa and they all after him.

282. Strolling went they forth, through the forest did they roam. Kṛṣṇa the flute kept playing, and at the sound love attacked the herd-damsels.

283. As they frolicked, madly did they frolic. Then, deceiving them, from their midst he hid himself, and one herd-damsel with him took.

284. (Bhāg. Pu. X, xxx.) Like unto poison was this to the other damsels, and bereft of reason did they become. Like mad women did they ask the trees, but no trace of Kṛṣṇa can they find.

285. Here 'tis as though his shadow appeared, and after it they ran; there find they the prints of Kṛṣṇa's feet, but find no sign of him. Footprint by footprint do they follow him, kissing each mark of Kṛṣṇa's feet.

286. Each footprint of Kṣṛṇa do they scan, and see the footprints of a woman with him, as among themselves distraught do they become.

287. 'There appeareth to be some herd-damsel with him; some happy fair hath gained his love. Who can she be that hath taken his heart away from us?'

288. Again they mark that the woman's footprints are no longer with him, in one place there is but the print of Kṛṣṇa's foot alone. Then made they no doubt but that he had on to his shoulder lifted her.

289. Elsewhere they came upon a weeping herd-damsel. They asked her, and quoth she, 'me hath he deceived, from me hath he gone; for at the thought that it was I who was his dearling I had been filled with self conceit.

290. So he abandoned me. What can I say to whom?' and with them too did she begin to run. Crazy were they all, nor can their madness be described.

kă̄h nād lāyihēs ta kă̄h gĕvihēs ta
kă̄h rōzi Krushna-dyān mani dörith
kă̄h batsh băr[1] băr[1] pān mārĕs ta
lāgas bŏh dasta dasta pampōsh. 291.

pānay biyĕ ākh pān wond[u]has ta
sārĕv[ü]y yikawaṭa nāla-mati roṭ[u]
prath kă̄h dapi mĕy mot[u] kor[u]mas ta. lāgas etc. 292.

tōshān ta khēlān khēla karanas ta
māyā Krushnüñ[ü] khēlān ös[ü]
khēlun[u] mani ākh rāsa-manḍalas ta. lāgas etc. 293.

manḍul karith ta lăg[i] khēlanas ta
Krushna-jyuv ta gōpī prath nakha ös[ü]
manz-bāg ti Krushna-jyuv wād tulanas ta. lāgas etc. 294.

shĕ-rĕts[ü] rāth gayĕ tath rātas ta
dēwatā söriy wuchanas ös[i]
Vishnu-māy yiyi na zi kaĭsi wuchanas ta. lāgas etc. 295.

dēwatā ta gandarwa ös[i] gĕwanas ta
Nārod[u] vīnā wāyān[1] ôs[u]
tih kĕh yiyi na zi kaĭsi wananas ta. lāgas etc. 296.

tawa pata biyĕ lăg[i] khēla karanas ta
nānā răng[i] pānavüñ[ü] khēlani lăg[i]
pör[i] pör[i] lăg[i]zēs prath khēlanas ta. lāgas etc. 297.

kuni gur[u] lögith guri khāranas ta
kuni host[u] lögith pakanāwanas
kuni pölikh zan pān tsānanas ta. lāgas etc. 298.

Shēnkara-yĕtshy ākh tath samayĕs ta
gōpiyĕ sārĕy gūr[i] hĕth gav
Krushnani atha gav mŏkti-dwāras ta. lāgas etc. 299.

jai-kār Krushna-jyuwanis khēlanas ta
jai-kār gōpiyĕn bāgĕwatiyĕn
jai-kār Shukadēwanis wananas ta. lāgas etc. 300.

---

1 The Gandharvas are the heavenly quiristers. Nārada is the musician of the gods. His special instrument is the lute.

2 According to the Bhāgavata Purāṇa his name was Śaṅkhacūḍa, and the carrying off took place subsequently. He was a demon, a Daitya, not a Yakṣa.

291. Some called to him, some sang to him; some, meditating upon Kṛṣṇa in their hearts, stood still; others beat their own bodies babbling and distraught.

292. Again himself he came to them, and to him did they their bodies dedicate; all came to him and together seized him in embrace; and each saith to herself, 'It is I alone who did embrace him.'

293. Rejoicing and frolicking did they make their sport. Kṛṣṇa's Illusive Form, too, sported with them, and into his mind came the frolic of the Rāsa dance.

294. They formed the circle and began the revel, and Kṛṣṇa (multiplied himself) and by the side of each herd-damsel (danced), while in the centre clapping his hands to time the dancing also Kṛṣṇa stood.

295. That single night became a night that lasted for six months, and all the gods were gazing at the scene, but by no one, not e'en by them, can all Viṣṇu's Illusive Power be seen.

296. The gods and the Gandharvas[1] songs did sing, Nārada was playing on his lute. But naught of that can any one describe.

297. Thereafter again began they to frolic, and mutually did they sport in varied manner. To each sport shouldst thou dedicate thyself.

298. (As Kṛṣṇa's childish pranks came to their minds) here damsels pretended to be horses and others to be their riders; there some pretended to be elephants while others drove them; there some pretended to make others enter palankeens.

299. (Bhāg. Pu. X,xxxiv.) At that hour came Śaṅkara[2] the Yakṣa, and he the herd-damsels and the herdsmen carried off; but by Kṛṣṇa's hand the door of salvation did he attain.[3]

300. Victory be to Kṛṣṇa's sporting, victory be to the herd-damsels highly blessed, and victory be to the telling of the tale by Śukadēva.[4]

---

[3] The door of salvation is death. As he was killed by Kṛṣṇa he necessarily received salvation.

[4] He was the original reciter of the Bhāgavata Purāṇa.

gōpiyĕn hīth ôs^u^ mŏkth karanas ta
lōla sūty sārĕy karĕn mŏkth
Vishnu-māyĕ yiyi na zi kĕ̄h ti tsēnanas ta
lāgas bŏh dasta dasta pampōsh. 301

yus lagi Krushna-jyuwanis nāwas ta
tas kari Krushna-jyuv sarŏ wŏpakār
yiti yĕsh nith ta wāti Vishnu-bawanas ta. lāgas etc. 302

pör^i^ pör^i^ Krushna-jyuwanis nāwas ta
pör^i^ pör^i^ tasandis autāras
pör^i^ pör^i^ tasandis shŏba tsarĕtas ta. lāgas etc. 303

XVI.

dŏha aki bŏcha lüj^ü^ Krushna-zīwas ta
khēli-bājĕn ti bŏcha sārĕn^i^ lüj^ü^
gara dūr^i^ ôsukh wanahan kas ta
lāgas bŏh dasta dasta pampōsh. 304.

Jamunāyĕ baṭhi ôs^u^ and wanas ta
rĕsh^i^ ös^i^ tath wani karān jag
Krushna-jyuv^i^ shur^i^ sūz^i^ yĕgñĕ-manḍalas ta. lāgas etc. 305.

lajyēy Krushnüñ^ü^ bŏcha wananas ta
'sôn^u^ Krushna-jyuv chuwa khyon^u^ mangān'
rĕshĕn gaṭakār ôs^u^ bōzanas ta. lāgas etc. 306.

'pröpyun^u^ zi hāwun chuh wŏñ yĕgñĕs ta
dēwa-bali-dān dith ta ada bōzav
gŏḍa kĕtha gōrĕn pazi dinas' ta. lāgas etc. 307.

bŏcha-hát^i^ phīrith ta āy Krushnas ta
rĕsh^i^-bāyĕn nishĕ biyĕ sūzin
rĕsh^i^-bāyau būz^u^ ta tsāyĕ tōshĕnas ta. lāgas etc. 308.

dŏyĕ atha haṭi-rath lajĕ wandanas ta
'Krushna-jyuv tūṭh^u^ asĕ pāna Bagawān'
myūṭh^u^ myūṭh^u^ khyon^u^ hĕth ta lāryēyĕs ta. lāgas etc. 309.

301. Al this was done that the herd-damsels might have salvation, and by their love saved by him became they all. (So beyond limit is) Viṣṇu's Illusive Power, that naught of it can reach the comprehension.

302. He who beareth in his heart the name of Kṛṣṇa, to him will Kṛṣṇa every favour render. In this world glory will he win, and thereafter the abode of Viṣṇu will he reach. To him posy and posy do I offer lotuses.

303. Ever dedicating myself to Kṛṣṇa's name, ever dedicating myself to his incarnation, ever dedicating myself to his auspicious deeds, posy and posy do I offer lotuses.

XVI. THE CHURLISH SAGES. (Bhāg. Pu. X, xxiii.)

304. Once on a day it happed that Kṛṣṇa hungry became, and so did all his playmates. Their home was far distant, and to whom should they tell their state ?

305. On the bank of the Yamunā was the forest's edge, and in that forest were certain sages busy on a solemn sacrifice. So to the sacrificial circle did Kṛṣṇa send the lads.

306. They began to tell them of Kṛṣṇa's hunger. 'From you doth our Kṛṣṇa ask for food.' But when they heard it, upon the sages did the darkness (of this world's illusion) fall.

307. 'Now must we present the offering of the sacrifice. When we have given our oblation to the gods, then will we list to you. How is it meet that we should offer gifts to cowherds first' ?

308. Hungry and faint did they return to Kṛṣṇa, and back he sent them to the sages' wives. Then gladdened, when they heard the tale, were these.

309. With both hands did they offer (as it were) the life-blood of their necks. 'Kṛṣṇa Bhagavān,' cried they, 'on us hath favour shown.' So took they up sweet food of many kinds, and forth they ran.

pādan tal pĕyĕ Rāma-Krushnas ta
tihandĕn bāgĕn namaskār
Krushna-jyuv tōṭhyōkh ta gayĕ harshĕs ta.
lāgas bŏh dasta dasta pampōsh. 310.

āgyā dits^{u}nakh ta gayĕ pānas ta
Krushna-rūpa ôsukh ḍĕka phŏlawun^{u}
Dayĕ-gath yiyi na zi kaīsi tsēnanas ta. lāgas etc. 311.

brāhmanau wuchĕ pĕy britsh baranas ta
tihandi rūpa ôs^{u} sūryun^{u} gāsh
dĕkh-kār karani lȧg^{i} pön^{i}-pānas ta. lāgas etc. 312.

dĕkh-kār tihandis agyānas ta
jai-kār ḍĕka-bajĕ titsha brāhmañĕn
namaskār Dayĕ-güts^{ü} ta Krushna-zīwas ta. lāgas etc. 313.

yus lagi Krushna-jyuwanis nāwas ta
tas kari Krushna-jyuv sarŏ wŏpakār
yiti yĕsh nith ta wāti Vishnu-bawanas ta. lāgas etc. 314.

pör^{i} pör^{i} Krushna-jyuwanis nāwas ta
pör^{i} pör^{i} tasandis autāras
pör^{i} pör^{i} tasandis shŏba tsarĕtas ta. lāgas etc. 315.

XVII.

Gōkula rīth ös^{ü} yĕgñĕ karanas ta
gūr^{i} sör^{i} Yindra-shānth karān ös^{i}
manza lȧg^{i} karanē tath yĕgñĕs ta.
lāgas bŏh dasta dasta pampōsh. 316.

Krushna-jyuv^{i} pryutshun Nanda-gōpas ta
'Yindra-shānth karanas kyāh hyuh^{u} chuh phal'
dop^{u}nas 'Yind^{a}r lagi rūd karanas' ta. lāgas etc. 317.

'rūd wāli gāsa zĕn prath wanas ta
lūkh sör^{i} ta gōv^{ü}-mājĕ baran sŏkh
asĕ ti āsi tawa āy baḍanas' ta. lāgas etc. 318.

dop^{u}nakh zi 'yus kari shānth Yindras ta
tami khŏta wāli na Bagawān rūd
kawa chiwa lȧg^{i}mȧt^{i} agyānas' ta. lāgas etc. 319.

310. At the feet of Rāma and Kṛṣṇa did they fall. Reverence be unto their happy lot! Kṛṣṇa on them showed pleasure, and filled did they become with joy.

311. He gave them leave to depart, and home they went. Happy was the good luck that blossomed forth for them on seeing Kṛṣṇa's form. To no man's comprehension reach the ways of God.

312. When they saw them the Brāhmaṇas began to send forth lamentations, for, as it were, the glory of the sun was caused by the beauty of their wives and to utter curses on themselves did they begin.

313. Shame be on their ignorance! Victory be to Brāhmaṇa women of such great good luck! To the ways of God and to Kṛṣṇa be reverence paid.

314. He who beareth in his heart the name of Kṛṣṇa, to him will Kṛṣṇa every favour render. In this world glory will he win, and thereafter the abode of Viṣṇu will he reach. To him posy and posy do I offer lotuses.

315. Ever dedicating myself to Kṛṣṇa's name, ever dedicating myself to his incarnation, ever dedicating myself to his auspicious deeds, to him posy and posy do I offer lotuses.

XVII. THE UPHOLDING OF GŌVARDHANA. (Bhāg. Pu. X, xxiv–xxvii.)

316. In Gōkula it was the custom of their sacrifices, that to appease Indra the cowherds all their supplications made, and therefore to him did they engage themselves in sacrifice.

317. Kṛṣṇa once of Nanda the cowherd asked, 'What profit cometh from thus to Indra offering propitiation?' Quoth Nanda in reply, 'To us Indra giveth rain'.

318. 'He causeth rain to fall, and in each forest herbs are born. Thus will prosper all the folk and the mother-kine, and thereby shall we too all live long.'

319. Then answered Kṛṣṇa, 'If a man Indra do propitiate, Bhagavān (who is the real giver) doth not cause more rain than before to fall. Why are ye fast bound in ignorance?

'Vishnuy chuh vyöpith tsar-atsaras ta
Vishnuy chuh razō-gŏna wālān rūd
Vishnuy chuh sattŏ-gŏna sūty pālanas' ta.
lāgas bŏh dasta dasta pampōsh. 320.

'dēwatā chih adīn tās^{i} Vishnas ta
pūz^{i}tōn suy ta kariwa sĕd
mŏk^{a}th prāwanīy chĕh Vishnu-baktas' ta. lāgas etc. 321.

'pūzā kar^{i}tav tas Vishnas ta
Gōwardana-parbuth pūzanövith'
lögin söriy brāhman pūzanas ta. lāgas etc. 322.

gōryau būz^{u}has tsākh manas ta
Yindra-sond^{u} mani bayĕ borukh na kĕh
yiy yiy dop^{u}nakh tiy tiy môn^{u}has ta. lāgas etc. 323.

Bagawān pāna ôs^{u} khēlanāwanas ta
tsarĕthāh hôwunakh nowuy now^{u}
pör^{i} pör^{i} lagahös prath tsarĕtas ta. lāgas etc. 324.

Yindras ti tsakh āyĕ gav kūpas ta
atshĕn dārāyi rūd wôl^{u}nakh
rūd ḍās karanas pĕv Gŏkulas ta. lāgas etc. 325.

Krushna-jyuv gōrĕn pĕv rachanas ta
Gōwardana-parbuth kisi dôrun
gūr^{i}-shur^{i} ti lōri sūty ḍokh^{u} tsānanas ta. lāgas etc. 326.

gūr^{i} sör^{i} khyol^{u} hĕth tsāy chapanas ta
Krushna-jyuv chuh parbuth kisĕ pĕṭh hĕth
yĕs rachi Bagawān māri kus tas ta. lāgas etc. 327.

satan dŏhan ôs^{u} Yindra-kūpas ta
kĕtha sana pōshihē Bagawānas
mandoch^{u} ta pānay pĕv pāyĕs ta. lāgas etc. 328.

---

1 Three qualities, or principles, exist in all creation, named respectively *sattva*, or goodness *per se*, *rajas*, or activity *per se* (said to predominate in air), and *tamas*,

320. 'Viṣṇu alone it be that pervadeth all that is,—the living beings and dead matter. Through his principle of Activity causeth Viṣṇu alone the rain to fall, and through his principle of Goodness doth Viṣṇu alone protect and cherish us.[1]

321. 'Of that Viṣṇu alone are the gods the thralls. He alone is of adoration worthy and will give to you success. Yea, it is by him who is devoted to Viṣṇu that salvation alone is to be won.

322. 'To that Viṣṇu offer ye adoration, but worship ye first Mount Gōvardhana. Let all the Brāhmaṇas engage in rites of holy worship.'

323. What the cowherds heard that into their hearts did enter, and into their hearts there came no manner of fear of Indra. So did they to all that Kṛṣṇa said agree.

324. It was Bhagavān Himself who was thus causing a sportive manifestation, and who showed to them a mighty deed, ever new and new in all its parts. To each mighty deed do I dedicate myself.

325. (Bhāg. Pu. X, xxv.) Then Indra's fury rose, and full of wrath did he become. In never ceasing floods caused he rain to fall on them. 'Twas to cause a devastation that on Gōkula the rain did fall.

326. Then fell it to Kṛṣṇa to protect the cowherds. Mount Gōvardhana on his little finger did he uplift, and with their clubs did the herd-lads help to hold it up.

327. Beneath it entered the cowherds and their herds for their protection, while Kṛṣṇa upholdeth it upon his little finger. Who can kill him whom Bhagavān protecteth ?

328. For seven days was Indra in his wrath, but how could he against Bhagavān prevail ? With himself became he ashamed and to his right mind did he come.

---

or darkness (the source of heaviness, ignorance, illusion, lust, anger, pride, sorrow, dulness, and stupidity). Viṣṇu is free from the last named.

wasith pĕṭh pĕv Krushna-pādas ta
dēwatā sör^{i} hĕth ta shĕran āv
'khĕmā mĕ kār^{i}tōm pāpa-pūrnas' ta
lāgas bŏh dasta dasta pampōsh. 329.

Krushna-jyuv^{i} asith war dyut^{u}nas ta
Yindra-rāza sŏrga-lūkh tōshān gav
gūr^{i} lȧg^{i} vĕṭhani ta lȧg^{i} thĕkanas ta. lāgas etc. 330.

akh shur^{u} dapi 'mĕ ti ḍokh^{u} tsôn^{u}mas ta'
akh dapi 'myāñĕy lōrĕ pĕṭh ôs^{u}'
gūr^{i} sör^{i} nānā-rȧṅg^{i} stutā karanas ta. lāgas etc. 331.

namaskār Krushna-jyuwanis tsarĕtas ta
namaskār gūr^{i}-ḍĕḳa-bajĕras tath
namaskār Shukadēwanis wananas ta. lāgas etc. 332.

yus lagi Krushna-jyuwanis nāwas ta
tas kari Krushna-jyuv sarŏ wŏpakār
yiti yĕsh nith ta wāti Vishnu-bawanas ta. lāgas etc. 333.

pör^{i} pör^{i} Krushna-jyuwanis nāwas ta
pör^{i} pör^{i} tasandis autāras
pör^{i} pör^{i} tasandis shŏba tsarĕtas ta. lāgas etc. 334.

XVIII.

bösh^{u}-dŏh Nanda-gūr^{u} woth^{u} snānas ta
Warunȧn^{i} sīwakh ös^{i} phĕrān
raṭith suh nishĕ nyūkh lūka-pālas ta
lāgas bŏh dasta dasta pampōsh. 335.

Krushna-jyuv būzith gav Warunas ta
brŏ̃ṭh yith ta Warun pādan pyōs
dop^{u}nas 'zagi rōzi yi-ti tsĕtaṣ' ta. lāgas etc. 336.

pūzā pölith stutā kür^{u}nas ta
Krushna-jyuv ti dŏda-bab sūty hĕth āv
wôt^{u} yĕli gara ta lȧg^{i} vĕṭhanas ta. lāgas etc. 337.

---

1 Varuṇa was the deity presiding over the western quarter of the universe. Nanda had been, as a good Hindū, fasting on the eleventh day of the fortnight, and on the twelfth bathed on the completion of the fast. He unfortunately bathed at

329. (Bhāg. Pu. X, xxvii.) Down did he descend, and fell at Kṛṣṇa's feet. With all the gods he came, and for mercy did he supplicate. 'Pardon thou me, for I am filled with sin.'

330. Then Kṛṣṇa smiled and gave to him the boon (that he implored). Well pleased went Indra back to heaven, the while the cowherds to exult and boast began.

331. Crieth one lad, 'I too helped the mountain to sustain;' another saith 'Nay, it was on my club that upheld it was,' and all the cowherds joined in varied hymns of praise to Kṛṣṇa.

332. Reverence be to the mighty deed of Kṛṣṇa, reverence be to the greatness of the cowherds' lot, and reverence be to the telling of the tale by Śukadēva.

333. He who beareth in his heart the name of Kṛṣṇa, to him will Kṛṣṇa every favour render. In this world glory will he win, and thereafter the abode of Viṣṇu will he reach. To him posy and posy do I offer lotuses.

334. Ever dedicating myself to Kṛṣṇa's name, ever dedicating myself to his incarnation, ever dedicating myself to his auspicious deeds, posy and posy do I offer lotuses.

XVIII. THE RESCUE OF NANDA FROM VARUṆA. (Bhāg. Pu. X, xxviii.)

335. On the twelfth day of the moon's fortnight, Nanda to bathe descended into the Yamunā. It happed that there certain servants of Varuṇa were wandering, and him they seized and brought before the Guardian of the Quarter.[1]

336. Kṛṣṇa heard this, and straightway went to Varuṇa, but (before he reached him) Varuṇa to meet him came, and at his feet he fell, crying, 'In the world's memory will ever this remain.'

337. Kṛṣṇa did he worship and to him sang he praises, and with his foster-father home returned Kṛṣṇa. When their home they reached, all to exult began.

---

an unlucky moment, when all was dark, and this gave Varuṇa's servants an excuse for seizing him.

gōryau būzith kor^{u} manas ta
    yih zi chuh pānay Shrī-Bagawān
asĕ wātanāvihē Vaikunṭhas ta
    lāgas bŏh dasta dasta pampōsh. 338.

mani kāmanā ākh Day pūranas ta
    tithay Vaikunṭh wôt^{u}mot^{u} ôs^{u}
wuchākh Krushna-jyuv pĕṭh prangas ta. lāgas etc. 339.

dēwatā söriy pūz karaṇas ta
    Nārod^{u} vīnā wāyĕnas ôs^{u}
gūr^{i} söriy ös^{i} dūri wuchanas ta. lāgas etc. 340.

dopukh zi 'asĕ kō-na bāgĕ baḍanas ta
    yiman chuh athi ta kŏchĕ gindun^{u}
Gōkul mộn^{u} tsor^{u} Vaikunṭhas' ta. lāgas etc. 341.

yus lagi Krushna-jyuwanis nāwas ta
    tas kari Krushna-jyuv sarŏ wŏpakār
yiti yĕsh nith ta wāti Vishnu-bawanas ta. lāgas etc. 342.

pör^{i} pör^{i} Krushna-jyuwanis nāwas ta
    pör^{i} pör^{i} tasandis autāras
pör^{i} pör^{i} tasandis shŏba tsarĕtas ta. lāgas etc. 343.

XIX.

Shiwa-sond^{u} dŏh āv Gōkulas ta
    söriy Shiv Shĕk^{a}th pūzani drāy
baḍi lōla bükts^{u} lág^{i} pūz karanas ta
    lāgas bŏh dasta dasta pampōsh. 344.

brȭṭh pĕv saruphāh Nanda-gōpas ta
    shwāsa aki Nanda-gūr^{u} nĕngalith nyūn
Krushnas sör^{i} lág^{i} zāra-pāras ta. lāgas etc. 345.

Krushna-jyuv^{i} lath dith zuv koḍ^{u}nas ta
    vidyādar ôs^{u} ta shāpa mŏkalyōv
pādan tal pĕv Krushna-zīwas ta. lāgas etc. 346.

---

1 Viṣṇu's heaven.

338 To themselves said the cowherds when the story they had heard, 'Of a surety this Kṛṣṇa must be Bhagavān himself, and us Vaikuṇṭha [1] may he cause to reach'?

339. The God (i.e. Kṛṣṇa in his ineffable form) came to fulfil the longing of their hearts, and to that very place itself Vaikuṇṭha came, and there saw they Kṛṣṇa seated on his throne.

340. Worshipping him were all the gods, and Nārada upon his lute was playing, while all the cowherds from afar upon them gazed.

341. Thus cried (the gods), 'Wherefore hath not our lot become so great as that of these cowherds? Here, in their hand and in their bosom sporteth he'. So deemed they Gōkula than Vaikuṇṭha blessèd more.

342. He who beareth in his heart the name of Kṛṣṇa, to him will Kṛṣṇa every service render. In this world glory will he win, and thereafter the abode of Viṣṇu will he reach. To him posy and posy do I offer lotuses.

343. Ever dedicating myself to Kṛṣṇa's name, ever dedicating myself to his incarnation, ever dedicating myself to his auspicious deeds, posy and posy do I offer lotuses.

XIX. NANDA SWALLOWED BY THE SERPENT. (Bhāg. Pu. X, xxxiv.)

344. When in Gōkula there came Śiva's day, they all went forth to worship his Energic Power, and with great love and faith began they their adorations.

345. A certain serpent happened before Nanda, and in a single breath down swallowed him. To Kṛṣṇa then they all began to wail.

346. Kṛṣṇa the serpent kicked, and so expelled his life. A Vidyādhara [2] was he, who thus from a curse became released, and prostrate before Kṛṣṇa's feet he fell.

---

[2] The Vidyādharas are a class of semi-divine beings.

Sŏdarshĕna path-kun nāv ôs^{u} tas ta
Angirasa-rĕsh^{i} ôs^{u} shāph dyut^{u}mot^{u}
prārān ôs^{u} Krushna-autāras ta
lāgas bŏh dasta dasta pampōsh. 347.

yus lagi Krushna-jyuwanis nāwas ta
tas kari Krushna-jyuv sarŏ wŏpakār
yiti yĕsh nith ta wāti Vishnu-bawanas ta. lāgas etc. 348.

prör^{i} prör^{i} Krushna-jyuwanis nāwas ta
prör^{i} prör^{i} tasandis autāras
prör^{i} prör^{i} tasandis shŏba tsarĕtas ta. lagas etc. 349.

XX.

Vrushabāsŏr tsāv manz Gōkulas ta
mada sūty kul^{i} kaṭ^{i} phuṭarani log^{u}
Krushnani vĕha sūty log^{u} grazanas ta
lāgas bŏh dasta dasta pampōsh. 350.

Krushna-jyuv^{i} brōṭh yith ta hĕng raṭ^{i}nas ta
dörith ta dyutun kala pĕṭh^{i} kin^{i}
sanmukha biyĕ biyĕ āv Krushnas ta. lāgas etc. 351.

mŏkth sapanun^{u} ôs^{u} tas rākhĕsas ta
Krushnani atha sūty mŏkalith gav
namaskār tasandis tath bāgĕs ta. lāgas etc. 352

yus lagi Krushna-jyuwanis nāwas ta
tas kari Krushna-jyuv sarŏ wŏpakār
yiti yĕsh nith ta wāti Vishnu-bawanas ta. lāgas etc. 353.

pör^{i} pör^{i} Krushna-jyuwanis nāwas ta
pör^{i} pör^{i} tasandis autāras
pör^{i} pör^{i} tasandis shŏba tsarĕtas ta. lāgas etc. 354.

XXI.

samay wôt^{u} yĕli tas Kansas ta
Nārada-mŏnīshŏr tshaḷ^{a}rani ās
dop^{u}nas 'tör^{ü} chĕy na kĕh ti maranas' ta
lāgas bŏh dasta dasta pampōsh. 355

347. In ancient days his name Sudarśana had been. By Angiras the sage had he been cursed, and for Kṛṣṇa's incarnation had he been waiting long.

348. He who beareth in his heart the name of Kṛṣṇa, to him will Kṛṣṇa every favour render. In this world glory will he win, and thereafter the abode of Viṣṇu will he reach. To him posy and posy do I offer lotuses.

349. Ever dedicating myself to Kṛṣṇa's name, ever dedicating myself to his incarnation, ever dedicating myself to his auspicious deeds, posy and posy do I offer lotuses.

XX. THE DEMON BULL. (Bhāg Pu. X, xxxvi.)

350. In the form of a bull did an Asura enter Gōkula, and in his madness began he to rend apart the trees and shrubs. Full of hatred against Kṛṣṇa loud he roared.

351. Kṛṣṇa came forward and by the horns he grasped him. He seized him and cast him head downwards on the ground. Again and again Kṛṣṇa did he attack.

352. It was that Demon's (happy) fate that he should thus gain salvation, and by (his death at) Kṛṣṇa's hand was he released from being born again. Reverence be to the blessed lot he so obtained!

353. He who beareth in his heart the name of Kṛṣṇa, to him will Kṛṣṇa every favour render. In this world glory will he win, and thereafter the abode of Viṣṇu will he reach. To him posy and posy do I offer lotuses.

354. Ever dedicating myself to Kṛṣṇa's name, ever dedicating myself to his incarnation, ever dedicating myself to his auspicious deeds, to him posy and posy do I offer lotuses.

XXI. NĀRADA VISITS KAṀSA. AKRŪRA'S MISSION. THE JOURNEY TO MATHURĀ. THE DEATH OF KAṀSA. (Bhāg. Pu. X, xxxvi, 16–xliv.)

355. When Kaṁsa's time was come, to lay a snare for him did Nārada approach him, and thus quoth he, 'Before thy death now is there no long delay'.

'Krushna-rūp^{i} kāl cyôn^{u} chuy zanmas ta
aiṭhyum^{u} santān Vasudēwun^{u}
wôt^{u}mot^{u} Nanda-gōrini zanmas' ta
lāgas bŏh dasta dasta pampōsh. 356.

'kūr^{ü} ös^{ü} zāmüts^{ü} Nanda-gōpas ta
anith ta Krushnani kani thüv^{u}hay
Krushn wuñĕ baḍyōy na ta dĕwa pōshĕhas' ta. lāgas
etc. 357.

hīth ôs^{u} taph sŏranāwun^{u} tas ta
taway Nārád^{i} shĕch^{i} wüñ^{u}nas
bŏḍ^{a}rana yitha yiyi aparādas ta. lāgas etc. 358.

Kansan tsakh kür^{ü} bēma māranas ta
Nāradan dop^{u}nas 'kawa wulaṭyōkh
kāl gŏḍa gāltan ada phērtas' ta. lāgas etc. 359.

'tsĕ hyuh^{u} balavīr chuna samayĕs ta
vīra-köm^{ü} karüñ^{ü} pazi vīra-pŏrashĕn
chuy-ĕy bal kĕh ta hāv Krushnas' ta. lāgas etc. 360.

'Krushn chuy bālukhāh ta kō-na pōshĕhas ta
tsĕ nishĕ kyāh tas bālakas pāy
cyāni bala bayĕ chuh tribuwanas' ta. lāgas etc. 361.

'söriy Yādav chih tsĕy^{i} athas ta
Wasudēv mārana kyāh wātiy
mör^{i}zĕn yus āsi tsor^{u} pānas' ta. lāgas etc. 362.

'Krushn-ay baḍiy ta kot^{u} pōshĕhas ta
wuñĕ chuy āyot^{u} gālahön kāl
kāl gölith rōz sŏkha pānas' ta. lāgas etc. 363.

'dapān chih "khēla chĕh tsarĕ Krushnas" ta
gāṭ^{ā}l^{i} zānan na shĕtras nyuk^{u}
tagiy-ĕy kĕh-ti tör^{ü} mata kartas' ta. lāgas etc. 364.

'Wasudēv tsāntan bŏd^{i}wānas ta
mĕtra-rūpa-shĕṭh^{a}r pazi pashĕnāwun
kāl^{ü}y gāltan ta pĕta pāyĕs' ta. lāgas etc. 365.

356. 'In Kṛṣṇa's body hath thy Death been born. The eighth child is he of Vasudēva, and in Nanda's house hath he arrived at birth.

357. 'To Nanda was a daughter born, and hither was she brought and for thee put in Kṛṣṇa's place. Kṛṣṇa is now grown up, nor against him is it likely that thou canst prevail.'

358. This was but a ruse to call to Kaṁsa his austerities to mind; and therefore Nārada to him spake this message, that he might plunge yet further into sin.

359. Then became Kaṁsa furious, and sought to kill his sister's spouse. Quoth to him Nārada, 'Why dost thou reverse the order of thy doings? First destroy thou thy Death, and then turn thou for revenge on Vasudēva.

360. 'At this present time no hero is thine equal. Only heroic acts should heroes do. If any might thou hast, then against Kṛṣṇa it do thou display.

361. 'Kṛṣṇa is but a lad, and how canst thou not prevail against him? Against thee what recourse can help the lad, for of thy dread might stand all the worlds in fear.

362. 'In thy hand alone lie all the Yādavas. From slaying Vasudēva to thee what profit will accrue? Only him shouldst thou slay who than thyself is mightier.

363. 'If Kṛṣṇa grow to manhood, how wilt thou prevail against him? Now is he at thy mercy, so speedily destroy thy Death. Then, when thy Death thou hast destroyed, in happiness abide at peace.

364. 'True, people say that Kṛṣṇa spends his time in divers childish pranks, but the wise ne'er think of an enemy as small. If the means thou ken, make no delay against him.

365. 'Into the prison cast thou Vasudēva, for to an enemy that poseth as a friend 'tis right to sorrow give. But, above all, to destroy thy Death seek out a plan.'

kȧh^{i}-tāñ tuj^{ü}nakh thaph māranas ta
dŏshĕwȧn^{i} paikȧr^{i} biyĕ kȧr^{i}nakh
tsönith ta thȧvin bŏ̃d^{i}wānas ta
lāgas bŏh dasta dasta pampōsh. 366.

ȧnin vīr sör^{i} nīth karanas ta
Kālañĕ shĕnkāyĕ kampas gav
anani wŏṭi log^{u} prath rākhĕsas ta. lāgas etc. 367.

Kēshāsŏras baḍis rākhĕsas ta
biyĕ Mushṭikas ta Tsönūras
biyĕ yim rākhĕs bȧḍ^{i} ös^{i} tas ta. lāgas etc. 368.

āgyā kür^{u}nakh kāl gālanas ta
'Krushna-rūp^{i} kāl myôn^{u} marinā-san'
samith sārĕv^{ü}y sath kür^{u}has ta. lāgas etc. 369.

pūzā kür^{ü}n Mahādēwas ta
mahādanu-danḍas pūzani log^{u}
su-ti ôs^{u} dyut^{u}mot^{u} Mahādīv^{i} tas ta. lāgas etc. 370.

āgyā kür^{ü}nakh jag karanas ta
mahādanu-danḍuk^{u} bal dyun^{u} tas
danu-danḍa-jagakis lȧg^{i} sanzas ta. lāgas etc. 371.

ranga-būmi-pĕnḍav log^{u} karanas ta
pānas ti shāyāh thazaras pĕṭh
'Krushn ti ȧn^{i}tōn bal wuchahas' ta. lāgas etc. 372.

Kuwalayāpīḍ nôm^{u} ôs^{u} host^{u} tas ta
mar^{a}ts khyöv^{i} khyöv^{i} korun mȧd^{i}
'diman zi gŏḍa brŏ̃ṭh host^{u} Krushnas' ta. lāgas etc.
373.

mongun Akrūr nishĕ pānas ta
'Krushn zi antan böyis sān
waharüc^{u} łāg hĕzi Nanda-gūris' ta. lāgas etc. 374.

'kuni pöṭh^{i} bram dizi tas Krushnas ta
"danushĕ-jaguk^{u} zi kor^{u}hawa sāl"
yi-na ḍar atsĕs ta lagi tsalanas' ta. lāgas etc. 375.

366. So somehow Kaṁsa raised his hand from killing Vasudēva and his spouse, and gyves put he upon them, and into prison cast he them and let them stay.

367. To hold counsel all his mighty men he called. In terror of his Death he trembled sore, and each Demon did he cause to leap up before him:—

368. Kēśâsura, the mighty Demon; Muṣṭika and Cāṇūra too, and again all who among his Demons mighty were.

369. To them the command he gave his Death to destroy. 'I dread that in Kṛṣṇa's body lieth my Death, and that he will surely kill me.' Then altogether did they hearten him.

370. To Mahādēva did he offer adoration, and to the great bow did he make worship—the bow that Mahādēva had given him himself.

371. The command he gave for making a great sacrifice. To the mighty bow an offering must be made. So, for the bow-sacrifices began they to make ready.

372. A wrestling ground and an altar began he to prepare, and for himself a place on high exalted. Then ordered he, 'Kṛṣṇa bring ye here, that I may see his might.'

373. An elephant had he, Kuvalayâpīḍa hight. Again and again on peppers did he feed it, so as to madden it. 'First,' quoth he, 'will I the elephant in front of Kṛṣṇa set.'

374. Akrūra summoned he, 'Hither bring thou Kṛṣṇa with his brother, and from Nanda the Cowherd collect thou the tax of the rainy season.

375. 'In one way or in other must thou beguile that Kṛṣṇa. Say to him "To the bow-sacrifice have they invited you." So thus will fear not enter him, and he will set out upon the way.

‘ yāñ wāti Mathurāyĕ rāza-dwāras ta
bala-vīra ! bram dith ta gālan kāl
kāl gölith ta rōza sŏkha pānas ’ ta
lāgas bŏh dasta dasta pampōsh. 376.

‘ tath pata nāsh kara Braja-lūkas ta
Yādav ti mārakh Wugrasēn hĕth
dād hĕma Dēwakiyĕ Wasudēwas ’ ta. lāgas etc. 377.

khasun^{u} panun^{u} ratha dyut^{u}nas ta
‘ rathas kĕth ȧn^{i}zĕn yitha zan wāv
tör^{ü} mata kartas kāl ananas ’ ta. lāgas etc. 378.

Akrūr shĕch^{i} hĕth drāv prātas ta
Krushna-Bagawānun^{u} dyān dörith
Krushna-bakth büḍ^{ü} ös^{ü} tath kŏlas ta. lāgas etc. 379.

Kēshāsŏr brōṭh gav Gōkulas ta
gurāh lögith Gōkulas tsāv
amōb boḍ^{u} ôs^{u} gur^{i}-pān tas ta. lāgas etc. 380.

Krushna-jyuv brōṭha gōs ös^{ü} roṭ^{u}nas ta
jilav dits^{ü}nas ta prān vĕlaryēs
phüṭ^{ü}s yĕḍ ta pĕv āganas ta. lāgas etc. 381.

mörith tas ta gav wanas ta
gūr^{i}-shur^{i} ta gōv^{ü}-khyol^{u} sūty hĕth kĕth
Krushna-jyuv gōv^{ü}-rôch^{u} athi chīr^{ü} tas ta. lāgas etc.
382.

Nārod^{u} nishĕ āv Krushna-zīwas ta
nĕshūk^{u} lôg^{u} tȧm^{i} gōv^{ü}-rachawȧn^{i}
shur^{u} kyāh-zi zānihē baḍis brāhmanas ta. lāgas etc.
383.

Nārada-mŏnīshŏr log^{u} tŏtanas ta
‘ ts^{a}y trĕn bŏwanan-hond^{u} swömī
sĕzi achi wuchtam nitĕ-sīwakas ’ ta. lāgas etc. 384.

‘ anth cyôn^{u} kus zāni nirantas ta
pāna chukh Yīshŏr ta wanay kyāh
būmi-bār kāsani ākh zanmas ’ ta. lāgas etc. 385.

376. 'No sooner than he reach in Mathurā the palace gate, will I, Great Hero, beguile him, and so destroy my Death. Then, with my Death destroyed, will I in happiness abide in peace.

377. 'Thereafter the folk of Vraja will I exterminate, the Yādavas with Ugrasēna will I slay, and on Dēvakī and Vasudēva will I my vengeance wreak.'

378. (Bhāg. Pu. X,xxxviii.) His own chariot gave he him on the which to ride, and thus spake he. 'In this chariot must thou like the wind him bring. Make no delay in bringing here my Death.'

379. At dawntide hied Akrūra with the message forth. On Kṛṣṇa Bhagavān the while he fixed his meditation, for in his tribe to Kṛṣṇa was there great devotion.

380. (Bhāg. Pu. X, xxxvii.) Ahead of him to Gōkula sped Kēśâsura, and in horse's form Gōkula did he enter. Very huge was his equine body.

381. Kṛṣṇa went forth to meet him. His face he seized. Then (mounting him) with his soles his flanks he crushed till consciousness he lost. His belly burst, and down in the courtyard he fell.

382. Then, having killed him, to the forest Kṛṣṇa hied with the herd lads and with the herd of kine; and in his hand, as guardian of the cows, a wand he bore.

383. Then Nārada to Kṛṣṇa did approach, and, in his rôle of herd lad, Kṛṣṇa made belief and showed no sign of awe; for how should a lad like him discern the mighty Nārada!

384. Then Nārada, the chief of sages, began to sing his praises. 'Of the three worlds art Thou alone the Lord. On me, Thy slave for aye, cast Thou a kindly glance.

385. 'Of Thee, the limitless, who can the limit comprehend? Thou art Thyself the all-knowing Lord, and therefore to Thee what need I say? Birth hast Thou taken the earth's sad burden to dispel.'

Krushna-jyuv mot^{u} gōmot^{u} khēlanas ta
Nārada-mŏnīshŏr tŏth karawun^{u}
yih karun^{u} ôsus sôr^{u} won^{u}nas ta
lāgas bŏh dasta dasta pampōsh. 386.

Krushna-jyuv chuh amōb mot^{u} gindanas ta
Nārod^{u} līlā karith gav
namaskār tas ta tath tŏtanas ta. lāgas etc. 387.

Krushna-jyuv shurĕn sūty log^{u} gindanas ta
Vyōmāsŏr ās shur^{u} lögith
aṭa-bārĕn ös^{i} khēla karanas ta. lāgas etc. 388.

aṭa-bāri khasān shur^{i} asŏras ta
gŏphi nith ta thavihēkh band kår^{i} kår^{i}
shur^{i} sör^{i} athi låg^{i} tsūri asŏras ta. lāgas etc. 389

Krushna-jyuv^{i} zônun ta nakhi khot^{u} tas ta
atiy rākhyus parbuthwāh gav
Krushna-jyuv^{i} mŏngil dith kala tsoṭ^{u}nas ta. lāgas etc.
390.

kaḍith gŏphi āv shur^{i} pānas ta
dēwatā pōshĕ-pūz karanē låg^{i}
gōv^{ü} hĕth phīrith āv pānas ta. lāgas etc. 391.

Akrūr yĕli drāv nishĕ Kansas ta
Krushnañi lōlari lārani log^{u}
Krushna-pāda-kamal log^{u} mani dāranas ta. lāgas etc.
392.

yitha ôs^{u} cākar tas asŏras ta
na-ta ôs^{u} boḍ^{u} bakth Nārānun^{u}
mani ôs^{u} dörith zan Kansas ta. lāgas etc. 393.

yihay ös^{ü} kāmanā tas manas ta
kar wāta brōṭh-kun Krushna-zīwas
wātawun^{u} wandahas muñĕ pādas ta. lāgas etc. 394

karān chuh bajĕ sütš^{u} mana-rāzas ta
bāgĕn tasandĕn jai-jai-kār
sārĕn^{ü}y zi brōṭh wāta bŏy darshĕnas ta. lāgas etc.
395.

386. In his childish sports Kṛṣṇa remained absorbed, the while Nārada, the chief of sages, sang his praises, and told him what was destined he should do.

387. In his childish sports Kṛṣṇa abode utterly absorbed, and Nārada having told his tale departed. Reverence be to the praises that he sang.

388. Kṛṣṇa went on playing with the lads, and there came Vyōmâsura, as a lad disguised, while they played pickaback.

389. On the demon mounted the lads pickaback, and into a cave he took them, and there one by one did them incarcerate. Thus, without their witting it, into his power fell there all the lads.

390. But Kṛṣṇa discerned this and on to his back he climbed. Then straightway into a mountain did the demon turn himself, but Kṛṣṇa, with a blow of his mace, open split his head.

391. Forth from the cave brought he the lads and led them home. The gods, the while, from heaven on him flowers rained, as with the kine he home returned.

392. (Bhāg. Pu. X, xxxviii.) As forth from Kaṁsa's presence Akrūra sped, with a soul full of love for Kṛṣṇa on his way he hurried, and all his thoughts were fixed on Kṛṣṇa's lotus-feet.

393. True was it that of Kaṁsa was he a servant (and him must needs obey): but natheless an earnest devotee was he of Nārâyaṇa, and (for obedience) kept him in his thoughts, even as he kept Kaṁsa.

394. In his thoughts was there but one desire,—'When shall I before Kṛṣṇa come? When there I come, to his foot would I dedicate the pupils of mine eyes.'

395. In the fancies of his heart great consolations found he. 'To his blessed lot be victory! May he reveal himself to me before all others.'

wôt^{u} yĕli nērinyūr^{u} Gōkulas ta
Krushna-pād dīṭhin mĕtsĕ lȧg^{i}mȧt^{i}
mĕtsĕ pĕṭh woth^{u} ta log^{u} ḍĕka g^{a}hanas ta
lāgas bŏh dasta dasta pampôsh. 396

tsĕh^{a}nau Vishnu-pād ās parzanas ta
dŏza ta ankushĕ tsakrākār
biyĕ yim tsĕh^{a}n ös^{i} Krushna-pādas ta. lāgas etc. 397

wôt^{u} yĕli wanas nishĕ Krishna-zīwas ta
shēr dörith rūd^{u} tsaranan pĕṭh
log^{u} ḍĕka g^{a}hanas ta mīṭh^{i} karanas ta. lāgas etc. 398

Krushna-jyuv^{i} tulith ta mot^{u} kor^{u}nas ta
nāla-mati dŏnawȧn^{i} yēkut^{u} gav
Haladar Rāman manz roṭ^{u}nas ta. lāgas etc. 399

athawās karith nyūn sūty pānas ta
gara tāñ mŏd^{a}rĕ katha ös^{i} karawȧn^{i}
'Bakta-watsal' nāv chuh Krushna-zīwas ta. lāgas etc. 400

gara wātanövith ta mān kor^{u}has ta
sŏna-sanzi cōkĕ pĕṭh bĕhanôwukh
khyon^{u} cyon^{u} myūṭh^{u} myūṭh^{u} ananôw^{u}has ta. lāgas etc. 401

Akrūr^{i} Kansüñ^{ü} shĕch^{i} vüñ^{ü}nas ta
'mahādanu-danḍuk^{u} chuh jag karawun^{u}
dop^{u}nawa sārĕn^{ü}y yun^{u} swālas' ta. lāgas etc. 402

Krushna-jyuv^{i} shĕch^{i} vüñ^{ü} Nanda-babas ta
'rāzan zi gör^{i}nawa pazi mānanas
jaga-swālas ti pazi pāna gatshanas' ta. lāgas etc. 403

Nanda-gūr^{i} shĕch^{i} kür^{ü} kūṭapālas ta
ḍanḍūr phiranöv^{ü}n nagaras
'sārĕṇ^{ü}y zi gatshun^{u} chuwa rāza-swālas' ta. lāgas etc. 404

samith ta söriy drāy prātas ta
gūr^{i} gūr^{i}-shur^{i} ta yim tati sör^{i} ös^{i}
'rāza-sünz^{u} āgyā zi pazi mānanas' ta. lāgas etc. 405

396. When to Gōkula he drew near, in the earth saw he the prints of Kṛṣṇa's feet, and there to the ground did he alight and on them humbly his forehead rub.

397. By the marks upon them,—by the banner, the driving-hook, the discus, and the other marks on Kṛṣṇa's feet,—as the footprints of Viṣṇu did he recognize them.

398. When to the forest he came, on Kṛsna's feet he laid his head, and on them his brow he rubbed and kissed them.

399. Kṛṣṇa raised him up and then embraced him, and by that same embrace the two one became, while Haladhara Rāma clasped him round the waist.

400. He took him by the hand and led him home, making sweet words until they reached the house, for Kṛṣṇa's name is 'He who loveth devotees.'

401. (Bhāg. Pu. X,xxxix.) With much honour did they conduct him to the house, and seat him on a golden couch. Sweet food and drink of varied kinds caused they to be laid before him.

402. Kaṁsa's message did Akrūra tell him, 'A sacrifice to the great bow is he a-making, and all of you hath he invited.'

403. To Nanda his [foster-] father did Kṛṣṇa convey the message. 'The king hath with an invitation honoured you, you should accept. Right is it for us ourselves to attend the sacrificial feast.'

404. To the Captain of the Town did Nanda send the news, and proclamation had he made by beat of drum that at the royal invitation all should go.

405. At dawn they all assembled and set forth. The cowherds and their lads and all were there, for right was it to obey the king's command.

Nanda-gūr^{i} lāg hĕts^{u} sūty pānas ta
shrī-Krushna-jyuv ta Haladar Rām
Akrūras sūty khàt^{i} rathas ta
lāgas bŏh dasta dasta pampōsh. 406.

Yĕshōdā ta gōpiyĕ tsāyĕ wadanas ta
'sahav kĕtha shrī-Krushnun^{u} dūrĕr'
sārĕn^{u}y Krushna-jyuv süts^{u} karanas ta. lāgas etc. 407.

drāy yĕli nagara ta làg^{i} lāranas ta
Akrūr manas tsēntani log^{u}
'mĕ zi kĕtha bram dyut^{u} bāla-Krushnas' ta. lāgas etc. 408

Vishnu-māyā ös^{u} māy hāwanas ta
tatiy gyān ta biyĕ agyān
prath kaīsi zön^{i} zön^{i} biyĕ mashĕhēs ta. lāgas etc. 409.

Yĕmunāyĕ pĕṭh wöt^{i} làg^{i} snānas ta
Akrūr snāna-sand karanē log^{u}
bram dyun^{u} Krushnas mani tsēntanas ta. lāgas etc. 410.

woth^{u} yĕli ḍung dini manz zalas ta
Krushna-jyuv sanmukha drēṭh tati ās
vishŏrūpa-darshun tati hôwanas ta. lāgas etc. 411.

dēwatā sör^{i} ös^{i} tŏtā karanas ta
mŏràlī wāyān pāna Bagawān
Akrūr wuch^{i} wuch^{i} gav harshēs ta. lāgas etc. 412.

zala manza khasith ta gav āshtsaras ta
Krushna-Bagawānas pādan pĕv
agyān tsolus ta phyūr^{u} sōras ta. lāgas etc. 413.

pakān gay tim ta wöt^{i} nagaras ta
gūr^{i} shur^{i} sör^{i} sūty-sūtin hĕth
Krushnani daira sūty ös^{i} dairas ta. lāgas etc. 414.

Akrūr lāryōv nishĕ Kansas ta
'söriy zi sọmb^{a}rith hĕth āsay'
kamph tsāv bōzana mani Kansas ta. lāgas etc. 415.

406. With himself Nanda brought his yearly tax and Kṛṣṇa and Haladhara Rāma, and with Akrūra did they mount the chariot.

407. To weep began Yaśōdā and the herd-wives, 'How shall we thole the distance far of Kṛṣṇa!', and to them did Kṛṣṇa comfort give.

408. When from the town they had issued, they made haste with speed, and in his heart to meditate Akrūra began, 'How came it that I deluded the boy Kṛṣṇa ?'

409. Viṣṇu's Illusive Power had shown to him illusion, and in that illusion no knowledge is there and no ignorance, for each one understood and forgot and anon understood and anon forgot again.

410. At the Yamunā did they arrive and to bathe did they begin. To make his evening ablution did Akrūra prepare, and then did Kṛṣṇa him to delude determine.

411. When Akrūra descended into the water that he might plunge therein, there there appeared before him Kṛṣṇa, who in that place revealed himself as All Creation.

412. There were all the gods his praises singing, Bhagavān himself his flute was playing, and Akrūra as he looked and looked again was filled with joy.

413. (Bhāg. Pu. xl.) Astonied did he rise from mid the waters, and at the feet of Kṛṣṇa Bhagavān he fell. Ignorance fled from him and he again to consciousness returned.

414. (Bhāg. Pu. xli.) So on the cowherds went and to the city came, with them in company all the lads. By Kṛṣṇa's courage were they filled with courage too.

415. To Kaṁsa Akrūra hastened, 'All of them have I together brought and come to thee', and as he heard these words into Kaṁsa's heart did trembling enter.

Krushna-jyuv gūr^{i} hĕth ta tsāv nagaras ta
Mathurāyĕ lūkh sör^{i} wuchanē drāy
dēv yāzani lȧg^{i} tath nagaras ta
lāgas bŏh dasta dasta pampōsh. 416.

hȧst^{i}-cāli pakān Krushna-jyuv asta
sör^{i} lūkh ās pata pata lārān
kāmĕ kŏcĕ trövith lȧg^{i} pata tas ta. lāgas etc. 417.

Kansun^{u} dọb^{u} pĕv gŏḍa brōṭha tas ta
söriy wast^{a}r lūṭith ta gōs
ditin gōrĕn lȧg^{i} vĕṭhanas ta. lāgas etc. 418.

kū̃h gūr^{i}-shur^{u} ganḍi pag khōras ta
kū̃h lāgi kurtañĕ-narĕ zangan
gūr^{i} kyāh zānan nāv wastras ta. lāgas etc. 419.

Bagawat-bakthāh wôt^{u} darshĕnas ta
Bāyĕka Wôwur^{u} ôsus nāv
Krushnas brō̃ṭha āv 'bŏy pairahas' ta. lāgas etc. 420.

Bāyĕk^{i} jāma gȧnḍ^{i} Krushna-zīwas ta
pāna gūr^{i}-shur^{u} zan zānihē na kē̃h
Bagawān chuh āyot^{u} prath baktis ta. lāgas etc. 421.

bāgyōday ôs^{u} bŏna Bāyĕkas ta
Krushna-jyuv wastrav sū̃ty pūrun
yih kē̃h wor^{u}nas tiy dyut^{u}nas ta. lāgas etc. 422.

Sŏdām brō̃ṭha wôt^{u} Krushna-zīwas ta
rambawañĕ pōshĕ-māla tani pairĕnas
baktan bakth^{ü}y war mong^{u}has ta. lāgas etc. 423.

Krushna-jyuv^{i} bŏk^{a}th mŏk^{a}th war dyut^{u}nas ta
'gyāna-yōga sū̃tin prazoluy ās
wŏdyot^{u} yiha-lūk^{i} para-lūkas ta.' lāgas etc. 424.

Kubzā wati mīj^{ü} Krushna-zīwas ta
tsandan-wörāh g^{ü}sh^{u}mŭts^{ü} hĕth
dyūṭhun Krushna-jyuv ta tani mol^{u}nas ta. lāgas etc.
425.

416. As Kṛṣṇa with the cowherds the city entered, all the folk of Mathurā came forth to see him, and in that city began they the gods to worship.

417. Kṛṣṇa went forward with the slow gait of a mighty elephant, and behind him followed running all the folk. Abandoning work and household toils they followed him.

418. The first one that he met was Kaṁsa's washerman. Him robbed he of all his burden of garments, and gave them to the cowherds to their huge delight.

419. One cowherd lad tieth a turban round his feet, another through the sleeves of a coat doth thrust his legs. What should cowherds know of a garment's name (or use)?

420. Thereon a devotee of Bhagavān came up to watch,—his name was Bhāyaka the weaver. Kṛṣṇa did he approach crying, 'Let me thee adorn.'

421. On Kṛṣṇa did Bhāyaka put apparel, and Kṛṣṇa himself, like a cowherd lad, seemed naught to understand; for to the service of each devotee is Bhagavān devoted.

422. Verily high rose Bhāyaka's good fortune that he himself should Kṛṣṇa with garments clothe, and whatsoever boon he asked, that Kṛṣṇa gave him.

423. Then did Sudāman [1] approach Kṛṣṇa, and with beauteous flowers did adorn his body, and, for a boon, asked this devotee for naught but pure devotion.

424. To him did Kṛṣṇa prosperity and salvation grant, 'With the grace of the true knowledge be thou illuminate. Exalted be thou in this world and in the world to come.'

425. (Bhāg. Pu. X, xlii.) On the road was Kṛṣṇa met by Kubjā, the hunchback girl. Bearing was she a vessel of powdered sandal. When she saw him, on his body did she apply it.

[1] For Sudāman, see further in chapter xlvii and also verse 253.

tsandun^{u} hĕth gatshi sa-ti Kansas ta
tsandunuy prath dŏha maṭi tas ôs^{u}
bāgĕ ās wŏdayĕs ta wöts^{ü} Krushnas ta
lāgas bŏh dasta dasta pampōsh. 426

Kubzāyĕ kaitsāh yĕtsh bür^{u}nas ta
kŏbi pāna bükts^{ü} sūty prasan gōs
nĕshūk^{u} khŏras khŏr thow^{u}nas ta. lāgas etc. 427.

hŏngañĕ zīr^{ü} dith ta kọb^{u} kôs^{u}nas ta
Kubzā sapüñ^{ü} sŏndarāh zan
kôtwāh lōl bor^{u} tami Krushnas ta. lāgas etc. 428.

yus mahādanu-danḍ ôs^{u} Kansas ta
tàth^{i} danu-danḍas nishĕ gŏḍa nyūkh
tulith athi kĕth ta khanḍ kor^{u}nas ta. lāgas etc. 429.

danu-danḍa-khanḍa sūty log^{u} māranas ta
yus yus Kansun^{u} brōṭha pĕyihēs
Kansan bala-vīr brōha dit^{i}nas ta. lāgas etc. 430.

atiy ās mad-host^{u} brōṭha Krushnas ta
dah sās hastĕn-hond^{u} tas bal
hàst^{i}-wöl^{i} host^{u} hĕth wath rüṭ^{u}nas ta. lāgas etc. 431.

mĕtsĕ-hond^{u} host^{u} āsi yitha bālakas ta
Krushna-jyuv^{i} host^{u} titha gilanôwun
khīcith mushti aki zuv koḍ^{u}nas ta. lāgas etc. 432.

mörith ta hastis dand koḍ^{u}nas ta
athi kĕth āyŏda kani hĕth gav
pakān syod^{u} gav ranga-manḍalas ta. lāgas etc. 433.

malla-daityau ḍyūṭh^{u} pĕy dōranas ta
Krushna-jyuv parbuth zan drēṭh ākh
zônukh zi pōshĕy na bāla-Krushnas ta. lāgas etc. 434.

sādu-zan wuchanas shānta-rūpas ta
triyi-zan wuchanas Kāmadēwas
gūr^{i} sọr^{i} ḍēshān gūr^{i}-shur^{u} tas ta. lāgas etc. 435.

426. To Kaṁsa is she the sandal taking,—for such was her duty day by day,—and high exalted was her fate that her to Kṛṣṇa led.

427. How wondrous was the longing that Kubjā bare for him! By the devotion of that hunchbacked form well-pleased was he, and resolutely on her foot he placed his foot.

428. To her chin gave he a push, and so banished he her crookedness. Kubjā, the hunchback, became a comely damsel. Wondrous was the love for Kṛṣṇa that filled her heart.

429. The great bow that Kaṁsa owned, to that verily first of all did they bring Kṛṣṇa. It did he raise and into fragments break.

430. With a broken piece of the bow he began to smite all those of Kaṁsa who before him came, the mighty men whom Kaṁsa had set to bar his way.

431. (Bhāg. Pu. X, xliii.) Then and there to oppose Kṛṣṇa came the maddened elephant. Of ten thousand elephants was his the might, and the drivers led him forth Kṛṣṇa's way to stop.

432. Like a clay elephant, a baby's toy, did Kṛṣṇa whirl him in the air. Then dragging it, with one fist-blow tore he out its life.

433. Then from the dead elephant tore he out its tusk, and for a weapon grasped he it in his hand. So into the arena did he stride.

434. The demon wrestlers saw him and upon him ran. Like an incarnate mountain to them he seemed, and then, I ween, did they understand, 'The boy Kṛṣṇa we shall ne'er o'ercome.'

435. To the quietists did he appear as incarnate Peace; as an incarnate Cupid did the women see him; and all the cowherds beheld but a cowherd lad.

bala-vīr drēṭh āv prath rāzas ta
tasandi rāza-tīza kōpani lȧg[i]
hyokhukh-na wuchith ta lȧg[i] kōpanas ta
lāgas bŏh dasta dasta pampōsh. 436.

Virāṭh drēṭh āv gyānawānas ta
yōgīshŏran yōguk[u] sār
gyāna-drēshṭi myul[u] gōkh Param-Brahmas ta. lāgas
etc. 437.

mahārāza drēṭh āv prath Yādawas ta
dēwan drēṭh āv pāna Bagawān
yĕm[i] yitha wuch[u] ta tȧm[i] tyuth[u] ḍyūṭh[u] ta. lāgas etc.
438.

Kāla-rūph drēṭh āv tas Kansas ta
thara thara tsāyĕs maranüñ[ü] hish[ü]
pör[i] pör[i] lȧg[i]zĕs prath vihas ta. lāgas etc. 439.

Mushṭikh ta Tsönūr brōṭha dit[i]nas ta
mushti aki Haladȧr[i] Mushṭikh môr[u]
Tsönūr mārun pĕv Krushnas ta. lāgas etc. 440.

yus vīr yiyihē brōṭha Krushnas ta
tas tas mushti aki karihē sūr
mārana sūty āyĕ tsakh Kansas ta. lāgas etc. 441.

Krushna-jyuv shur[i] hĕth log[u] natsanas ta
Kansas wölinj[ü] dazanē lüj[ü]
āgyā kür[ü]nakh dūr karanas ta. lāgas etc. 442.

khüts[ü]s tsakh ta log[u] wŏthanas ta
thazra pĕṭha ôs[u] kraka lāyān
dapān chuh 'rȧṭ[i]tōn dād hĕmahas' ta. lāgas etc. 443.

āgyā kür[ü]nakh gūr[i] raṭanas ta
'möryūkh söriy biyĕ Yādav
mörith Dēwakīyĕ Vasudēwas' ta. lāgas etc. 444.

---

1 A mystic Being. In the Vedānta philosophy he is the Supreme Intellect loca-

436. To each king seemed he a mighty man of war, and at his royal fury did they tremble, trembling they dared not look at him.

437. To those who had the true knowledge appeared he as Virāj[1], the Essence of the asceticism of the great ascetics, who by the eye of knowledge with the Supreme Bráhma become one.

438. To each Yādava as a mighty monarch did he appear; to the gods did he appear as Bhagavān Himself. As each one looked, so did he seem to him.

439. To Kaṁsa did he appear as incarnate Death. Quaking and shaking like that of death did enter him. To each form that Kṛṣṇa took do I dedicate myself.

440. (Bhāg. X, xliv.) Muṣṭika and Cāṇūra set he to oppose him. By one fist-blow by Haladhara was Muṣṭika slain, and Cāṇūra's fate it was by Kṛṣṇa to be killed.

441. Each valiant man that to meet Kṛṣṇa came, him with one fist-blow did Kṛṣṇa turn to dust, and at their slaughter high mounted Kaṁsa's wrath.

442. With the lads began Kṛṣṇa to dance, and up blazed Kaṁsa's heart. The command gave he forth that they should far away be driven.

443. High rose his wrath. Uprose he, and from on high forth did he cry, 'Seize ye him, seize ye him, vengeance will I take.'

444. Command gave he to seize the cowherds. 'Also let all the Yādavas be slain, after Dēvakī and Vasudēva ye have first done to death.

---

ted in the aggregate of created beings. The Sanskrit name is Virāj (Nom. sing. Virāṭ).

'māranas Dēwakas ta Wugrasēnas ta
raṭyūn Krushn ta Haladara-rām'
kraka dith rath khot^u kôtwāh tas ta
lāgas bŏh dasta dasta pampōsh. 445.

wŏthith Krushna-jyuv^i wŏṭh lŏy^ü nas ta
thadi ôs^u Kans ta wötith pyōs
khar^i-khara gav ta wọṭh^u laḍanas ta. lāgas etc. 446.

ḍāl ta tar^a wār athi Kansas ta
Krushṇas sanmukha laḍanē log^u
Kansun^u bayĕ ôs^u söris bŏwanas ta. lāgas etc. 447.

Kansan athi dyut^u na pān Krushnas ta
ōr yōr wŏṭa-wŏṭh log^u karanē
kuni pöṭh^i zi pōshĕ-nā bāla-Krushnas ta. lāgas etc. 448.

Krushna-jyuv^i tīzāh praḳh^a ṭôwunas ta
kŏrōra-sūrĕn hyuh^u camakān
wuna pĕyĕ Kansas ta ōṭ^ü rüṭ^ü nas ta. lāgas etc. 449

raṭith lati aki tāj trôw^u nas ta
khaḳh^a ri hĕri pĕṭha bŏn wôlun
prān gös nīrith ta pĕv āganas ta. lāgas etc. 450.

hāhā-kār wọṭh^u rāza-dwāras ta
rākhĕs söriy chāg^a ri gay
dēv lág^i söriy pōshĕ-warshĕnas ta. lāgas etc. 451.

rākhĕs aiṭh böy^i ös^i Kansas ta
aiṭhaway mīlith yŏddas drāy
Haladár^i aiṭhaway tim mör^i nas ta. lāgas etc. 452

Kansañĕ rañĕ drāyĕ nanga Krushnas ta
aiṭhan-hanza rañĕ biyĕ sārĕy
vilāph tihond^u na zi yiyi wananas ta. lāgas etc. 453.

Krushna-jyuv^i māmañĕn maṭha kor^u nas ta
māman dāha-kriy karanöv^ü nakh
māman-handi dŏkha pĕv wadanas ta. lāgas etc. 454

445. 'That ye may slay Dēvaka and Ugrasēna, seize ye Kṛṣṇa and Haladhara Rāma.' As he cried out, the blood in torrents rose into his face.

446. Kṛṣṇa arose and leaped upon him. On high was Kaṁsa as he came before him, and with the courage of despair he rose to fight.

447. Shield and sword grasped Kaṁsa in his hand, and face to face with Kṛṣṇa began he to contend. The whole earth was filled with fear of him.

448. Kaṁsa his body set not within reach of Kṛṣṇa's arms. Backwards and forwards gave he leap on leap, thinking, 'In some way shall I not the boy Kṛṣṇa overcome?'

449. Then his own glory showed forth Kṛṣṇa. Dazzling became he like ten million suns. On Kaṁsa blindness fell, and Kṛṣṇa seized him by the apple of his throat.

450. As he thus seized him, with one kick down dashed he his diadem. From his high place along the ground he dragged him low. Forth fled his life, and in the courtyard dead he lay.

451. In the palace arose there a wail of woe. Far abroad were all the Demons scattered, and all the gods sent down a rain of flowers.

452. Kaṁsa had eight brethren, Demons all, and these came forth together to the combat; but the whole eight did Haladhara slay.

453. Then came forth Kaṁsa's queens uncovered before Kṛṣṇa, and eke all the queens of the brethren eight, nor of their lamentations can the tale be told.

454. To his aunts did Kṛṣṇa consolation tend, and for his uncles'[1] obsequies ritely did he prescribe. In sorrow for his uncles did he himself lament.

---

[1] I.e. Kaṁsa and his eight brothers.

namaskār Kansanis tath tapas ta
namaskār tasandis tath mānas
Krushnani atha ġav mŏkti-dwāras ta.
lāġas bŏh dasta dasta pampōsh. 455

yus laġi Krushna-jyuwanis nāwas ta
tas kari Krushna-jyuv sarŏ wŏpakār
yiti yĕsh nith ta wāti Vishnu-bawanas ta. lāġas etc. 456.

pör[i] pör[i] Krushna-jyuwanis nāwas ta
pör[i] pör[i] tasandis autāras
pör[i] pör[i] tasandis shŏba tsarĕtas ta. lāġas etc. 457.

XXII.

tawa pata nishĕ āv mājĕ babas ta
parzan ākh na zi 'nĕcyuw[u] chuh sôn[u]'
bāsyōkh pūrna-Brahma-rūph manas ta.
lāġas bŏh dasta dasta pampōsh. 458.

Krushna-jyuv mölis āv bōlanas ta
'asĕ kō-na ġŏbaran chiwa parzanān
môl[u] möj[ü] ös[i]tan prath bālakas' ta. lāġas etc. 459.

'mĕ zi pazi tuhünz[ü]y sīwā karanas ta
mölis-ta-mājĕ-hond[u] kĕtha wasi rĕn
shēr dāra tuhandis pāda-kamalas' ta. lāġas etc. 460.

paikår[i] phuṭarith sath kür[ü]nas ta
sŏra āv Wasudĕv vĕṭhanē log[u]
wŏthith nāla-måt[i] mīṭh[i] kår[i]nas ta. lāġas etc. 461.

Dēwakī-mājĕ pĕv pāda-kamalas ta
gāsh hyuh[u] ās ta lüj[ü] vĕṭhanē
dŏda-baba āyĕs srĕh baranas ta. lāġas etc. 462.

dŏshĕway pānavüñ[ü] låg[i] tōshĕnas ta
dŏshĕwån[i] ġari ġari mīṭh[i] karawån[i]
Haladara-rāmas ta Krushna-zīwas ta. lāġas etc. 463.

---

[1] This is explained by the Bhāg. Pu. Dēvakī and Vasudēva recognized the incarnate Deity in their two sons, and instead of embracing them, as would have been natural, humbly saluted them. Kṛṣṇa then sent forth his illusion, so that

455. Reverence be to Kaṁsa's austerities ascetic, and eke to his haughty pride be reverence paid, for 'twas (through them) that he at Kṛṣṇa's hand obtained salvation.

456. He who beareth in his heart the name of Kṛṣṇa, to him will Kṛṣṇa every favour render. In this world glory will he win, and thereafter the abode of Viṣṇu will he reach. To him posy and posy do I offer lotuses.

457. Ever dedicating myself to Kṛṣṇa's name, ever dedicating myself to his incarnation, ever dedicating myself to his auspicious deeds, posy and posy do I offer lotuses.

XXII. KṚṢṆA RELEASES HIS PARENTS, AND REINSTATES UGRASĒNA ON HIS THRONE. THE DISMISSAL OF NANDA. (Bhāg. Pu. X, xlv.)

458. Thereafter Kṛṣṇa approached his mother and his father, but him they did not recognize that he was their son, for to their minds he seemed a form of the Supreme Bráhma in all its fulness.

459. Then quoth Kṛṣṇa to his father, 'Wherefore dost thou not recognize us as thy sons? Each child should have a father and a mother.[1]

460. 'Meet is it for me to do you service, else how can the debt to father and to mother e'er be repayed? At your lotus-feet do I humbly lay my head.'

461. Their gyves he burst asunder and consoled he them. Then did Vasudēva call to mind (the birth of his son), and he exulted as he arose and kissed him.

462. At the lotus-feet of Dēvakī his mother did Krsna fall, and as though light had come to her (in darkness) began she to exult. Filled became she with a yearning love, and from her bosom milk welled forth.

463. Filled were the pair with mutual content, again and yet again do they fondle Haladhara-Rāma and Kṛṣṇa with their kisses.

---

they forgot their temporary recognition of the truth, and looked upon the boys as actually their sons in the flesh.

dôd^{u} tsol^{u} Dēwakiyĕ Wasudēwas ta
dôd^{u} tsol^{u} Dēwakas ta Wugrasēnas
dôd^{u} tsol^{u} Yādawan ta biyĕ nagaras ta.
lāgas bŏh dasta dasta pampōsh. 464.

Wugrasēn dyūn^{u} zan āv Krushnas ta
pādan pĕṭh rūd^{u} shēr dörith
rāza-dwārüc^{ü} kunz^{ü} athi dits^{u}nas ta. lāgas etc. 465.

Krushna-jyuv^{i} rājy dith Wugrasēnas ta
'Yādawan zyuṭh^{u} sôn^{u} ts^{a}y sārĕn^{ü}y
söriy ösin tsĕy mānanas' ta. lāgas etc. 466.

Krushna-jyuv^{i} sath kür^{u} prath Yādawas ta
sārĕn^{i} byon^{u} byon^{u} ranzawani log^{u}
Yādawa-kŏl sôr^{u} tsāv tōshĕnas ta. lāgas etc. 467.

yim ös^{i} tsāl^{i}māt^{i} par nagaras ta
Kansāsŏranē ḍara Yādav
tim tim sör^{i} āy Mathurā-nagaras ta. lāgas etc. 468.

köm^{ü} mŏkalövith āv Nandas ta
'dŏda-baba! sôruy cyônuy chum
tsĕy^{i} nakhi kŏchi yūt^{u} wātanôw^{u}thas' ta. lāgas etc.
469.

'cyāniy dŏda thañi ās balas ta
māy cyöñ^{ü} mana nishĕ mashĕm na zāh
tŏhĕ ti pazi na maṣh^{e}rāwanas' ta. lāgas etc. 470

dŏshĕway khōran pĕy Nandas ta
'asĕ wŏñ öhiyāh karān ās
Yĕshōdā-mātāyĕ kyāh wanahas' ta. lāgas etc. 471.

'rōzi na asĕ rost^{u} man kuni tas ta
sāni kani ös^{i}zēs süts^{ü} karawun^{u}
yi-na kē̃h bari ta āsi shūkas' ta. lāgas etc. 472.

'asĕ wŏñ āgyā pazi karanas ta
mölis-ta-māje-hond^{u} kāsav rĕn
tŏhĕ ti ös^{i}nawa sŏkh baḍanas' ta. lāgas etc. 473.

464. Pain fled from Dēvakī and Vasudēva. Pain fled from Dēvaka and Ugrasēna. Pain from the Yādavas and from the city fled.

465. Before Kṛṣṇa as humble suppliant came Ugrasēna, and with his head on Kṛṣṇa's feet he lay, as into his hand he gave the palace keys.

466. But the kingdom to Ugrasēna did Kṛṣṇa give. 'Thou alone art the chief of all us Yādavas. To thy command let all of us be subject.'

467. To each Yādava did Kṛṣṇa consolation give (for all that he had tholed at Kaṁsa's hand), and each and all did he delight, so that with content was filled the whole tribe of Yādavas.

468. Those Yādavas who in fear of Kaṁsa had fled to distant lands, all one by one came back to Mathurā.

469. When all his task was finished, to Nanda Kṛṣṇa came, 'My foster father, all that I have I owe to thee. 'Tis thou alone, who on thy shoulder, in thy lap, brought me to my present state.

470. 'On thy milk and on thy butter to vigour am I come; ne'er from my heart shall be forgot thy love, nor mayst thou ever me forget.'

471. At Nanda's feet the two brothers fell. 'Fain would we that thy blessing thou wouldst on us bestow. What wilt thou say to Mother Yaśōdā?

472. 'Apart from us in no way will her soul remain at peace, and therefore on our account be thou her consoler, so that no grief at all she need experience.

473. 'And now 'tis meet that us thou bid depart; the debt we owe our father and our mother, that must we repay. And may, for aye, thy happiness increase!'

bōzana murtshā phīr^{ü} Nandas ta
andakār zan pyōs bē-sŏr gav
Krushna-jyuv^{i} wāra wāra süts^{ü} karĕnas ta.
lāgas bŏh dasta dasta pampōsh. 474.

bram sôr^{u} samsār kyāh wanihēs ta
ruma ruma wuch^{i} wuch^{i} harshĕni log^{u}
wŏthith nāla-måt^{i} ta mīṭh^{i} kår^{i}nas ta. lāgas etc. 475.

ŏhiyāh kür^{u}nas yitsh^{ü} pazihēs ta
'prazol^{u} zi sārĕn^{ü}y pĕṭh-kun ās
kuni kuni asĕ ti ån^{i}zi manas' ta. lāgas etc. 476.

Wasudēwa-rāzan ti süts^{ü} karĕnas ta
mĕtra-bāwa pānavün^{u} tōshĕni låg^{i}
ŏhiyĕ karani låg^{i} Krushna-Rāmas ta. lāgas etc. 477.

Krushna-jyuv^{i} dana dyār küt^{i} dit^{i}nas ta
hata-bod^{u} gurĕn yyūt^{u} wôt^{u} tyūt^{u}
timan gotsh^{u} na kēh rost^{u} Krushnas ta. lāgas etc.
478.

wadān ta gūr^{i} gay gara pānas ta
Krushnun^{u} dūrĕr chi-na z^{a}rawān
Krushnun^{u} dyān låg^{i} mani dāranas ta. lāgas etc. 479.

Yĕshōdā vilāph lüj^{ü} karanas ta
'kuni kuni wuchahŏn Shrī-Bagawān'
sārĕy garacĕ kāmĕ machĕs ta. lāgas etc. 480.

yus lagi Krushna-jyuwanis nāwas ta
tas kari Krushna-jyuv sarŏ wŏpakār
yiti yĕsh nith ta wāti Vishnu-bawanas ta. lāgas etc.
481.

pör^{i} pör^{i} Krushna-jyuwanis nāwas ta
pör^{i} pör^{i} tasandis autāras
pör^{i} pör^{i} tasandis shŏba tsarĕtas ta. lāgas etc. 482.

XXIII.

Wasudēv gŏbaran log^{u} rachanas ta
darmuk^{u} samskār sôr^{u} kor^{u}nakh
zara-kāsanas ta yōñĕ-tshunanas ta.
lāgas bŏh dasta dasta pampōsh. 483.

474. When Nanda heard these words, into a swoon he fell. 'Twas as though darkness fell on him, and without sense he swooned, as o'er and o'er again him Kṛṣṇa comforted.

475. Delusive error is all this universe, and what could he say (to Kṛṣṇa in reply)? As he looked and looked again on each and every hair (of his dearling) happiness began to come to him. He rose and took him in his arms, and sweet kisses gave he him.

476. He gave him every blessing that was meet. 'Above all shine thou illustrious! and now and again must thou call us to the mind.'

477. King Vasudēva also did him console. As loving friends made they each the other content, and to Kṛṣṇa and Rāma gave they both their blessings.

478. Countless the possessions and the coined money that Kṛṣṇa gave to him, so much was it as would be the burden of hundreds of horses. Nanda and Yaśōdā received all that they needed saving only Kṛṣṇa.

479. Weeping the Cowherds returned to their home,—weeping, for they could not endure that Kṛṣṇa should be far away. Their hearts they set to meditate on him.

480. Lamentations began Yaśōdā, 'When shall I ever see Śrī Bhagavān?' and all her household duties she forgot.

481. He who beareth in his heart the name of Kṛṣṇa, to him will Kṛṣṇa every favour render. In this world glory will he win and thereafter the abode of Viṣṇu will he reach. To him posy and posy do I offer lotuses.

482. Ever dedicating myself to Kṛṣṇa's name, ever dedicating myself to his incarnation, ever dedicating myself to his auspicious deeds, to him posy and posy do I offer lotuses.

XXIII. THE EDUCATION OF THE BROTHERS, THE PRECEPTOR'S FEE, THE DEATH OF ŚAṄKHÂSURA, AND THE RESCUE OF THE PRECEPTOR'S SON FROM YAMA'S LIMBO. (Bhāg. Pu. X, xlv, 29ff.)

483. So Vasudēva took the charge of bringing up his sons. For each he carried through the holy sacraments,—the Cutting of the Hair, and the Vesting with the Sacramental Thread.

Garga-rĕsh[1] gāyĕtrī zaph dyut[u]nas ta
Krushna-jyuv snān sand log[u] karanē
pāṭhas pūzi log[u] yitha pazihēs ta.
lāgas bŏh dasta dasta pampōsh. 484.

bārȧn[i] sūzin tsāṭahālas ta
Sŏndīpan nömis gŏras nish
tsŏhaiṭh vidyāyĕ log[u] paranas ta. lāgas etc. 485.

tsŏhaiṭhan dŏhan sand dits[ü]nas ta
tsŏhaiṭhay vidyāyĕ hĕchith gav
jai-kār tasandis paranāwanas ta. lāgas etc. 486.

jai-kār Krushna-jyuwanis paranas ta
namaskār kara-nā Krushnañē bŏz[ü]
namaskār Shukadēwanis wananas ta. lāgas etc. 487.

vidyā-dakhĕnā gŏr[i] münj[ü]nas ta
'pŏth[a]r sôn[u] chuh phoṭ[u]mot[u] samudras manz
mā̃gayi-wŏnda chum tȧs[i] pŏtras' ta. lāgas etc. 488.

yüts[ü] kāl wātsākh pŏtra-shūkas ta
Bagawān zönith mang kür[ü]has
gŏra-bāwa Krushna-jyuv[i] maṭi hyot[u]nas ta. lāgas etc. 489.

Krushna-jyuv bôy[u] hĕth khot[u] rathas ta
samudra pĕṭh gōra-bôy[u] tshāḍani drāy
manŏshĕ-rūp[i] Samudra pyōs pādas ta. lāgas etc. 490.

Krushna-jyuv[i] wŏṭh löy[ü] manz sŏdras ta
Shĕnkhāsŏras tati mörith drāv
wacha andra Pāntsazañ shĕnkh koḍ[u]nas ta. lāgas etc. 491.

Pāntsazañ shĕnkh yus Bagawāṇas ta
suy tȧm[i] asŏran on[u]mot[u] ôs[u]
hīth ôs[u] suy shĕnkh athi ananas ta. lāgas etc. 492.

tati pĕṭha gatshān chuh Darmarāzas ta
nĕb[a]ray shĕnkhuk[u] shĕbd kor[u]nas
Darmaröz[i] shĕbd būz[u] gav harshĕs ta. lāgas etc. 493.

---

1 See verse 129.

2 According to Hindū ideas, a preceptor is a second father. His son is there-

484. Garga[1] the Sage was he who chanted the Gāyatrī. Kṛṣṇa began duly to bathe and to perform the Evening Rite, and, as was meet, worship did he and holy texts recited.

485. Then to school did Vasudēva send the brothers, to a preceptor named Sāndīpani, and he to them of the sixty-four sciences the lore read forth.

486. Sixty-four days gave he him instruction, and so the four and sixty lores he taught. To his tuition Victory be ascribed!

487. To Kṛṣṇa's studies too be victory ascribed! To his discerning wit shall I not offer reverence! Reverence be to the telling of the tale by Śukadēva.

488. Then the preceptor asked of them his teacher's fee, 'In the Ocean hath our son been drowned, and for that son, and him alone, make I my longing prayer.'

489. For many a day had they, the teacher and his wife, been homed with sorrow for their son. Kṛṣṇa they held as Bhagavān, and so they made to him this prayer. So Kṛṣṇa, in duty to his preceptor bound, upon his shoulder took the task.

490. He and his brother on their chariot mounted, and to the Ocean forth they sallied in quest of their teacher-brother[2]. There did the Ocean, taking human form, at their feet prostrate himself.

491. Into the Ocean Kṛṣṇa took a leap, and came forth thence, there having Śaṅkhâsura slain, and from his breast tore he the conch named Pañcajanya.

492. This Pañcajanya conch to Bhagavān had in elden time belonged, but it that demon once had carried off. (And that had been permitted with but) this object that into Kṛṣṇa's hand the conch should come.

493. Thereafter goeth he to Yama, the Regent (of the Limbo of the Dead), and still outside the palace sounded he the conch. Then, when he heard the blast, did Yama, the Lord of Justice, in his heart rejoice.

---

fore a brother to his pupils, and is called in Kāshmīrī a *gōra-bôy*ᵘ, or 'Teacher-brother.'

brõṭha drās nana-wāth pād nám^{i}nas ta
tsönith pūzanas vĕdi-vĕz^{ü} log^{u}
gōra-bôy^{u} anith ta sũty dyut^{u}nas ta.
lāgas bŏh dasta dasta pampōsh. 494.

hīth ôs^{u} Narakák^{i} mŏkalāwanas ta
Pāntsazañĕ-shĕnkha-shĕbda mŏkalith gay
gōra-bôy^{u} sũty hĕth ta āv pā^{n}as ta. lāgas etc. 495.

gōras ách^{i}-gāshĕr dyut^{u}nas ta
gōr-mājĕ gŏras paran pĕv
öhiyāh nith ta āy tati pānas. lāgas etc. 496.

yus lagi Krushna-jyuwanis nāwas ta
tas kari Krushna-jyuv sarŏ wŏpakār
yiti yĕsh nith ta wāti Vishnu-bawanas ta. lāgas etc. 497.

pör^{i} pör^{i} Krushna-jyuwanis nāwas ta
pör^{i} pör^{i} tasandis autāras
pör^{i} pör^{i} tasandis shŏba tsarĕtas ta. lāgas etc. 498.

XXIV.

kal rūz^{ü} Gōkul kun Krushnas ta
Nanda-gūr^{u} Yĕshōdā ti tsĕtas pyēs
gōpiyĕn-hond^{u} srĕh log^{u} sŏranas ta.
lāgas bŏh dasta dasta pampōsh. 499.

Wuddav sūz^{u}nakh sath karanas ta
gyānüc^{ü} sand dith man raṭanas
tsintā tröv^{i}tan sör^{ü} manas ta. lāgas etc. 500.

Wuddav wôt^{u} yĕli Gōkulas ta
Nanda-gūr^{u} pŏtra-dādi bōwala zan
Yĕshōdāyĕ-hond^{u} yiyi na zi wananas ta. lāgas etc. 501.

gūr^{i}-shur^{i} gūr^{i}-bāyĕ söriy d^{a}yanas ta
'Krushna, Krushna,' karith wŏsh trāwān
walana ās sör^{i} Krushna-nāwas ta. lāgas etc. 502.

Nanda-gūr^{u} gari gari log^{u} pritshanas ta
'mölis ta mājĕ chwā karān sīwā
lás^{i}tan ta biyĕ dĕwa ani tsĕtas' ta. lāgas etc. 503.

494. Barefoot came he forth to meet him, and to his feet he bowed himself; within he led him, and duly worshipped him. The teacher-brother brought he, and to Kṛṣṇa gave he him.

495. All this was done that all in Limbo might be saved; for at the sound of the blast of the Pañcajanya conch salvation gained they all. So with his teacher-brother Kṛṣṇa went his way.

496. To his preceptor gave he the light of his eyes, and at the feet of his teacher-father and his teacher-mother did he fall. Then he their blessing took and home returned.

497. He who beareth in his heart the name of Kṛṣṇa, to him will Kṛṣṇa every favour render. In this world glory will he win, and thereafter the abode of Viṣṇu will he reach. To him posy and posy do I offer lotuses.

498. Ever dedicating myself to Kṛṣṇa's name, ever dedicating myself to his incarnation, ever dedicating myself to his auspicious deeds, to him posy and posy do I offer lotuses.

XXIV. UDDHAVA'S MISSION. (Bhāg. Pu. X, xlvi.)

499. Longing for Gōkula to Kṛṣṇa came. To his mind came a memory of Nanda and Yaśōdā and of the love the herd-damsels bare him.

500. To comfort them sent he Uddhava, and to hearten them by the teaching of the true knowledge. 'Let them', quoth he, 'abandon all anxiety of mind.'

501. When Uddhava to Gōkula came, Nanda found he as though crazed by sorrow for his son, and of Yaśōdā naught can be described.

502. The herd-lads and the herd-wives all were sad distraught. Sighing 'Kṛṣṇa, Kṛṣṇa' all were wrapt in Kṛṣṇa's name.

503. Ever and anon would Nanda ask, 'To his father and his mother doeth he now suit and service? Long may he live! Again will he ever call us to his mind?

'dŏda-mȫj^{u} pĕwān chĕsa kuni tsĕtas ta
yĕs ôs^{u} rāth-dŏh karān laḍa
khēlan-bȫj^{i} ti chisa tana manas' ta.
lāgas bŏh dasta dasta pampōsh. 504.

Krushnȧn^{i} tsarĕth yāñ lȧg^{i} tsĕntanas ta
tsēntān söriy vismrĕth gay
zônun 'gatshan mā prān trāwanas' ta. lāgas etc. 505.

apoz^{u} wanun pĕv Wuddawas ta
'Krushna-jyuv zi mĕ pata yiwāṅ chuh'
būzukh tih biyĕ tsākh zuv pānas ta. lāgas etc. 506

Yĕshōdāyĕ dŏda-baba āyĕ baranas ta
Krushnun^{u} yun^{u} yāñ kanan gōs
atshĕn dārāyĕ lüj^{u} wadanas ta. lāgas etc. 507.

Wuddȧv^{i} zĕv küḍ^{u} gyān wananas ta
gōpiyĕn ta biyĕ mājĕ Yĕshōdāyĕ
'lȧg^{i}tav söriy Paramātmas' ta. lāgas etc. 508.

'ātma chuh vyöpith tsar-atsaras ta
ruma ruma ramān gyānawānan
tana mana lȧg^{i}tav Nishkalas' ta. lāgas etc. 509

gōpiyĕn tsās na kēh gyān manas ta
Krushnani prīma āsa britsha barān
kētha kēh phōrihē tas Wuddawas ta. lāgas etc. 510.

lagahön Krushnañĕ khēla wananas ta
Krushnun^{u} wanān rōzihēkh na sŏr
sārĕy wandān pān Krushnas ta. lāgas etc. 511.

öhiy mangani lajĕ Wuddawas ta
'Krushnunuy prīm asĕ mani bȧḍ^{i}tan
Krushn^{ü}y āsav nĕth sŏranas' ta. lāgas etc. 512.

---

1 I.e., the philosophy of the Vēdânta, based on knowledge, as contrasted with loving faith in God. The whole teaching of the Bhakti-mārga, of which the Bhāgavata Purāṇa is the great textbook, is that salvation can be gained only by loving

504. 'To his mind doth ever come his foster-mother, she in whose arms he was wont to frolic struggling night and day? Have his playmates since those days been in his heart?'

505. When on Kṛṣṇa's deeds they began to think, as they thought they lost all consciousness, and to Uddhava it seemed that soon will they abandon life.

506. Words void of truth was he compelled to tell them, 'After me doth Kṛṣṇa follow on,' and, when that they heard, life again their bodies entered.

507. When the tale of Kṛṣṇa's coming came upon her ears, the bosom of Yaśōdā filled with milk, and tears in floods to weep did she begin.

508. To the herd-damsels and to Yaśōdā did Uddhava put forth his tongue to tell the way of Knowledge,[1] 'To the Soul Supreme be ye devoted all.

509. 'That Self which pervadeth all that moveth and all that moveth not, that Self that abideth in each hair of them that Knowledge have, to that Self indiscrete, body and soul do ye yourselves devote.'

510. But into the mind of the herd-damsels naught entered of his knowledge. For love of Kṛṣṇa lamentations poured they forth. How could speech issue from their mouths to Uddhava?

511. They would begin to tell him of Kṛṣṇa's frolics, and as they spake of him, all consciousness would they lose. To Kṛṣṇa each and all did they dedicate themselves.

512. From Uddhava began they to implore a blessing. 'Ever may love for Kṛṣṇa, and him alone, in our hearts wax more and more, and him alone may we ever in our memories keep.'

---

faith. No system of dry philosophy can bring the seeker to it. Uddhava tries to console them by philosophy, but soon finds his error, and is converted by them to the Way of Love.

gyānuk^{u} ahambāv tsol^{u} Wuddawas ta
dopun 'bakth ay ta gōpiyĕn-hünz$^{\breve{i}}$
gōpiyĕn sārĕn^{ü}y pĕv pādas ta.
lāgas bŏh dasta dasta pampōsh. 513.

hāwun bŏna ôs^{u} tas Wuddawas ta
prīm ta bakth kitsh^{ü} gatshi āsüñ^{ü}
kami lōla lȧg^{i}zĕs Bagawānas ta. lāgas etc. 514.

Wuddav phyūr^{u} yĕli pān wond^{u}has ta
thüñ^{ü} dŏd Krushnas kyut^{u} dyut^{u}has
thañĕ-dŏda-pray ös^{ü} bāla-Krushnas ta. lāgas etc. 515.

wôt^{u} Krushnas nishĕ sôr^{u} won^{u}nas ta
'gōpiyĕ sārĕn^{ü}y pĕṭh-kun chĕh
titsh^{ü}y bakth āsi prath baktis' ta. lāgas etc. 516.

yus lagi Krushna-jyuwanis nāwas ta
tas kari Krushna-jyuv sarŏ wŏpakār
yiti yĕsh nith ta wāti Vishnu-bawanas ta. lāgas etc. 517.

pör^{i} pör^{i} Krushna-jyuwanis nāwas ta
pör^{i} pör^{i} tasandis autāras
pör^{i} pör^{i} tasandis shŏba tsarĕtas ta. lāgas etc. 518.

XXV.

Wuddav boḍ^{u} bokt^{u} bǫw^{u} Krushnas ta
sārĕy kāmĕ āsa maṭi tȧm^{i}s^{ü}y
prath kĕh āgyā ôs^{u} pālanas ta
lāgas bŏh dasta dasta pampōsh. 519.

dŏha aki mani āv Krushna-ziwas ta
tĕli zi Kubzāyĕ ditsām wātsh
tasond^{u} gara pazi shūb^{a}rāwanas ta. lāgas etc. 520.

kuni chuna parwāy Bagawānas ta
bükts^{ü} nishĕ āyot^{u} sadā bǫw^{u}
bükts^{ü} suh warihē mĕ ti abalas ta. lāgas etc. 521.

513. Then from Uddhava did the egoism of knowledge flee. Cried he, 'If such a thing as loving devotion be, then that is what the damsels of the herd possess,' and at their feet he fell.

514. For sooth to that Uddhava had it to be shown how great the love and how great the devotion are that must be cherished, and with what yearning for Bhagavān he should be full filled.

515. When Uddhava turned back to go to Mathurā to him did they dedicate themselves. Butter and milk for Kṛṣṇa did they give him, for butter and milk had the boy Kṛṣṇa loved.

516. To Kṛṣṇa did he come and tell him all. 'Exalted above all be the herd damsels. May every devotee have such devotion.'

517. He who beareth in his heart the name of Kṛṣṇa, to him will Kṛṣṇa every favour render. In this world glory will he win, and thereafter the abode of Viṣṇu will he reach. To him posy and posy do I offer lotuses.

518. Ever dedicating myself to Kṛṣṇa's name, ever dedicating myself to his incarnation, ever dedicating myself to his auspicious deeds, to him posy and posy do I offer lotuses.

XXV. THE VISIT TO KUBJĀ. (Bhāg. Pu. X, xlviii.)

519. Thus became Uddhava with great devotion for Kṛṣṇa filled. On his shoulder lay the burden of all Kṛṣṇa's businesses, and each order that was given him, that did he obey.

520. Once on a day it came to Kṛṣṇa's mind, 'That day to Kubjā a promise did I give, and I must go, and with my presence make her house adorned.'

521. No need for cark or care concerning Bhagavān. To true devotion ever hath he been the slave. To me, the feeble wight, true devotion may he too vouchsafe.

Kubzāyĕ ǵara āv wöñ^{ü} pālanas ta
Wuddawa-baktis sŭ̄ty hĕth kĕth
bakti-bāv hāwun ôs^{u} Wuddawas ta.
lāǵas bŏh dasta dasta pampōsh. 522.

wātawun^{u} Kubzāyĕ pān wond^{u}nas ta
lōla sŭ̄ty pādan dörith ta shēr
bakth prīm kôtwāh lüj^{ü} baranas ta. lāǵas etc. 523.

pūzā kür^{ü}nas yitha pazihēs ta
khĕnüc^{ü} ta cenüc^{ü} kath kyāh ös^{ü}
tana mana Krushna-rūph lüj^{ü} wuchanas ta. lāǵas etc. 524.

rāth dŏh lagith Krushna-dyānas ta
tas vina ôsus na kĕ̄h bāsān
sath nĕth kiʦh^{ü} āsi Bagawānas ta. lāǵas etc. 525.

Wuddawa-baktis ti yĕʦh bür^{ü}nas ta
sīwā kaiʦāh karanē lüj^{ü}
Wuddav wuch^{i} wuch^{i} pĕ̄v sŏranas ta. lāǵas etc. 526.

yiʦh^{ü}y bakth yĕs āsi baktis
sadā Waikunṭh tasonduy thān
bakth^{ü}y ʦür^{ü} kắr^{i}zi Bagawānas ta. lāǵas etc. 527.

namaskār Krushnanis dayĕ gaʦhanas ta
Kubzāyĕ bāǵĕ-bajĕ namaskār
ʦandana-ṭūrĕ kyāh phal dyut^{u}nas ta. lāǵas etc. 528.

yus lagi Krushna-jyuwanis nāwas ta
tas kari Krushna-jyuv sarŏ wŏpakār
yiyi yĕsh nith ta wāti Vishnu-bawanas ta. lāǵas etc. 529.

pör^{i} pör^{i} Krushna-jyuwanis nāwas ta
pör^{i} pör^{i} tasandis autāras
pör^{i} pör^{i} tasandis shŏba ʦarĕtas ta. lāǵas etc. 530.

XXVI.

dŏha aki ǵara āv Akrūras ta
Haladar Rām ta Wuddav hĕth
Bagawān chuh baktis āyĕʦāras ta
lāǵas bŏh dasta dasta pampōsh. 531.

522. To Kubjā's house came he, his promise to fulfil, and with him took he Uddhava, his devotee: for fain to Uddhava would he show the nature true of devotion.

523. E'en as he reached her door, to him did Kubjā dedicate herself; in yearning upon his feet her head she laid. Mighty was the love and mighty the devotion that her heart full filled.

524. As meet, she duly to him offered worship. What need is there to tell the meat and drink she offered. With body and with soul on Kṛṣṇa's form she gazèd fain.

525. Night and day on Kṛṣṇa had she been pondering. Apart from him naught was apparent to her eyes. Wondrous is the hope that can for aye on Bhagavān be placed.

526. To Uddhava the devotee showed she also honour great. How great was the service that she did to him! And to Uddhava, as he looked and looked, fell understanding.

527. The devotee who hath such devotion and it alone, for aye in Vaikuṇṭha his abode will be. Therefore to Bhagavān offer thou plenteous devotion.

528. To Kṛṣṇa's graciousness be reverence paid, reverence be to Kubjā's blessed lot. For but a jar of sandal so wondrous a reward to her was granted.

529. He who beareth in his heart the name of Kṛṣṇa, to him will Kṛṣṇa every favour render. In this world glory will he win, and thereafter the abode of Viṣṇu will be reach. To him posy and posy do I offer lotuses.

530. Ever dedicating myself to Kṛṣṇa's name, ever dedicating myself to his incarnation, ever dedicating myself to his auspicious deeds, to him posy and posy do I offer lotuses.

XXVI. AKRŪRA'S MISSION TO DELHI. (Bhāg. Pu. X, xlviii-ix.)

531. Once on a day came he to Akrūra's house, and with him Haladhara and Uddhava; for Bhagavān is of his devotees the slave.

Akrūr^{i} kaitsāh bakth kür^{u}nas ta
bāgĕs tasandis jai-jai-kār
yĕs wari Bagawān tsor^{u} kus tas ta
lāgas bŏh dasta dasta pampōsh. 532.

āgyā sōpün^{u} Akrūras ta
Kaurawan ta Pānḍawan hĕnē shŏd
mônun bāgy ta log^{u} pakanas ta. lāgas etc. 533.

Akrūr yĕli wôt^{u} tath nagaras ta
sārĕv^{ü}y ādar ta mān kor^{u}has
rāza Duryōdan ôs^{u} madas ta. lāgas etc. 534.

Kuntiyĕ mātāyĕ shĕch^{i} pritsh^{u}nas ta
manuk^{u} shūkh lüj^{ü} tas wananē
'sôn^{u} ār yiyi-nā Krushna-zīwas' ta. lāgas etc. 535.

'wuch-ta tas myōn^{i} shur^{i} bōy^{i} wātanas ta
pit^{a}rĕn-handi atha dŏkh bājan
bōy^{i}cār pazihēs wŏndi ananas' ta. lāgas etc. 536.

Kuntī pŏph ōs^{u} Krusḥna-zīwas ta
Pāndav santān Kuntiyĕ-hánd^{i}
wár^{i} tami hĕt^{i}mát^{i} Pantsa-daiwatas ta. lāgas etc. 537.

Darmarāzas ta Yindra-rāzas ta
byākh hyot^{u}mot^{u} Wāwa-lūkapālas
Mŏdriyĕ Ashwinī-dēwa-jōras ta. lāgas etc. 538.

Yindraprastha-rājy ôs^{u} Pānḍu-rāzas ta
Drĕtarāshṭr on^{u} rājy karihē kyāh
Duryōdan zāv Drĕtarāshṭras ta. lāgas etc. 539.

Pānḍu-rāza yĕli gav maranāntas ta
Yudishṭhir rāza tath taktas byūṭh^{u}
Duryōdan rājy kĕtha z^{a}ravihas ta. lāgas etc. 540.

532. What manifold devotion did Akrūra pay to him! To his good fortune be there victory! What greater man is there than he to whom Bhagavān a boon doth grant!

533. To Akrūra a command gave he of the Kauravas and of the Pāṇḍavas to bring the news. His happy lot Akrūra recognized, and straightway he set forth.

534. At the city (of Delhi) did Akrūra arrive, and to him all showed honour and respect. Full of mad pride was King Duryōdhana.

535. From Mother Kuntī did he ask the news, and sorrow filled her heart as the tale she told, 'On us will not the pity of Kṛṣṇa fall?

536. 'Behold the happenings to my sons, his brethren.[1] Sorrow sup they at their cousins' hands. Into his heart should he recall their brotherhood.'

537. Of Kṛṣṇa's father, Kuntī was the sister, of Kuntī were the Pāṇḍavas the sons, in boon from the Five Gods had she obtained them.

538. On her had they been begotten by Dharma-rāja (i.e. Yama), by Indra, and again by Vāyu the Lōkapāla, and again, on (her co-wife) Mādrī, by the twin Aśvin gods.

539. The kingdom of Indraprastha to King Pāṇḍu did belong, for blind was (his elder brother) Dhṛtarāṣṭra, and therefore rule he could not, and to Dhṛtarāṣṭra was Duryōdhana born.

540. When died the Pāṇḍu king, upon the throne sat Yudhiṣṭhira (his eldest son), and his rule how could Duryōdhana endure?

---

[1] I.e. cousins, as explained in the next verse.

Pānḍawan hīta hīta log^{u} khīdas ta
pit^{a}r^{i} gālanas pĕṭh pyōmot^{u}
hath böy^{i} biyĕ tas hih^{i} pānas ta
lāgas bŏh dasta dasta pampōsh. 541.

Pānḍawan khīd ôs^{u} prath samayĕs ta
shĕtruth ôsukh karahŏn kyāh
hĕkahŏn na z^{a}ravith ös^{i} shūkas ta. lāgas etc. 542.

Akrūr nishĕ gav Drĕtarāshṭras ta
dop^{u}nas ‘ rājy karta vĕtsāra sān
som^{u} wuch ta pŏtras biyĕ bābath^{a}ras ’ ta. lāgas etc.
543.

lajyāv Krushnañi zĕvi wananas ta
tas ôs^{u} na pānas āyĕtsār kĕh
dop^{u}nas zi ‘ pör^{i} laga Krushna-pādas ’ ta. lāgas etc.
544.

‘ kyāh kara, chim na shur^{i} athi āyĕtas ta
na ta chim bābath^{a}r ach^{i}-gāshĕr
pōshĕ na pŏtras ta kyāh dapa kas ’ ta. lāgas etc. 545.

Akrūr wuchith nishĕ āv Krushnas ta
Pānḍawan ta Kaurawan-hond^{u} won^{u}nas
Kuntiyĕ mātāyĕ-hond^{u} ti won^{u}nas ta. lāgas etc. 546.

Krushna-jyuv ti zāgān ôs^{u} hītas ta
butarötsü-hond^{u} bār kāsun^{u} chus
hīta aki Kaurav gay nāshĕs ta. lāgas etc. 547.

yus lagi Krushna-jyuwanis nāwas ta
tas kari Krushna-jyuv sarŏ wŏpakār
yiti yĕsh nith ta wāti Vishnu-bawanas ta. lāgas etc.
548.

pör^{i} pör^{i} Krushna-jyuwanis nāwas ta
pör^{i} pör^{i} tasandis autāras
pör^{i} pör^{i} tasandis shŏba tsarĕtas ta. lāgas etc. 549.

XXVII.

Magad-rājy ôs^{u} Zarāsandas ta
kōrĕ z^{a}h zāmatsa tas rākhĕsas
timay ditsamatsa tàm^{i} Kansas ta
lāgas bŏh dasta dasta pampōsh. 550.

541. On pretext here and pretext there the Pāṇḍavas he harassed. Though of his own father's kin sought he to destroy them; and like himself had he a hundred brothers.

542. Time and time again the Pāṇḍavas he harassed, yet could they not to him show enmity. His tyranny they could not thole, and filled were they with sorrow.

543. To Dhṛtarāṣṭra then Akrūra went. Quoth he, 'Prithee in justice do thou rule. Look equally upon thy son and on thy nephew.'

544. With Kṛṣṇa's tongue began he then to speak, for for himself had he no power to raise his voice, and to him Dhṛtarāṣṭra made reply, 'To Kṛṣṇa's feet I dedicate myself.'

545. 'What can I do? my lads are out of hand, nor are my nephews of my eyes the light. Upon my sons prevail I cannot, what can I say to whom?'

546. Thus did Akrūra see the doings there, and back to Kṛṣṇa did he return. To him of the Pāṇḍavas and Kauravas the tale he told, and of the plaint that Mother Kuntī made.

547. For a pretext was Kṛṣṇa seeking that the burden of the earth he might relieve; and through one pretext to destruction went the Kauravas.

548. He who beareth in his heart the name of Kṛṣṇa, to him will Kṛṣṇa every favour render. In this world glory will he win, and thereafter the abode of Viṣṇu will he reach. To him posy and posy do I offer lotuses.

549. Ever dedicating myself to Kṛṣṇa's name, ever dedicating myself to his incarnation, ever dedicating myself to his auspicious deeds, to him posy and posy do I offer lotuses.

XXVII. THE WAR WITH JARĀSANDHA. (Bhāg. Pu. X, l, li.)

550. Of Magadha was Jarāsandha king, a demon he, and two daughters he possessed. Them to Kaṁsa in wedlock had he given.

Krushna-jyuv phor^{u} yĕli tas Kansas ta
Zarāsandas ṭôṭh^{u} dŏkh pĕv
mŏnḍa kōrĕ gatshith ta dôd^{u} won^{u}has ta
lāgas bŏh dasta dasta pampōsh. 551.

'tsĕ hyuh^{u} zi rāza chu-na yith samayĕs ta
balāy cyŏnis rājy karanas
gūr^{i}-shur^{i} laz pöv^{ü}nay rājĕs' ta. lāgas etc. 552.

laz pöv^{ü}has tas baḍis rākhĕsas ta
tr^{a}h akshauhinī sūty hĕth ta drāv
laḍani lāryōv Krushna-zīwas ta. lāgas etc. 553.

Mathurāyĕ kamph tsāv prath Yādawas ta
Zarāsand^{i} yĕli sīnā sūz^{ü}
'Krushna, Krushna, trāhi, trāhi' låg^{i} karanas ta. lāgas etc. 554.

ḍīṭh^{i} yĕli Krushnan log^{u} sŏranas ta
ratha z^{a}h ākāshĕ brōṭh-kun ās
sŏna ratna jår^{i}måt^{i} hih^{i} sūrĕs ta. lāgas etc. 555.

akis āyŏd yus Krushnas ta
biyis ti āyŏd Haladaranis
jĕba-jāma rathawöl^{i} sūty rathas ta. lāgas etc. 556.

dŏshĕway jĕba-jāma låg^{i} ganḍanas ta
dŏnaway bārån^{i} rathan bīṭh^{i}
kĕh Yādav ti nīkh sūty pānas ta. lāgas etc. 557.

sanmukh sampån^{i} yĕli yŏddas ta
Krushna-jyuv rākhĕsañi sīnāyi gyūr^{u}
Zarāsand bōlani log^{u} Krushnas ta. lāgas etc. 558.

'nĕcivi, bōz myôn^{u}, tsal pānas ta
'na-ta zān zi myāni atha kĕh chuy na pāy
Haladara-rāmas kĕtha patsas' ta. lāgas etc. 559.

Krushna-jyuv^{i} dop^{u}nas 'wanakh pānas ta
sīnā sör^{ü}y mūmüts^{ü} zān
ts^{a}y yôt^{u} trāwath zinda-pānas' ta. lāgas etc. 560

551. When Kṛṣṇa Kaṁsa of his life had robbed, dear (i.e. extreme) grief on Jarāsandha fell, as his widowed daughters came and to him unfolded of their woes the tale.

552. 'In these days like to thee there is no king. On thy rule be shame! On thy rule the cowherd lads have cast disgrace.'

553. On that great demon cast they shame. With thirty armies all complete then marched he forth, and hastened on with Kṛṣṇa to contend.

554. In Mathurā trembling entered every Yādava when Jarāsandha his host dispatched, and 'Kṛṣṇa! Kṛṣṇa! Save us! save us!' began they to implore.

555. When Kṛṣṇa saw them, then he became attent, and from the sky there came before him two chariots studded with gold and jewels like the sun.

556. In one were weapons that for Kṛṣṇa were, the other for Haladhara held the arms. With each were armour and a charioteer.

557. The brothers twain their armour donned. Then sat they in their chariots, and a few Yādavas took they with themselves.

558. When to the battle front they came, the host of demons Kṛṣṇa did surround, and thus to him did Jarāsandha speak.

559. 'Boy, hearken to my rede, and flee thou home. If thou wilt not, then know that from my hand no shift can save thee. On Haladhara, too, (if him I slay not), how can I have trust?'

560. Kṛṣṇa replied, 'Say that to thyself. Know that thine army is as good as dead, and thee alone shall I let go alive.'

krūd khot^{u} asŏras ta log^{u} laḍanas ta
yĕkh-lakh sārĕv^{ü}y atha korukh
danu-danḍ tulun^{u} pĕv Shrī-Krushnas ta
lāgas bŏh dasta dasta pampōsh. 561

danu-danḍa-shĕbda sūty lág^{i} maranas ta
Haladara-rāman ti mārán^{i} hĕt^{i}
samhār samponukh tath kshĕnas ta. lāgas etc. 562.

ratacĕ kŏla lajĕ bajĕ wahanas ta
narĕ zanga gāḍa zan āṣa phērān
Zarāsand kun^{u} zon^{u} rūd^{u} laḍanas ta. lāgas etc. 563.

Haladár^{i} raṭith nyūn Krushna-zīwas ta
'daph-tam zi, Krushna-jyuwa. karas kyāh'
āgyā kür^{ü}nas atha trāwanas ta. lāgas etc. 564.

'sĕṭhāh zi kāmĕ chĕh wuñĕ maṭi tas ta
yīts^{ü} biyĕ phiri yiyi sīnā hĕth
sŏrith ta lūkh ös^{i} sör^{i} tsalanas' ta. lāgas etc. 565.

atha tala trôwun ta log^{u} tsalanas ta
mandachani log^{u} ta karihē kyāh
pananĕv sārĕv^{ü}y süts^{ü} karĕhas ta. lāgas etc. 566

Krushna-jyuv Mathurāyĕ āv pānas ta
Yādav pānavüñ^{ü} wadạvĕn lág^{i}
dēwatā söriy pōshĕ-warshĕnas ta. lāgas etc. 567

ánikh brāhman vēd paranas ta
gara gara wŏtsav sōpanani log^{u}
kaitwāh dana lág^{i} dān dinas ta. lāgas etc. 568.

yih kĕh dana ās athi lūṭas ta
dyutun tih athi rāja Wugrasēnas
söriy zayĕ sūty lág^{i} vĕṭhanas ta. lāgas etc. 569.

sadāhi phiri biyĕ biyĕ yiyihas ta
zönith zi 'chum na kuni pōshĕn pāy'
sör^{ü}y sīnā biyĕ mör^{ü}nas ta. lāgas etc. 570

561. Wrath seized the demon and he advanced to fight. All the host joined in combat hand to hand, and Kṛṣṇa saw that he must raise his bow.

562. At the bow's mere twang, to die did they begin, and Haladhara too set to to slay. Then in that single moment on them fell destruction.

563. Great rivers of blood began to flow. In them, like fishes, round and round floated arms and legs, and on the battlefield Jarāsandha alone remained.

564. Him Haladhara seized and before Kṛṣṇa brought. 'Tell me, O Kṛṣṇa, what shall I do to him?' And to release him Kṛṣṇa gave command.

565. 'Of many a deed to do on his shoulder lieth still the burden. Again will he come with such a host as this, when he remembereth that all his men (to-day) have fled.'

566. Him he set free, and so away he fled, cast down with shame. But what else could he do? So all his folk to him gave consolation.

567. To Mathurā did Kṛṣṇa then return. With gratulations did the Yādavas mutually give him welcome, and from heaven showered down the gods a rain of flowers.

568. To read the Vēdas Brāhmaṇas they brought, in every house held they high festival. Uncounted wealth in gifts did they distribute.

569. The wealth that to his hand as plunder came, that gave he all to Ugrasēna the king, as full of exultation all cried victory.

570. Again, again, full seventeen times kept Jarāsandha coming, knowing full well 'ne'er over him shall I prevail,' and each time was his host by Kṛṣṇa slaughtered.

su-ti ôs^{u} tayār biyĕ laḍanas ta
na-ta ôs^{u} gŏḍañiy mŏkalyōmot^{u}
būmi-bār kāsun^{u} ôs^{u} Krushnas ta
lāgas bŏh dasta dasta pampōsh. 571.

Zarāsandas gav yĕli manas ta
'phiri aki myāni atha kyāh tsalihē'
kāman barihē tsür^{ü} manas ta. lāgas etc. 572.

dŏha aki Nārod^{u} wôt^{u} rākhĕsas ta
darshĕna tȧm^{i}-sandi zuv tsāv tas
'kāmanā zi nērĕm nishĕ Nāradas' ta. lāgas etc. 573.

Zarāsȧnd^{i} pūzā kür^{ü} Nāradas ta
kāmanā pūranuk[1] war mong^{u}nas
Nāradan bükts^{ü} sũty tiy môn^{u}nas ta. lāgas etc. 574.

Zarāsȧnd^{i} wāc hĕth sôr^{u} won^{u}nas ta
'bŏh zi chus prath vizi lazi tsalanas
pōshān zāh chus-na Krushna-gōpas ta. lāgas etc.
575.

'wŏpāyāh wantam tas tsalanas ta
su-ti aki laṭi nishĕ tsalihē mĕ
cyāniy wāka pazi tiy bananas' ta. lāgas etc. 576.

Nārada-munīshŏr^{i} war dyut^{u}nas ta
'yimi phiri pānay lagi tsalanē
cyāni ḍarạ gara kari manz samudras' ta lāgas etc.
577.

wŏpakār kor^{u}nas ta wath hôw^{u}nas ta
'Kāliyĕwan Kôbuluk^{u} rāzā boḍ^{u}
tas kũh pōshi-na tath balas' ta. lāgas etc. 578.

'Rudran dits^{ü}-müts^{ü} chĕh tsür^{ü} wath tas ta
asandi atha atsi Yādawan kŏph
hĕki-na mōra yith Krushna-jyuv tas' ta. lāgas etc.
579.

'yŏddas sũty hĕth suy pānas ta
Krushna-jyuv pānay lagi tsalanē
ma-ta karta tör^{ü}, shĕch^{i} karta rāzas' ta. lāgas etc.
580.

---

1 The Text spells the name *Kāliyavana*, but the Viṣṇu Purāṇa has *Kālayavana*.

571. Again the war to wage did he make ready. (This was allowed) that Kṛṣṇa might relieve the burden of the earth; else at the first would he (by death) salvation have received.

572. When into Jarāsandha's mind it came, 'Will he once more from out my hand escape,'—for such was the longing that greatly filled his heart,—

573. Once on a day to the demon king came Nārada, and at his sight life, as it were, did Jarāsandha enter, as he thought, 'Surely through Nārada will my longing meet success.'

574. To Nārada did Jarāsandha offer reverence meet, and of the fulfilment of his longing craved the boon. Then Nārada with courtesy consented.

575. So Jarāsandha took up his parable and said, 'Time after time disgraced I flee from him. Ne'er over that cowherd, Kṛṣṇa, do I aught prevail.

576. 'Tell me some means for putting him to flight, that he but once from me may flee. Thy word must necessarily be fulfilled.'

577. Nārada, Prince of Sages, granted him the boon. 'This time will he himself before thee flee; in fear of thee, the ocean will he make his home.'

578. Thus him he favoured, and the way he showed. 'Of Kābul is Kālayavana[1] a puissant king; against his power can no one e'er prevail.

579. 'Rudra hath given him a mighty course; quaking will enter the Yādavas at his hand, nor will it be in Kṛṣṇa's power to confront him.

580. 'If with thyself thou takest him to battle, Kṛṣṇa himself will fain betake to flight. Make no delay, but send a message to the king.'

---

[1] The Bhāgavata Purāṇa generally calls him simply *Yavana*.

Zarāsandas yĕli tsāv manas ta
Nāradas phīrith ta dapanē log^{u}
'ġŏra, zi köm^{ü} cyŏñ^{ü} chĕh, biyĕ dapa kas' ta
lāgas bŏh dasta dasta pampōsh. 581.

Nārada-munīshŏr^{i} ti-ti mộn^{u}nas ta
tasünz^{ü}y shĕch^{i} hĕth ta Kộbul^{u} gav
tithay wột^{u} yi-na kũh ḍēshihē tas ta. lāgas etc. 582.

sŏgand tsor^{u} ộs^{u} tas kanṭhas ta
pārizāta-pōshĕ-mālan-handi sũty
parzana ākh tami pādi nom^{u}has ta. lāgas etc. 583.

Kāliyĕwan^{i} shĕchi-bŏd sör^{ü} pritsh^{ü} tas ta
Nārad^{i} Zarāsandun^{u} won^{u}nas
'shĕran cĕy öy, pazi pālanas' ta. lāgas etc. 584.

Kāliyĕwan mana-kin^{i} log^{u} vĕṭhanas ta
'rāza Zarāsand-hyuh^{u} zi shĕranē pyōm
shĕranāgath āv, pazi rachanas' ta. lāgas etc. 585.

'wŏdyōg karun^{u}' pĕv Kāliyĕwanas ta
sīnā sör^{ü} hĕth ta Kộbula drāv
gur^{i}-m^{a}tra nadiyĕ lajĕ pakanas ta. lāgas etc. 586.

Krushna-jyuv dapān Balabadras ta
'Kāliyĕwan wŏñ zi āv, mŏkha nērus,
Zarāsand yiyi mā pata nagaras' ta. lāgas etc. 587.

sọrun samud^{a}r ās pādas ta
Dwārakāyĕ-kits^{ü} tas münj^{ü}n shāy
bāh yōzan hộkh^{u} boṭh^{u} samudras ta. lāgas etc. 588.

sampüñ^{ü} āgyā Vishŏkarmas ta
Dwārakā nagarāh sampanāwun^{u}
tamic^{ü} warnanā yiyi-na wananas ta. lāgas etc. 589.

---

1 This is a tree which grows in Indra's paradise. Its flowers have an unearthly fragrance. Nārada commonly wears a garland of them. See also verses 772 ff.

581. As these words entered Jarāsandha's mind, to Nārada thus made he his reply, 'O Mentor mine, thine is this work, I trow. Who other is there to whom the tale to tell?'

582. Also to this did Nārada consent, and so to Kābul he his message took. There so did he arrive that no one marked his coming.

583. But from the garland of Pārijāta[1] flowers, fragrance exceeding from his neck exhaled. So was he recognized, and at his feet the king bowed down.

584. From him did Kālayavana the news inquire, and Nārada the plight of Jarāsandha told. 'Upon thy mercy hath he thrown himself, and thus it be thy duty to protect him.'

585. Then in his heart did Kālayavana rejoice. 'A monarch great as Jarāsandha with me refuge seeketh. When one hath come to seek for refuge, then sheltered must he be.'

586. Then himself did Kālayavana bestir, from Kābul set he forth with all his host; from but the urine of his horses whole rivers 'gan to flow.

587. To Balabhadra then doth Kṛṣṇa say, 'Now hath come Kālayavana. If thou go forth to meet him, who knoweth but Jarāsandha may behind thee against the city come.'

588. Then called he the Ocean to his mind and at his feet he fell. From him he begged a site for Dvārakā,—for twelve leagues of the dry ocean shore.

589. To Viśvakarman[2] gave he a command. 'A city, Dvārakā must thou cause to be.' (So was it made, nor) can its glory be described.

---

[2] He was the artificer of the gods.

ġara kyuth^{u} pazihē Baġawānas ta
rājĕs naġarāh kyuth^{u} shūbihēs
sŏna mŏkta hīra-ratna sôr^{u} pūr^{u}nas ta
lāġas bŏh dasta dasta pampōsh. 590.

Yindras Kuvēras ta biyĕ Warunas ta
biyĕ yim söriy dēwa-lūkas
sōzun^{u} bôg^{u} pyōkh tath naġaras ta. lāġas etc. 591.

gör^{ü}n Māyā, shĕch^{i} wüñ^{ü}nas ta
Mathurāyĕ-hȧnd^{i} sör^{i} Dwārakāyĕ nīn
rātas shŏngith ta wŏth^{i} prātas ta. lāġas etc. 592.

wuch^{ü}kh Dwārakā baṭhi samudras ta
Mathurāyĕ-pĕṭha ös^{i} tot^{u} wöt^{i}mȧt^{i}
Māyāyĕ pör^{i} lȧg^{i} Baġawānas ta. lāġas etc. 593.

Mathurāyĕ Krushn drāv Kāliyĕwanas ta
tsatur-bŏza-darshun^{u} gŏḍa hôw^{u}nas
Garġanis pŏtras kō-na tōshĕhēs ta. lāġas etc. 594.

parzanana Krushn āv Kāliyĕwanas ta
hȧth^{i}yār trövith ta darshĕnas āv
tana mana sũty log^{u} Krushna-dyānas ta. lāġas etc.
595.

darshun^{u} hövith log^{u} tsalanas ta
Kāliyĕwan pata pata lārani log^{u}
mani chĕs kāmanā zi thaph karahas ta. lāġas etc.
596.

wātĕs atha tāñ pān dōravĕs ta
Kāliyĕwan pata pata biyĕ lārĕs
yāñ wôt^{u} Krushna-jyuv nishĕ parbatas ta. lāġas etc.
597.

tati tsāv ġŏphi ta pān khoṭ^{u}nas ta
Mutsukunda-rāza ôs^{u} tati shŏngith
tȧs^{i}-pĕṭh Krushnüñ^{u} shĕ̄kh ġayĕ tas ta. lāġas etc.
598.

---

[1] Garga was Kṛṣṇa's family priest and Guru, or spiritual preceptor. See verse 127. Kṛṣṇa therefore was bound to be polite to his son, and could not kill him

590. What sort of home for Bhagavān is fit? For his kingdom, how glorious should the city be! With gold and pearls and diamond-jewels did he fill it.

591. To Indra, to Kuvēra, and to Varuṇa, yea, to all them in heaven who abide, tribute to pay to Dvārakā there fell.

592. Then called he lovingly Illusion to his mind. To her a message he spake, and all the folk of Mathurā to Dvārakā she brought. At night went they to sleep at Mathurā. At dawn in Dvārakā they woke.

593. Then saw they Dvārakā on Ocean's shore; there had they all arrived from Mathurā, and to Bhagavān's Illusive Power themselves they dedicated.

594. (Bhāg. Pu. X, li.) From Mathurā went forth Kṛṣṇa Kālayavana to meet, and first (in graciousness) revealed he himself to him in his four-armed form. To Garga's [1] son how could he not show grace?

595. By Kālayavana was Kṛṣṇa recognized. Away he threw his weapons and, to show respect, advanced. Body and soul in meditation on Kṛṣṇa was he absorbed.

596. Having thus shown himself in wondrous guise Kṛṣṇa began to flee and Kālayavana after him pursued, for in his heart his longing was to grasp him with his hand.

597. Or ever his hand reached him, Kṛṣṇa increased his speed, and Kālayavana after him pursued, until a mountain Kṛṣṇa reached.

598. There entered he a cave and hid himself, where Mucukunda, the king, lay sunk in sleep, but Kālayavana thought that he was Kṛṣṇa.

---

with his own hands. The account of Kālayavana's birth will be found in verses 614ff.

ot^{u}-tāñ shŏd bŏd ös^{ü}s tas ta
gŏphi manz rākhyus yŏddas āv
zônun zi wôtus pata shĕtras ta
lāgas bŏh dasta dasta pampōsh. 599.

mada-sān rākhĕsan kraka ditsanas ta
wudus-na ta lath lāyēnas
'wŏth, laḍ, kawa tsākh tshĕpa dinas' ta. lāgas etc. 600

nẹ̆nd^{a}r tami tsüj^{ü} Mutsukundas ta
nitrav tasandĕv oğun drāv
tami-sūty basm ğav Kāliyĕwanas ta. lāgas etc. 601.

hīth ôs^{u} tshāḍun^{u} Bağawānas ta
gŏra-bôy^{u} ôsus kĕtha mārihēs
kāl pyōs tshāḍun^{u} kami pöṭh^{i} tas ta. lāgas etc. 602.

Mutsukund rāza ôs^{u} satĕ-yŏgas ta
dēwatā söriy artsān ôs^{u}
kĕ̃h kāl gatshith rūd^{u} dēwa-lūkas ta. lāgas etc. 603.

waīsi bajĕ ṫaṫ^{i} ôs^{u} kĕ̃h na sŏr tas ta
ṗaṫ^{i}-kin^{i} sôruy kŏl gol^{u}mot^{u}
tati drāv dīv laġ^{i} war dini tas ta. lāgas etc. 604.

dop^{u}nakh zi 'kĕ̃h chĕm-na kā̃kshā manas ta
nẹ̆nd^{a}rāh karahö khŏr wahörith
yuth^{u} na kā̃h wŏzanāvi mĕ shŏnganas' ta. lāgas etc. 605.

dēwatav prīti tiy war dyut^{u}has ta
'dwāpara-yŏğ tāñ nẹ̆ndr^{ü}y kar
Krushna-autāra gatsh mŏkti-dwāras' ta. lāgas etc. 606.

samay suy wôt^{u} Mutsukundas ta
kami hīta kami pöṭh^{i} sapon^{u} mŏkth
bŏd kuni wāti na Krushna-tsarĕtas ta. lāgas etc. 607.

---

1 Kālayavana, being the son of Garga, Kṛṣṇa's spiritual teacher, was therefore Kṛṣṇa's 'Teacher-brother'. See note to verse 490.

2 According to Hindū chronology there are four *yugas*, or ages., viz. the *Satya*, or Golden, Age, lasting 1,728,000 years, followed by the *Trēta*, or Silver, Age, lasting 1,296,000 years, then the *Dvāpara*, or Copper, Age, lasting 864,000 years, and then

599. Up to that time his senses had been clear. Into the cave the demon came to fight, 'For now,' thought he, 'I have mine enemy.'

600. In pride the demon gave forth a roar, but still King Mucukunda ne'er awoke, and Kālayavana kicked him with the shout, 'Arise and fight! Why hast thou entered here to hide thyself?'

601. Then, through that kick, did sleep flee from Mucukunda, and from his eyes there issued fire. Therewith to ashes was Kālayavana consumed.

602. For needs must Bhagavān a pretext seek, for how could he himself his Teacher-brother [1] slay, and how else compass his destruction?

603. Now Mucukunda in the Golden Age was king, and all the gods did he duly worship. Once, for a space, he went and dwelt in the gods' heaven itself.

604. There to a great age did he live, and (of his earthly life) lost memory. Thereafter was his entire family destroyed, and when at last from heaven he departed, granted the gods to him a boon.

605. Quoth he to them, 'Now no desire have I in my heart, and fain would I my legs stretch out and sleep, secure that no man e'er will wake me from my slumber.'

606. The gods in their love gave him that very boon. 'Naught shalt thou do but sleep until the Copper Age.[2] Then, through incarnate Kṛṣṇa, enter thou Death, the gateway of salvation.'

607. That time at length to Mucukunda came. How wondrous were the pretext and the mode by which salvation he attained! Man's intellect to Kṛṣṇa's deeds will ne'er attain.

---

the *Kali*, or present Iron, Age, lasting 432,000 years. As Kṛṣṇa lived at the end of the Dvāpara Age, Mucukunda must have slept during a part of the Satya Age, through the whole of the Trēta Age, and through the greater part of the Dvāpara Age, and his sleep must have lasted for more than two million years.

Mutsukund wŏthith pĕv āshtsaras ta
yih zi kus ôs^{u} ta banyōs kyāh
Dayĕ-gath kyāh-sana ös^{ü} bananas ta
lāgas bŏh dasta dasta pampōsh. 608.

wuchun ta Krushna-jyuv pata-kani tas ta
ạgnas hyuh^{u} zan prazalān ôs^{u}
pryutsh^{u}nas ta Krushna-jyuv^{i} sôr^{u} won^{u} tas ta.
lāgas etc. 609

būzun tih ta pĕv Krushna-pādas ta
pādan rūdus shēr dörith
bük^{ü}ts^{ü} sān kaitsāh tŏtā kür^{u}nas ta. lāgas etc. 610.

Krushna-jyuv tōṭhyōs ta war dyut^{u}nas ta
Mutsukund bakt^{ü}y mangani log^{u}
Krushna-jyuv^{i} bakth ti ta mŏkth dits^{ü}nas ta.
lāgas etc. 611.

labith war ta tāñ gav pānas ta
wŏttarāpath kun taph tsaranē
tana mana lagith Krushna-dyānas ta. lāgas etc. 612.

pör^{i} pör^{i} Krushna-jyuwanis nāwas ta
pör^{i} pör^{i} tasandis bakth waranas
pör^{i} pör^{i} Krushna-jyuwanis dyānas ta. lāgas etc. 613.

XXVIII.

Kāliyĕwanun^{u} zanm yiyi wananas ta
Garga-ryosh^{u} môl^{u} tas kĕtha-kin^{i} bọw^{u}
gŏra-bôy^{u} kĕtha āv lāri Krushnas ta
lāgas bŏh dasta dasta pampōsh. 614.

Garga-ryosh^{u} purōhĕth Yādawa-kŏlas ta
nētra-rost^{u} ôs^{u} brahma-tsarĕtas
Yādav tshāḍān thĕth purōhĕtas ta. lāgas etc. 615.

nētras kun pray karahönas ta
brahma-tsör^{i} Garga-ryosh^{u} māni na kĕh
kuni pöṭh^{i} pūshis na möñ^{e}rāwanas ta. lāgas etc. 616.

608. Arose then Mucukunda, and astonied cried, 'Who may this be, and what is this that happed? What manner of God's way hath thus been destined?'

609. He looked behind him then and Kṛṣṇa saw. Like fire blazing bright did Kṛṣṇa shine. Him did he ask, and Kṛṣṇa told him all.

610. The tale heard he and fell at Kṛṣṇa's feet, there did he rest with head upon his feet, and with devoted love unbounded praise he offered.

611. Kṛṣṇa to him showed grace and gave a boon. Only for holy love did Mucukunda pray, and to him such love and eke salvation Kṛṣṇa gave.

612. The boon received, forth did he depart in northern lands to live as anchorite, body and soul on Kṛṣṇa meditating.

613. Ever dedicating myself to Kṛṣṇa's name, ever dedicating myself to his incarnation, ever dedicating myself to his auspicious deeds, to him posy and posy do I offer lotuses.

XXVIII. THE HISTORY OF KĀLAYAVANA. (Viṣṇu Purāṇa,[1] V, xxiii.)

614. The birth of Kālayavana must now be told,—how Garga the sage became his sire, and how, being Teacher-brother, he came Kṛṣṇa to pursue.

615. Garga the sage was clan-priest of the Yādavas. Under a rule of chastity ne'er had he marriage made, but natheless sought the Yādavas the family of their clan-priest to establish.

616. They desired that he should marry, but being under the rule of chastity he heeded not, nor could they any wise persuade him to agree.

[1] This legend is not told at length in the Bhāgavata Purāṇa.

dŏha aki kathi-pĕṭh ṭhaṭha kor^{u}has ta
‘ triy yā napumsakh chuh purōhĕth sôn^{u}
na-ta kō-na āsihēs pray nētras’ ta.
lāgas bŏh dasta dasta pampōsh. 617.

tatiy krūd khot^{u} Garga-rĕshis ta
mani gōs zi ‘ nĕcivwāh wŏpadāwahön
yĕsond^{u} bayĕ atsi Yĕdu-kŏlas ’ ta. lāgas etc. 618.

Kôbula nĕb^{a}r^{i} ôs^{u} thān Rudras ta
totuy gatshith ta tsaryōn taph
Shĕnkàr^{i} darshun tati dyut^{u}nas ta. lāgas etc. 619.

monḍun yiy war tas Rudras ta
‘ pŏth^{a}rāh ladtam boḍ^{u} balawān
yus bayĕ tsānihē Yĕdu-kŏlas ’ ta. lāgas etc. 620.

Mahādēv tōṭhyōs ta tiy dyut^{u}nas ta
labith war āv Kôbulas manz
tasandi tīza pĕv gwāh nagaras ta. lāgas etc. 621

Yauwanāsh Kôbula ôs^{u} rājĕs ta
nĕpŏth^{a}r ösith ôs^{u} shūkas
Garga-ryosh^{u} ḍĕshana gav harshĕs ta. lāgas etc. 622

pŏtra-kăchi push^{ĕ}r^{ü}n kūr^{ü} Gargas ta
‘ rājĕc^{ü} thĕth dēwa pata ṭhaharĕm ’
Gargas ti kăch ös^{ü} kō-na mānihēs ta. lāgas etc. 623.

kĕh köl^{i} gŏbur zāv tati Gargas ta
Kāliyĕwan gŏbaras korukh nāv
Garg āv nīrith ta log^{u} tapas tą. lāgas etc. 624.

buḍ^{i}-bab yĕli mūd^{u} Kāliyĕwanas ta
Kôbuluk^{u} rājy wôt^{u} tás^{i} vīras
Rudra-wara sūtin hyuh^{u} na kăh tas ta. lāgas etc.
625.

samay wôtus ta wôt^{u} Krushnas ta
Krushnani darshĕna mŏktiyĕ gav
pŏr^{i} pŏr^{i} Krushna-jyuwanis darshĕnas ta. lāgas etc.
626.

617. One day, as they conversed, they mocked at him, 'Our priest is or a woman or a eunuch, or wherefore doth he not desire to wed.'

618. Then anger hot in Garga's heart arose, and to beget a son his mind he fixed,—a son whose fear should strike the Yadu clan.

619. On Kābul border sacred to Rudra was a holy spot, thither he went and made austerities till Śaṅkara[1] revealed himself to him.

620. From Rudra then only this boon he craved, 'Grant thou to me a very mighty son, who will cause fear to strike the Yadu clan.'

621. Gracious to him was Mahādēva, and granted he that selfsame boon. Acquiring it to Kābul did he wend, and, through his god-inspired energy, in the city glory shone.

622. In Kābul Yauvanâśva was the king. Sonless was he, and so was filled with woe, but, at the sight of Garga, into joy he came.

623. In longing for a son, to Garga his daughter did he give, 'For thereby will my kingdom be established.' Moreover such was Garga's wish, and how could he refuse?

624. After due time a son was born to Garga, and Kālayavana his name was called. Then Garga did depart, and to an anchorite's life again betook himself.

625. When the heroic Kālayavana's grandfather died, into his hand there passed the rule of Kābul. Through Rudra's boon no one his equal was.

626. To him came his (fated) time, and Kṛṣṇa did he meet, and when to him did Kṛṣṇa himself reveal, then did Kālayavana obtain salvation. To the revelation of Kṛṣṇa ever do I dedicate myself.

---

[1] Rudra, Śaṅkara, and Mahādēva are all names of Śiva.

tas pata sīnā sör^{u} mör^{u}nas ta
hīta hīta būmi ôs^{u} bār kāsawun^{u}
anta-rost^{u} dana āv tati Krushnas ta
lāgas bŏh dasta dasta pampōsh. 627.

tawa pata mŏkha āv[1] Zarāsandas ta
ḍyūṭhukh yāñ tāñ lȧg^{i} tsalanē
Nāradun^{u} wākh āv poz^{u} karanas ta. lāgas etc. 628.

akis parbatas khȧt^{i} tŏngas ta
Zarāsand pata pata lārān ôs^{u}
wuchun zi bārȧn^{i} khȧt^{i} tŏngas ta. lāgas etc. 629.

shĕrāh mani drāv Zarāsandas ta
'mĕ ti nishĕ aki phiri Krushna-gūph tsol^{u}'
tana mana mānani log^{u} Nāradas ta. lāgas etc. 630

Zarāsȧnd^{i} parbatas nār dyut^{u}nas ta
dŏshĕway zi manz-bāg ȧt^{i} zālakh
Krushna-jyuv^{i} khōra-nyŏṭh dyut^{u} tŏngas ta. lāgas etc.
631.

wasith tŏng gav Pātālas ta
wŏṭh löyith ta gay sŏkha pānas
Dwārakāyĕ wötith ta byūṭh^{u} pānas ta. lāgas etc. 632.

Zarāsand phīrith ta log^{u} vĕṭhanas ta
sŏkhith rājyāh log^{u} karanē
wuñĕ ös^{u} tör^{u} tas kāla-pŏrashĕs ta. lāgas etc. 633.

yus lagi pör^{i} pör^{i} Krushna-zīwas ta
tas kari Krushna-jyuv sarŏ wŏpakār
yiti yĕsh nith ta wāti Waikunṭhas ta. lāgas etc. 634.

XXIX.

Raiwata-nôm^{u} ôs^{u} rāza rājĕs ta
Rēwatī kūr^{u} ös^{u} tas rāzas
dits^{u}n kūr^{u} tȧm^{i} Balabadras ta
lāgas bŏh dasta dasta pampōsh. 635.

---

[1] V. l. vil āyĕ.

627. (Bhāg. Pu. X, lii.) Thereafter did Kṛṣṇa Kālayavana's entire host destroy, and thus by this means and by that did he from its load of woe the earth relieve, the while he from the plunder endless wealth did gain.

628. And next Jarāsandha did he confront, and as they saw him, so did Jarāsandha's troops to flight betake themselves. But natheless must Kṛṣṇa Nārada's pledge redeem.[1]

629. Upon a mountain peak did he and Haladhara ascend, as Jarāsandha after them pursued and marked the brothers how upon the peak they clomb.

630. And like an arrow to Jarāsandha's mind there came percipience. 'For once hath the cowherd Kṛṣṇa fled before me,' and body and soul to Nārada made he reverence.

631. The mountain then did Jarāsandha set on fire, 'So amid this will I the twain consume.' But Kṛṣṇa laid his toe upon the peak.

632. And down to hell descended then the peak, while he and Haladhara gave an easy leap and so departed. Thence reached they Dvāraka and in their home abode.

633. To his own home returned Jarāsandha jubilant, and full of happiness resumed his rule, for now delay had come to him who was his Death.

634. He who beareth in his heart the name of Kṛṣṇa, to him will Kṛṣṇa every favour render. In this world glory will he win, and thereafter the abode of Viṣṇu will he reach. To him posy and posy do I offer lotuses.

XXIX. BALABHADRA WEDS RĒVATĪ. THE RAPE OF RUKMIṆĪ.

(Bhāg. Pu. X, lii-liv.)

635. Of a certain kingdom was there a king hight Raivata, and he had a daughter Rēvatī by name. As spouse to Balabhadra did he the damsel give.

---

[1] See verse 580.

kūr^{ü} ös^{ü} vĕṭh^{ü} pūṭh^{ü} baḍi-yāwanas ta
Haladar Rām ôs^{u} bāla-bāwas
bāla-rūpa sampüñ^{ü} bāgĕ āyĕs ta
lāgas bŏh dasta dasta pampōsh. 636.

kaitwāh dana tas sūty dyut^{u}nas ta
ratha gur^{i} håst^{i} tsŏnza pūrith kĕth
wŏtshuwāh sōpon^{u} zi kyāh wån^{i}zĕs ta. lāgas etc. 637.

gŏḍañuk^{u} nēth^{a}r chuh Krushna-zīwas ta
Baktĕv, swāl chuwa, dör^{i}tav kan
kam kam tsarĕth āy pråy^{i} Krushnas ta. lāgas etc.
638.

Vidarba-dīsh ôs^{u} Bīshma-rāzas ta
Rukminī kūr^{ü} ös^{ü} tas rāzas
yutshun zi ' kūr^{ü} dima Krushna-zīwas ' ta. lāgas etc.
639.

gŏbaran Rukman na zi môn^{u}nas ta
' Shishupāl shūbi asĕ, boḍ^{u} suy chuh '
shĕch^{i} pāna sūz^{ü}n Shishupālas ta. lāgas etc. 640.

môl^{u} möj^{ü} band böy^{i} pĕy d^{a}yĕnas ta
' Rukminī zi shūbihē Krushna-jyuwas^{ü}y '
kuni pūsh^{i} na Rukmas tas mūrkhas ta. lāgas etc.
641.

Rukminī chĕh Låkh^{i}mī autāras ta
āmüts^{ü} chĕh Krushnani putshy zanmas
lüz^{ü}n tsūri-pöṭh^{i} shĕch^{i} Krushnas ta. lāgas etc. 642.

brôhmunāh anith ta shĕch^{i} wüñ^{ü}nas ta
panani atha paṭrāh līkhith kĕth
brāhmanas dith ta rūz^{ü} wata wuchanas ta. lāgas etc.
643.

brôhmun yĕli wôt^{u} Krushna-zīwas ta
porun paṭh^{a}r ta log^{u} sanzas
brāhmanas ādara dravy dit^{i}nas ta. lāgas etc. 644.

tithay sūzun shĕch^{i} kür^{ü}nas ta
'mĕ zi zān sārĕn^{ü}y brōṭh wôt^{u}mot^{u}'
dop^{u}nas zi ' wāra pöṭh^{i} sath kår^{i}zĕs ' ta. lāgas etc.
645.

636. Plump was the damsel, in the prime of youth, and Haladhara still was but a boy. Thus to him came the budding maiden as his fated wife.

637. The dowry given with her who can count? Chariots, horses, elephants, maid-slaves all adorned. High festival was held, and how can tongue describe it?

638. Now must be told of Kṛṣṇa the first espousals. Lo, to the feast, ye Faithful, are ye called. Lend ye your ears. Each deed of Kṛṣṇa cometh full of love.

639. Of the land of Vidarbha was Bhīṣmaka the king. He had a daughter namèd Rukmiṇī, and her did he desire to give to Kṛṣṇa.

640. But his son Rukma did not to this assent. 'King Śiśupāla of us is worthy, he alone is great,' and he himself to Śiśupāla did a message send.

641. Then Rukma's father, mother, kin, and brethren all deplored. 'Worthy is Rukmiṇī of Kṛṣṇa and of him alone,' but o'er the brainless Rukma could they not prevail.

642. Behold, of Lakṣmī is Rukmiṇī the incarnation. For Kṛṣṇa only hath she come to birth. So secretly to Kṛṣṇa sent she news.

643. A Brāhmaṇa brought the letter, and quoth he, 'By her own hand was this epistle writ. To me, a Brāhmaṇa, hath she given it, and (for an answer) doth she scan the roads.'

644. When before Kṛṣṇa came the Brāhmaṇa, Kṛṣṇa the letter read and forthwith armour donned, while to the Brāhmaṇa honour did he show and gifts of money gave.

645. (Bhāg. Pu. X, liii.) At once home was he dispatched and with him by Kṛṣṇa was this message sent. 'Know thou that first of all will I arrive.' Then said he to the Brāhmaṇa, 'To her must thou the fullest consolation give.'

phīrith brôhmun nishĕ wôt^{u} tas ta
yishāra sūtin wüñ^{u}nas shĕch^{i}
namaskār kor^{u}nas ta sôr^{u} wôt^{u} tas ta
lāgas bŏh dasta dasta pampōsh. 646.

thĕkith Shishupāl āv nētras ta
Zarāsand biyĕ rāza sūtin hĕth
Rukminī chĕh Krushnañĕ wata wuchanas ta. lāgas etc. 647.

Krushna-jyuv gara drāv maza wuchanas ta
Vidarba-dīshĕs wötith pĕv
Rukminīyĕ būz^{u} ta tsāyĕ vĕṭhanas ta. lāgas etc. 648.

Haladar Rām āv pata Krushnas ta
'kyāh zön^{i}zi har mā sōpani kĕh'
tsōr baḍ^{i} rāza sūty Shishupālas ta. lāgas etc. 649.

mazāh wuchun^{u} zan ôs^{u} Krushnas ta
nētruk^{u} pairun Shishupālas
Krushna-jyuv brōṭh wôt^{u} Shishupālas ta. lāgas etc. 650.

Bīshma-rāza nishĕ gav Shrī-Krushnas ta
pūzā kür^{u}nas yitha pazihēs
pāy kĕh ôsus na kyāh wanihēs ta. lāgas etc. 651.

Shishupāl yĕli wôt^{u} tath nagaras ta
Rukman lūkh sör^{i} brōṭha sūz^{i}nas
tshaṭ^{a}jĕ wāw^{a}jĕ lag^{i} karanas ta. lāgas etc. 652.

Rukminī tsartsanas chĕh Krushna-zīwas ta
Krushna-jyuw ti yōra-kani tsartsān ôs^{u}
zāgān ti kami tshala hĕth tsalas ta. lāgas etc. 653.

rīth ös^{ü} Dīviyĕ bal gatshanas ta
gōḍa drāyĕ mahārĕñ Dīviyĕ bal
Shishupāl rāza hĕth rūd^{u} prāranas ta. lāgas etc. 654

Rukminiyĕ Dīviyĕ war mong^{u}nas ta
'Krushna-jyuv wår^{i}tan mĕ pāna Bagawān
chāg^{ü}r^{ü} kartas Shishupālas' ta. lāgas etc. 655.

646. To Rukmiṇī the Brāhmaṇa returned, and by a beck the answer-message told. Then bowed she down to him, and to her full (understanding) came.

647. In boasting mood to the nuptials did Śiśupāla come, and with him brought he Jarāsandha too, as Rukmiṇī for Kṛṣṇa scanned the roads.

648. From his abode went Kṛṣṇa forth as though the wedding festival to see, and in due course Vidarbha-land he reached. Rukmiṇī heard the news, and with joy was she full filled.

649. Now Haladhara Rāma followed Kṛṣṇa, 'Who knoweth but some fighting might have place,' and four great kings with Śiśupāla came.

650. Kṛṣṇa was there as though a mere spectator of the festival and of the wedding robes of Śiśupāla; and, ere Śiśupāla came, did he arrive.

651. To Kṛṣṇa did Bhīṣmaka draw near, and to him ritely reverence proffer. [Against Śiśupāla] had he no resort, so what could he to Kṛṣṇa say?

652. When at the city arrived Śiśupāla, Rukma to meet him sent out all the folk, and *chowries* and fans waved he before him.

653. Rukmiṇī for Kṛṣṇa doth expectant wait, and from the other side for her did Kṛṣṇa wait, watching to see by what wile he should bear her off.

654. A customary rite there was to go to Dēvī's temple, and thither first of all went forth the bride, while Śiśupāla, with the kings that bare him company, stood awaiting her.

655. From Dēvī cravèd Rukmiṇī a boon, 'May Kṛṣṇa, Bhagavān himself, for his bride take me. To Śiśupāla may'st thou dire confusion give.'

Rukminī hēri yĕli lüj^{ü} wasanas ta
nīrith ōr yōr hāwān pān
wuchān Krushna-jyuv kĕtha wātĕs ta
lāgas bŏh dasta dasta pampōsh. 656.

murtshā gayĕ tas Shishupālas ta
tīzaki pratāpa bēsŏr gav
biyĕ rāza-lūkh gay sör^{i} muhas ta. lāgas etc. 657.

Krushna-jyuv^{i} nishĕ yith khör^{ü} rathas ta
Rukminī ti ṭ^{a}ka-ṭ^{a}kh lüj^{ü} karanē
yāñ gay nīrith ta lȧg^{i} tsalanas ta. lāgas etc. 658.

Krushna-jyuv^{i} zay lob^{u} ta gav harshĕs ta
Rukminī pānas vĕṭhanē lüj^{ü}
Shishupāl sŏra phyūr^{u} ta log^{u} lāranas ta. lāgas etc.
659.

Haladar mōra ākh ta log^{u} māranas ta
taṭ-kshĕn lūkan kor^{u}nas khĕy
lacha-bȧd^{i} mūdis ta kam rūdis ta. lāgas etc. 660.

Shishupāl mandachith ta log^{u} tsalanas ta
s^{a}ha-sanzi ūhawöñ^{ü} shāl zan gav
kĕh rāza bȧḍ^{i} hih^{i} sūty lȧg^{i} tas ta. lāgas etc. 661.

Rukmas dör^{ü} zan āyĕ kāsanas ta
mandachi hyokun na z^{a}ravith kĕth
lāryōv Krushnas pata yŏddas ta. lāgas etc. 662.

Krushna-jyuv^{i} phīrith ta sör^{i} mör^{i}nas ta
raṭith ta Rukmas log^{u} māranē
lüj^{ü}s Rukminī zāra-pāras ta. lāgas etc. 663.

trövith atha ta dör^{ü} kös^{ü}nas ta
Rukm ti mandachith phīrith gav 664.
nĕbar rūzith log^{u} d^{a}yĕnas ta. lāgas etc.

Krushna-jyuv Dwārakāyĕ gav pānas ta
Lȧkh^{i}mī bāgĕ āyĕ Nārānas
Dwārakāyĕ manz sanz log^{u} khāndaras ta. lāgas etc.
665.

656. As Rukmiṇī to descend the steps began, and from the temple issued, showing herself to the folk standing round, looking was she to see how her could Kṛṣṇa reach.

657. By giddiness was seized Śiśupāla, senseless did he become before the puissance of her glory, and all the kings that bare him company did lose their wit.

658. Then near did Kṛṣṇa come and into his chariot her uplift, and Rukmiṇī too began swift haste to make, till from the crowd the horses had emerged, and they could speed away.

659. Thus Kṛṣṇa gained the victory and rejoiced, and Rukmiṇī in her heart exulted, as Śiśupāla again to senses came, and forthwith after them pursued.

660. (Bhāg. Pu. X, lxiv.) Him did Haladhara confront and him defeat, and in the moment routed all his folk. Hundreds of thousands of them died, and there escaped but few.

661. Crest-fallen Śiśupāla fled, as flees the jackal at the lion's roar, and with him fled a many mighty kings.

662. To Rukma 'twas as though had been shaved off his beard, nor could he in his shame thole the disgrace, and to the battle after Kṛṣṇa did he run.

663. Kṛṣṇa turned back, and all his troops he slew. Rukma he seized and him would fain have killed, but Rukmiṇī for him did hard entreaty make.

664. Off shavèd he his beard and let him go; so Rukma humbled and ashamed turned back. Without the city did he stay, and there lamented.

665. Unhindered Kṛṣṇa to Dvārakā returned, and Lakṣmī thus became Nārāyaṇa's bride, the while in Dvārakā was the spousal festival prepared.

anīkh brāhman vēd paranas ta
pāṇigrah Krushnas Rukminiyĕ sūty
Lȧkh^{i}miyĕ Nārān atha-wāsas ta
lāgas bŏh dasta dasta pampōsh 666.

yus lagi Krushna-jyuwanis nāwas ta
tas kari Krushna-jyuv sarŏ wŏpakār
yiti yĕsh nith ta wāti Vishnu-bawanas ta. lāgas etc.
667.

pör^{i} pör^{i} Krushna-jyuwanis nāwas ta
pör^{i} pör^{i} tasandis autāras
pör^{i} pör^{i} tasandis shŏba tsarĕtas ta. lāgas etc. 668.

XXX.

dŏyum^{u} nēth^{a}r chuh Krushna-zīwas ta
Zāmbawanta-wānarüñ^{ü} ḍĕka-büḍ^{ü} kūr^{ü}
kētha pöṭh^{i} bāgȧn^{i} āyĕ Krushnas ta
lāgas bŏh dasta dasta pampōsh. 669.

Shĕtruzith[1]-nôm^{u} log^{u} taph karanas ta
Sūrĕ-sünz^{ü} āradan log^{u} karanē
Yādav ôs^{u} ta boḍ^{u} mān tas ta. lāgas etc. 670.

tūṭhus Sūrĕ ta raṭ^{a}n dyut^{u}nas ta
aiṭh bör^{i} sŏna tath raṭnas phal
Sūrĕ-sond^{u} cĕmakun^{u} ôs^{u} raṭnas ta. lāgas etc. 671.

Krushna-jyuv^{i} dop^{u}nas 'kyāh karahas ta
yih zi shūbi rāzas Wugrasēnas'
suh kĕtha trāvihē ta roṭun pānas ta. lāgas etc. 672.

dŏha aki bôy^{u} ās hĕth raṭnas ta
phērani wanas tath hĕth gav
tati môr^{u} s^{a}han ta raṭ^{a}n nyūnas ta. lāgas etc. 673.

---

1 *V.l. Sutrājith*, but only here. Elsewhere as above.

2 According to all other authorities Jāmbavat was king of the bears, not of the monkeys. Similarly, in the Kāshmīrī Rāmāyaṇa, the word *ponz^{u}*, which ordinarily means 'monkey,' is used to mean 'bear.'

666. Many were the Brāhmaṇas who the Vēdas recited at the wedding of Kṛṣṇa and of Rukmiṇī, when Nārāyaṇa of Lakṣmī took the hand.

667. He who beareth in his heart the name of Kṛṣṇa, to him will Kṛṣṇa every favour render. In this world glory will he win, and thereafter the abode of Viṣṇu will he reach. To him posy and posy do I offer lotuses.

668. Ever dedicating myself to Kṛṣṇa's name, ever dedicating myself to his incarnation, ever dedicating myself to his auspicious deeds, to him posy and posy do I offer lotuses.

XXX. THE SYAMANTAKA. THE MARRIAGES WITH JĀMBAVATĪ AND SATYABHĀMĀ.

(Bhāg. Pu. X, lvi, lvii.)

669. Kṛṣṇa hath made a second marriage. The damsel of high fortune was of Jāmbavat, the monkey-king,[2] the daughter, and this is how she Kṛṣṇa's fated spouse became.

670. A certain man named Satrājit[3] did great austerity, and paid devotion to the Sun. He was a Yādava, held in honour high.

671. Gracious to him became the Sun, and to him [the Syamantaka], a jewel, gave. Eight loads of gold a day did it produce, and its sheen was like unto the splendour of the sun.

672. Quoth to him Kṛṣṇa, 'What with it wilt thou do? King Ugrasēna would this well befit.' But how could he give it up? For himself he kept it.

673. Once on a day his brother [Prasēna] came to him and took the jewel, and with it in the forest wandered. There did a lion slay him and the jewel carry off.

---

[3] So the name is spelt in the usual texts and in the Sanskrit Dictionaries. According to our author, it was Śatrujit, and, in the Viṣṇu Purāṇa there is a variant reading with this spelling. In the translation I adhere to the customary form.

tatiy Zāmbawān wôt^{u} s^{a}has ta
capāth dith ta zuv koḍ^{u}nas
rạt^{a}n nyūnas ta gav pānas ta
lāgas bŏh dasta dasta pampōsh. 674.

Shĕtruzit^{i} hātsh löj^{ü} Krushna-zīwas ta
'bôy^{u} myôn^{u} zi mörith rạt^{a}n hĕth gōs'
lūkh sör^{i} chih mandachān zĕvi hĕnas ta. lāgas etc. 675.

tih phal ôs^{u} tsōrüm^{ü} tsandramas ta
Bādrapȧd^{i} Krushna-jyuv^{i} ḍyūṭh^{u}mot^{u} ôs^{u}
taway hātsh lüj^{ü} Krushna-zīwas ta. lāgas etc. 676.

Krushna-jyuv^{i} būz^{u} ta drāv tshāḍanas ta
'wucha zi ath kyāh wanan sampüñ^{ü}'
wan gav tshāḍani sör^{i} pata tas ta. lāgas etc. 677.

wuchukh suh mūd^{u}mot^{u} manz wanas ta
s^{a}ha-sȧnd^{i} panzĕ ös^{i} lȧg^{i}mȧt^{i} tas
s^{a}h ti tȧt^{i} mūd^{u}mot^{u} pĕy āshtsaras ta. lāgas etc. 678.

wuchukh wå̄dur pūsh^{u}mot^{u} tas ta
Zāmbawanta-wå̄darañĕ gŏphi pĕṭh gay
Krushn tsāv gŏphi ta biyĕ prāranas ta. lāgas etc. 679.

Zāmbawȧnt^{i} ḍyūṭh^{u} yĕli tsakh āyĕs ta
manŏshāh zönith hara-hür^{ü} drāv
Krushnañi thapi sŭty trān gav tas ta. lāgas etc. 680.

tsyūnun zi Rāma-jyuv chuh Krushn-zanmas ta
'Rāma, Rāma,' karān tŏtanē log^{u}
lōl ās mutsarana pyōs pādas ta. lāgas etc. 681.

Krushna-jyuv^{i} asith atha ḍôl^{u}nas ta
trān biyĕ tsās ta log^{u} vĕṭhanē
nānā-prakör^{i} bakth kür^{u}nas ta. lāgas etc. 682.

---

1 Compare Crooke, *Introduction to the Popular Religion and Folklore of Northern India*, p. 9. Whoever looks at the new moon of the month Bhādrapada (August-September) 'will be the victim of false accusations during the ensuing year. The only way to avoid this is to perform a sort of penance by getting someone to shy brickbats at your house, which at other times is regarded as an extreme form of

674. There verily did Jāmbavat upon the lion hap, and with a single cuff tore out his life. The jewel took he up and went his way.

675. Against Kṛṣṇa did Satrājit an accusation bring, 'My brother hath he slain, and the jewel hath he ta'en away.' And all the folk to take it on their tongue ashamèd are.

676. Now Kṛṣṇa the fourth moon of Bhādrapada had looked upon,[1] and this was the fruit thereof, that a false charge was brought against him.

677. This Kṛṣṇa heard, and forth a-seeking went he. 'Fain would I see what of this the outcome was.' Followed by all the folk a-seeking went he to the forest.

678. There in the forest saw he Prasēna lying dead, and on him of the lion's claws the marks. And all astonied were to see the lion too lie dead.

679. They saw that a monkey [? a bear] the lion had overcome, and to the cave of Jāmbavat, the monkey-king, they went. Within the cave went Kṛṣṇa, and without did all the others tarry.

680. When Jāmbavat saw him, filled became he with rage. Thinking him but a man, to struggle with him went he forth, but even as Kṛṣṇa seized hold of him gained he understanding.

681. That Rāma-chandra[2] had been born again as Kṛṣṇa did he perceive, and crying 'Rāma, Rāma' began he to extol him. Unfettered did for him his love become, and at his feet he fell.

682. Then Kṛṣṇa smiled and stroked him with his hand. To Jāmbavat again came understanding and to rejoice did he begin. In many and many a way to him devotion did he offer.

---

insult and degradation. There is a regular festival held for this purpose at Benares on the fourth day of Bhādon [i.e. Bhādrapada] (August), which is known as the *Ḍhēlā chauth mēlā* or "the clod festival of the fourth." '

2 Jāmbavat was a devoted friend and helper of Rāma-candra, who was also an incarnation of Viṣṇu before Kṛṣṇa.

Zāmbawatī kūr^{u} ös^{u} Zāmbawantas ta
say kūr^{u} push$^{\ddot{u}}$r$^{\ddot{u}}$n Krushna-zīwas
Zāmbawatī bāgĕ āyĕ Krushna-zīwas ta
lāgas bŏh dasta dasta pampōsh. 683

suy rạt^{a}n mahārĕñĕ dāj dyut^{u}nas ta
biyĕ sôruy kĕh yih tati ôs^{u}
dŏyum^{u} nēth^{a}r wôt^{u} Krushnas ta. lāgas etc. 684

yüts^{u} kāl gŏphi manz log^{u} Krushnas ta
Yādav söriy phīrith ta gay
Krushn āv kŏlayāh hĕth pānas ta. lāgas etc. 685

rạt^{a}n lodun tas Yādawas ta
suh ti log^{u} mandachani tath būzith
dopun zi ‘ bŏh ti dima kūr^{u} Krushnas ’ ta. lāgas etc. 686.

Satĕbāmā nöm^{u} kūr^{u} ös^{u} tas ta
push$^{\ddot{u}}$r$^{\ddot{u}}$n rạtna sān Krushna-zīwas
Krushna-jyuv^{i} rạt^{a}n biyĕ tūr^{i} dyut^{u}nas ta. lāgas etc. 687.

trĕh wöt^{i} nēth^{a}r Krushna-zīwas ta
Rukminī ta Zāmbawath Satĕbāmā
tsarĕtas tasandis pān wandahös ta. lāgas etc. 688.

XXXI.

môl^{u} mūd^{u} Pāṇḍawan wonukh Krushnas ta
Krushna-jyuv Pāṇḍawan mēlani gav
pata Shĕtruzith Shĕtadȧnv^{i} môr^{u}nas ta
lāgas bŏh dasta dasta pampōsh. 689.

rạtna putshy kāl wôt^{u} Shĕtruzitas ta
Satĕbām pata gayĕ Krushna-zīwas
phīrith biyĕ pĕv yun^{u} Krushnas ta. lāgas etc. 690.

Shĕtadȧnv^{i} būzun ta log^{u} tsalanas ta
push^{e}rith rạt^{a}n gav Akrūras
suh gav Köshiyĕ hĕth rạtnas ta. lāgas etc. 691.

---

1 According to the Bhāgavata Purāṇa, the visit of Kṛṣṇa was occasioned, not by Pāṇḍu's death, but by the attempted murder of the Pāṇḍavas in the famous lac

683. Jāmbavatī the daughter was of Jāmbavat, and her on Kṛṣṇa did he bestow, and thus of Kṛṣṇa did she become the spouse.

684. To Kṛṣṇa gave he that jewel as the dower of the bride, and also there all else that was, that too he gave. So thus the second nuptials of Kṛṣṇa came to pass.

685. A great while in that cave stayed Kṛṣṇa. The waiting Yādavas all returned home, and Kṛṣṇa, bringing his spouse, by himself came back.

686. Kṛṣṇa to Satrājit, the Yādava, the jewel gave, and he, on hearing the true tale, was filled with shame. Quoth he, 'I also to Kṛṣṇa will my daughter give.'

687. He had a daughter Satyabhāmā hight, and, with the jewel, on Kṛṣṇa did he her bestow, but Kṛṣṇa took not the jewel, and to him gave it back.

688. Thus came to pass Kṛṣṇa's espousals three, to Rukmiṇī, to Jāmbavatī, and to Satyabhāmā, and to his mighty deeds do I myself as offering devote.

XXXI. ŚATADHANVAN AND THE SYAMANTAKA. (Bhāg. Pu. X,lvii.)

689. Pāṇḍu, the father of the Pāṇḍavas died,[1] and of it told they Kṛṣṇa. So Kṛṣṇa went the Pāṇḍavas to visit. After that (while he was still away), Śatadhanvan slew Satrājit.

690. 'Twas for that jewel's sake that death came to Satrājit, so Satyabhāmā (to Delhi) followed Kṛṣṇa (and told him of her father's fate), and thus had Kṛṣṇa to return home again.

691. This Śatadhanvan heard, and straightway away he fled, but first the jewel made he over to Akrūra, and to Kāśī did Akrūra take it.

---

house (*Jātugṛha*—the *Jauhar* of the Rājputānā of later times).

Banārasa Akrūr log^{u} dānas ta
    aiṭh bör^{i} sŏna ôs^{u} dān karawun^{u}
dānüc^{ü} shĕch^{i} gayĕ prath dīshĕs ta
    lāgas bŏh dasta dasta pampōsh. 692

Krushna-jyuv pata gav Shĕtadanwas ta
    raṭith pôwun ta kala tsoṭ^{u}nas
wuchun ta rạt^{a}n kuni ôs^{u} na tas ta. lāgas etc. 693.

Haladar Rām-jī log^{u} rōshĕnas ta
    rạt^{a}n zi Satĕbāmi dyut^{u} Krushnan
sa ti rūṭh^{ü} zi dyutun Balabadras ta. lāgas etc. 694.

Akrūrun^{u} būzukh chuh dān karanas ta
    zônukh zi rạt^{a}n wôt^{u} Akrūras
Krushna-jyuv^{i} shĕch^{i} lüz^{ü} Akrūras ta. lāgas etc. 695.

Akrūr rạt^{a}n hĕth āv Krushnas ta
    sārĕn^{ü}y sör^{u}y shĕnkā tsüj^{ü}
Dwārakāyĕ vig^{a}n lảg^{i} sör^{i} tsalanas ta. lāgas etc. 696.

yus lagi Krushna-jyuwanis nāwas ta
    tas kari Krushna-jyuv sarŏ wŏpakār
yiti yĕsh nith ta wāti Vishnu-bawanas ta. lāgas etc.
697.

pör^{i} pör^{i} Krushna-jyuwanis nāwas ta
    pör^{i} pör^{i} tasandis autāras
pör^{i} pör^{i} tasandis shŏba tsarĕtas ta. lāgas etc. 698.

XXXII.

tsūryum^{u} nĕth^{a}r chuh Krushna-zīwas ta
    Kaurawan ta Pānḍawan mēlani āv
tati āv kŏlayāh hĕth pānas ta
    lāgas bŏh dasta dasta pampōsh. 699.

Dili ôs^{u} biyĕ yun^{u} Krushna-zīwas ta
    tĕli ṭ^{a}ki gayāv mēlana-rost^{u}
āv Dili biyĕ ta brŏṭha drās tas ta. lāgas etc. 700.

---

1 Kāśī and Benares are two names of the same city.

2 So also Haladhara Rāma and Bala-bhadra are both names of Kṛṣṇa's elder brother.

3 The poet glosses over the part taken by Akrūra. This pious gentleman was one of the persons who incited Śatadhanvan to commit the murder. We read in

692. There, in Benares,[1] began he to make pious gifts, each day the eight loads of gold gave he in charity, and of his gifts to all countries sped the news.

693. Kṛṣṇa on Śatadhanvan followed hard. He caught him, felled him, and his head cut off. Then sought he, but nowhere on him could he find the jewel.

694. Then Haladhara Rāma wroth became, thinking that Kṛṣṇa had given the jewel to Satyabhāmā, and wroth did she too become, thinking that he had given it to Bala-bhadra.[2]

695. Then heard they that Akrūra pious gifts was giving, and so they knew that into his hand had the jewel come. So Kṛṣṇa sent a message to Akrūra.[3]

696. To Kṛṣṇa did Akrūra bring the jewel, all the anxiety of everyone departed, and all the calamities of Dvārakā took to flight.

697. He who beareth in his heart the name of Kṛṣṇa, to him will Kṛṣṇa every favour render. In this world glory will he win, and thereafter the abode of Viṣṇu will he reach. To him posy and posy do I offer lotuses.

698. Ever dedicating myself to Kṛṣṇa's name, ever dedicating myself to his incarnation, ever dedicating myself to his auspicious deeds, posy and posy do I offer lotuses.

XXXII. THE MARRIAGE WITH KĀLINDĪ. (Bhāg. Pu. X, xlviii.)

699. There be yet a fourth espousal of Kṛṣṇa. To visit the Kauravas and the Pāṇḍavas did he go, and thence with a wife did he return.

700. (Beside the visit just set forth[4]) he had again to go to Delhi, for on that occasion he had had to depart without meeting (his relations). So again went he to Delhi, and forth came they to welcome him.

the Bhāgavata Purāṇa how famine and other calamities overtook Dvārakā when Akrūra took away the jewel to Benares. Wherever it went there the land had bounteous rain. On its return to Dvāraka all the calamities occasioned by its absence disappeared. This is referred to in the next verse.

[4] At the beginning of the preceding chapter.

samith sārĕv^{u}y pūz kür^{u}has ta
nānā-ráng^{i} bakth lág^{i} karanē
sārĕn^{u}y mīlith ta drāv sailas ta
lāgas bŏh dasta dasta pampōsh. 701.

Arzŏn sŭty hĕth gav sailas ta
Jamunāyĕ boṭh^{u} pĕṭh trēsh cĕni gav
dŏshĕw^{u}y trēsh cĕyĕ lág^{i} phēranas ta. lāgas etc. 702.

wuch^{u}kh kañĕkhāh tati tapas ta
sa kūr^{u} Sūrĕ-dēwatā-sünz^{u} ös^{u}
Kālindī-dēwatā nāv ôs^{u} tas ta. lāgas etc. 703.

yüts^{u} kāl wātsās tati tapas ta
bükts^{u} sŭty taph tsor^{u} tsarān ös^{u}
'bāgani yimahö zi Shrī-Krushnas' ta. lāgas etc. 704.

ḍiṭh^{u}n ta warüñ^{u} pĕyĕ Krushna-zīwas ta
warawun^{u} waradā chuh pāna Bagawān
saphal war gōs ta wöts^{u} Krushnas ta. lāgas etc. 705.

Dili-kani phīrith āv pānas ta
sārĕn^{i} bāndawan mīlith kĕth
āshĕñāh sŭty hĕth gav pānas ta. lāgas etc. 706.

yus lagi Krushna-jyuwanis nāwas ta
tas kari Krushna-jyuv sarŏ wŏpakār
yiti yĕsh nith ta wāti Vishnu-bawanas ta. lāgas etc.
707.

pör^{i} pör^{i} Krushna-jyuwanis nāwas ta
pör^{i} pör^{i} tasandis autāras
pör^{i} pör^{i} tasandis shŏba tsarĕtas ta. lāgas etc. 708.

XXXIII.

bĕñāh ös^{u} Awantī-pura-rāzas ta
tas Mitrabadrā ôsus nāv
sŏyĕmwar yitshi kor^{u} tami Krushnas ta
lāgas bŏh dasta dasta pampōsh. 709.

---

1 The Bhāgavata Purāṇa calls her Mitravindā.

2 A *svayaṁvara* is the selection of a husband by a princess at a public assembly

701. They all assembled and ritely worshipped him. In many a varied way did they show to him devotion, and then, having saluted each, he went forth on a stroll.

702. With Arjuna his companion strolled he forth, and to the Yamunā bank he went to quench his thirst. When the two had so quenched their thirst around did they begin to walk.

703. There saw they a damsel in austerities absorbed. She was the daughter of the sun, Kālindī hight.

704. Many a day had run its course in her austerities, which with devotion she had practised resolute, praying that she might be the spouse of Kṛṣṇa.

705. Her did he see, and thus it was her lot to become chosen of Kṛṣṇa, he who himself is Bhagavān, the Chooser and the Boon Bestower. The boon he gave her had its fulfilment due, and thus she came to Kṛṣṇa as his spouse.

706. When all his kinsmen he had visited, from Delhi he set forth, and home returned bringing there a wife.

707. He who beareth in his heart the name of Kṛṣṇa, to him will Kṛṣṇa every favour render. In this world glory will he win, and thereafter the abode of Viṣṇu will he reach. To him posy and posy do I offer lotuses.

708. Ever dedicating myself to Kṛṣṇa's name, ever dedicating myself to his incarnation, ever dedicating myself to his auspicious deeds, to him posy and posy do I offer lotuses.

XXXIII. THE MARRIAGE WITH MITRABHADRĀ. (Bhāg. Pu. X,lviii,31.)

709. Of Avantīpura was there a certain king. He had a sister Mitrabhadrā[1] hight, and she, in her desire for Kṛṣṇa held a *svayaṁvara*.[2]

---

of suitors. On this occasion she signified her choice by scattering saffron over the selected one.

rāza wöt^{i} söriy sŏyĕmwaras ta
Krushna-jyuv ti sŏyĕmwara-sabāyĕ gav
chüc^{ü}n kŏng-ṭūr^{ü} tami Krushnas ta
lāgas bŏh dasta dasta pampōsh. 710.

pŭntsyum^{u} nēth^{a}r wôt^{u} Krushnas ta
āshĕñāh hĕth ta Dwārakāyĕ gav
prath kạ̄h chuh tōshān tath zayĕs ta. lāgas etc. 711.

yus lagi Krushna-jyuwanis nāwas ta
tas kari Krushna-jyuv sarŏ wŏpakār
yiti yĕsh nith ta wāti Vishnu-bawanas ta. lāgas etc.
712.

pör^{i} pör^{i} Krushna-jyuwanis nāwas ta
pör^{i} pör^{i} tasandis autāras
pör^{i} pör^{i} tasandis shŏba tsarĕtas ta. lāgas etc. 713.

XXXIV.

Ayōdyāyĕ Krushna-jyuv gav phēranas ta
tatyuk^{u} rāza ôs^{u} Nagnazith nôm^{u}
būzith brō̃ṭha drāv Krushna-zīwas ta
lāgas bŏh dasta dasta pampōsh. 714.

rāza-dwār tsönith ta mān kor^{u}nas ta
vĕdi-vĕz^{ü} pūzā log^{u} karanē
wŏtsav sampon^{u} rāza-dwāras ta. lāgas etc. 715.

Satyā kūr^{ü} ös^{ü} tas rāzas ta
jarōga-pĕṭha drāyĕ maza-wuchanē
ḍyūṭhun Krushna-jyuv man log^{u} tas ta. lāgas etc.
716.

mangani ŏhiy lüj^{ü} ta Dayĕs ta
'ditam zi darmuk^{u} karmuk^{u} phal
bāgĕ zi yimahŏ Krushna-zīwas' ta. lāgas etc. 717.

Krushna-jyuv^{i} kāmanā sĕd kür^{ü}nas ta
antaryōmī chuh pāna Bagawān
münj^{ü}n rāzas ta kō-na mānihēs ta. lāgas etc. 718.

bāgĕ môn^{u} rāzan ta pādi nom^{u}nas ta
kēntshāh manz-bāg tör^{ü} thüv^{ü}nas
'pratigyā myöñ^{ü} ti zi pazi pālanas' ta. lāgas etc.
719.

710. To the *svayaṁvara* came all the kings, and to the assembly there came Kṛṣṇa too, and on him scattered she the saffron box.

711. A fifth espousal thus to Kṛṣṇa came, and with a wife returned he to Dvārakā, where every one at his victory rejoiced.

712. He who beareth in his heart the name of Kṛṣṇa, to him will Kṛṣṇa every favour render. In this world glory will he win, and thereafter the abode of Viṣṇu will he reach. To him posy and posy do I offer lotuses.

713. Ever dedicating myself to Kṛṣṇa's name, ever dedicating myself to his incarnation, ever dedicating myself to his auspicious deeds, to him posy and posy do I offer lotuses.

XXXIV. THE MARRIAGE WITH SATYĀ. (Bhāg. Pu. X,lviii, 32.)

714. To Ayōdhyā once did Kṛṣṇa wend his way. Of there the king was named Nagnajit, and when he heard the news, forth went he to welcome Kṛṣṇa.

715. Through the palace gate did he lead him. Honour to him did he show, and ritely to him did he offer worship. Thus in the palace rose high festival.

716. The monarch had a daughter, Satyā hight. She from the roof-pavilion issued forth to see the festival. On Kṛṣṇa fell her gaze, and to him did she lose her heart.

717. So then from God a blessing did she crave, 'Grant me the fruit of virtuous acts and of my deeds in lives long past, that Kṛṣṇa's spouse I may become'.

718. Kṛṣṇa fulfilled the longing of her soul. He is himself Bhagavān, the Inward Monitor. From the king did he ask her, and how could he not consent.

719. Great good fortune deemed it the Rājā, and at Kṛṣṇa's feet he bowed himself. But meanwhile somewhat of delay did he impose, 'I have a vow, and that vow must I keep.'

sath dā̆d thȧv^{i}mȧt^{i} tȧm^{i} shĕrtas ta
‘yus yikawaṭa raṭi kŏmi dörith
tȧs^{i} balavīras kūr^{ü} dimahas’ ta
lāgas bŏh dasta dasta pampōsh. 720

yüts^{ü} rāza mandachith gay pānas ta
sath dā̆d yikawaṭa kus raṭihē
prārān bŏna ôs^{u} Shrī-Krushnas ta. lāgas etc. 721.

rāza log^{u} mānanā tsür^{ü} karanas ta
‘tsĕ zi nishĕ pazihē na kē̆h wananas
darma-wākh ti pazi mā poz^{u} karanas’ ta. lāgas etc. 722.

sath dā̆d kyāh nishĕ Krushna-zīwas ta
yĕs ös^{i} sath lūkh āyĕtsāras
sath rüz^{ü} rāzas ta sath won^{u}nas ta. lāgas etc. 723.

dop^{u}nas zi ‘kāstam shūkh manas ta
darmüc^{ü} āgyā pālanāvtam
kōrĕ myāñĕ bāgĕ ös^{i} bŏna baḍanas’ ta. lāgas etc. 724.

sath rū̆ph sō̆pȧn^{i} Krushna-zīwas ta
sataway yikawaṭa nishĕ ȧn^{i}nas
sath gayĕ rāzas ta log^{u} vĕṭhanas ta. lāgas etc. 725.

vĕwāh karith kūr^{ü} dits^{u}nas ta
vĕdi-vĕz^{ü} pazihē yitha rāzan
grünz^{ü}-rost^{u} dana raṭ^{a}n dāj dyut^{u}nas ta. lāgas etc. 726.

tsŏnza hȧst^{i} sāsa-bȧd^{i} sū̆ty dit^{i}nas ta
lacha-bȧd^{i} ratha ta gur^{i} sū̆tin
zāmatur^{u} Bagawān kō-na diyĕs ta. lāgas etc. 727.

Arzŏn-dīv ôs^{u} sū̆ty Krushnas ta
bāyau manza ôs^{u} ṭôṭh^{u} suy tas
suh ti ôs^{u} satĕ-bāwa dās zan tas tā. lāgas etc. 728.

drāv yĕli Krushna-jyuv gara pānas ta
wati ās biyĕ rāza thŏth karanĕ
söriy zēnȧn^{i} pĕy Arzŏnas ta. lāgas etc. 729.

720. Seven bulls had he fixed as the condition of consent. 'He who at the one time may hold them to his breast, only to such a hero can I the damsel give.'

721. Many a king had homeward gone ashamed, for who could seven bulls seize at once? 'Twas as though he had been waiting for Kṛṣṇa (to carry out the task).

722. To Kṛṣṇa did the king show deference great, 'In thy presence to say aught it is not meet, but, of a surety, am I not bound a solemn oath to keep?'

723. Before Kṛṣṇa what were seven bulls, he to whom subject are the seven worlds? High were the Rājā's hopes, and he spake truth to him.

724. Quoth he to him, 'Drive sorrow from my heart, and, prithee, of my duty the command obey. Then of my daughter high will rise the happy lot.'

725. Kṛṣṇa then multiplied himself in seven-fold form, and so to himself brought near the seven bulls. Thus to the king came solace and joyful did he wax.

726. The damsel gave he him in wedlock with all due rite as befitteth kings, and dowry gave he countless wealth and jewels.

727. With her gave he thousands of maid-servants and of elephants, hundreds of thousands of chariots and of horses. When Bhagavān was his son-in-law, how could he not bestow them?

728. Arjuna Dēva Kṛṣṇa had accompanied. Of all the brother [Pāṇḍavas] was he to him most dear, and as it were a loyal slave to him.

729. When Kṛṣṇa set forth upon his journey home, on the road came there other kings to stop his way, and it was Arjuna's destiny to vanquish each and all.

Badrā ti sŏyĕmwara wöts^{ü} Krushnas ta
biyĕ Lȧkh^{i}manāyĕ ti wor^{u} pānay
aiṭh paṭa-röniyĕ wātsa Krushnas ta
lāgas bŏh dasta dasta pampōsh. 730.

namaskār tihandis tath bāgĕs ta
namaskār Krushna-zīwanis tsarĕtas
prath tsarĕtas bŏh ti pān wandahas ta. lāgas etc.
731.

yus lagi Krushna-jyuwanis nāwas
tas kari Krushna-jyuv sarŏ wŏpakār
yiti yĕsh nith ta wāti Vishnu-bawanas ta. lāgas etc.
732.

pör^{i} pör^{i} Krushna-jyuwanis nāwas ta
pör^{i} pör^{i} tasandis autāras
pör^{i} pör^{i} tasandis shŏba tsarĕtas ta. lāgas etc. 733.

XXXV.

kēh köl^{i} nĕcyuwāh zāv Krushnas ta
ṭika zāv gŏḍañiy Rukminiyĕ-hond^{u}
Pradyumn zātaka nāv kor^{u}has ta
lāgas bŏh dasta dasta pampōsh. 734.

suh ti ös^{u} Kāmadĕv autāras ta
Lȧkh^{i}miyĕ Kāmadēv santān bọw^{u}
Rukminī chĕh Lȧkh^{i}mī, suy zāv tas ta. lāgas etc.
735.

Shĕmbara-daity ös^{u} nishĕ samudras ta
dŏha aki Pradyumn tsūri hĕth gav
dyutun dörith manz samudras ta. lāgas etc. 736.

nĕngol^{u} gāḍi, tati āyĕ zālas ta
āyur^{u} Shĕmbaras gŏḍ^{ü} hĕth gav
Shĕmbar^{i} wāzas dits^{ü} rananas ta. lāgas etc. 737.

phösh^{ü}n nĕcyuwāh drāv wāzas ta
wāzan sīvakiñĕ kun push^{o}run
Ratī sa-ti ös^{ü} tshāḍān tas ta. lāgas etc. 738.

730. (Bhāg. Pu. X, lviii, 56,57.) By *svayamvara*[1] came Bhadrā to Kṛṣṇa as a spouse, and, again, was he himself chosen by Lakṣmaṇā. Thus eight chief queens to Kṛṣṇa came.

731. Reverence be to that blessed lot of their's. Reverence to the exploits of Kṛṣṇa. To each exploit do I also as a sacrifice offer myself.

732. He who beareth in his heart the name of Kṛṣṇa, to him will Kṛṣṇa every favour render. In this world glory will he win, and thereafter the abode of Viṣṇu will he reach. To him posy and posy do I offer lotuses.

733. Ever dedicating myself to Kṛṣṇa's name, ever dedicating myself to his incarnation, ever dedicating myself to his auspicious deeds, to him posy and posy do I offer lotuses.

XXXV. THE ADVENTURES OF PRADYUMNA. (Bhāg. Pu. X,lv.)

734. In course of time to Kṛṣṇa was born a son. First, like a crest-jewel, was he born of Rukmiṇī, and in keeping with his horoscope named they him Pradyumna.

735. In him did Kāmadēva (the Indian Cupid) become incarnate, for Kāmadēva the offspring was of Lakṣmī, who was one with Rukmiṇī, and he was born of her.

736. There was a demon dwelling by the sea named Śambara. Once on a day Pradyumna did he steal away, and into the ocean cast he him.

737. There was he swallowed by a fish. That fish in a net was caught. It did the fisherman to Śambara bring. To his cook did Śambara give it to prepare his meal.

738. When the cook cut it open, from it before him issued forth a lad. Him did the cook make over to a servant-maid. Now she was Rati (the Indian Psyche) taking human form to seek her spouse.

[1] See verse 709.

Pradyumn Kāmadēv autāras ta
Ratiyĕ ôs^{u} Mahādīv^{i} war dyut^{u}mot^{u}
bartā zi labahön nishĕ Krushnas ta
lāgas bŏh dasta dasta pampōsh. 739.

ot^{u} tāñ Rath ös^{ü} tshāḍān tas ta
yĕna-shut^{u} Mahādēv basmith gav
kȧh^{i}-tāñ bartā athi āv tas ta. lāgas etc. 740.

Rati ḍyūṭh^{u} nĕcyuwāh pĕy^{e} āshtsaras ta
bāh sūrĕ rūpa tsor^{u} prazalān ôs^{u}
Nārod^{u} āv ta sôr^{u} won^{u}nas ta. lāgas etc. 741.

Rukminiyĕ ti gatshith sath kür^{u}nas ta
'nĕcyuw^{u} wātiy pön^{i}-pānay
pānay-pāna āsi khēla karanas' ta. lāgas etc. 742.

Rati yĕli bartā āv athas ta
baḍi srĕha yitshi tas pālani lüj^{ü}
dŏda gĕyĕ anna-bala bal kor^{u}nas ta. lāgas etc. 743.

sŏra āv Rati sūty sôr^{u} won^{u}nas ta
'ts^{a}h zi myôn^{u} bartā bŏh zi cyōñ^{ü} triy
Shĕmbor^{u} mārun ta gatshav pānas' ta. lāgas etc.
744.

dŏha aki Shĕmbaras gōla dit^{i}nas ta
Shĕmbȧr^{i} būzith yŏddas drās
Pradyumnan söriy lūkh mör^{i}nas ta. lāgas etc. 745.

tawa pata raṭith kala tsoṭ^{u}nas ta
bāra-böts^{ü} Dwārakāyĕ lạg^{i} gatshanē
Rath rūz^{u} wāhana Pradyumnas ta. lāgas etc. 746.

wuḍith ākösh^{i} nini lüj^{ü} tas ta
yāñ Dwārakāyĕ wöt^{i} darthiyĕ pĕy
āyĕ triyĕ-bāwas ta tsor^{u} rūph tas ta. lāgas etc. 747.

---

1 Mahādēva had reduced Kāmadēva to ashes with a single look of his terrible eye, because Kāmadēva had endeavoured to excite love in him. Rati was inconsolable, and is represented as continually wandering in search of him. The servant-

739. Pradyumna was incarnate Kāmadēva, and to Rati had Mahādēva given the boon, that through Kṛṣna should she again obtain her lord.[1]

740. From the time that Mahādēva had him to ashes burnt, from that time ever had she been making quest, that somehow into her hand her lord might come.

741. Then Rati marvelled when she saw the lad. In form more glorious was he than a dozen suns. Then came to her Nārada and told her all the truth.

742. Also to Rukmiṇī went he, and bade her be of good cheer. 'Thy son, in very self, will come to thee. In very self will he near thee frolic.'

743. When into Rati's hand thus came her lord, with mickle love and longing did she cherish him, and his strength revive on aliment of milk and ghī.

744. When with Rati into consciousness he came, the whole tale did she tell him. 'Thou art my lord, and here thy wife am I. Śambara must thou slay, then safe can we depart.'

745. Once on a day at Śambara hurled Pradyumna cannon-balls, and Śambara learning (who had done this) came forth to fight him. Then all his army did Pradyumna slay.

746. Thereafter cut he off the demon's head, and husband and wife set forth to Dvārakā, while Rati served as chariot for Pradyumna.

747. Into the sky flew she and carried him, and when to Dvārakā they came, down on the ground did they alight. Then took she a woman's form of peerless beauty.

---

maid was named Māyāvatī (Bhāg. Pu. lv.) According to the Vishṇu Purāṇa, she was Śambara's wife, not a maid-servant, (Trans. Wilson-Hall, V, pp. 73ff.). The Bhāg. Pu. does not say who she was.

bāra-böts^{u} Dwārakāyĕ tsāy pānas ta
māji̯ĕn zānana āyāv na kĕh
sampadā chĕh sūtin Rath Krushnas ta
lāgas bŏh dasta dasta pampōsh. 748.

sārĕy kāmĕ āsa maṭi Nāradas ta
sôruy tsarĕth wanith ta gōkh
Rukminiyĕ parzanôw^{u} ta lūj^{u} vĕṭhanas ta. lāgas etc.
749.

mājĕ lajĕ tōshĕni nŏshi-gŏbaras ta
sārĕv^{u}y yith ta nālamati roṭ^{u}
nŏshi ti nālamat^{i} sārĕ karanas ta. lāgas etc. 750.

dahan^{u}y dŏhan-hond^{u} zāmot^{u} tas ta
Rukminiyĕ Shĕmbar^{i} yĕli nyūnas
jai-kār bŏyin tas vīra-pŏrashĕs ta. lāgas etc. 751.

Dwārakāyĕ wŏtsav log^{u} sapananas ta
söriy Yādav lag^{i} tōshĕnē
Krushna-jyuv chuh tōshān nŏshi-gŏbaras ta. lāgas
etc. 752.

yus lagi pör^{i} pör^{i} Krushna-zīwas ta
tas kari Krushna-jyuv sarŏ wŏpakār
yiti yĕsh nith ta wāti Vishnu-bŏwanas ta. lāgas etc.
753.

XXXVI.

Baumāsŏr ôs^{u} rājy karanas ta
samudra-ṭŏpis manz āsān
dēwan ta manŏshĕn ôs^{u} khīdas ta
lāgas bŏh dasta dasta pampōsh. 754.

taph yĕli asŏras āv antas ta
wŏthith gatshith pĕv Yindra-rāzas
kana-wöli nīnas mājĕ Yindras ta. lāgas etc. 755.

Yindra-rāza nishĕ āv Shrī-Krushnas ta
Baumāsŏrun^{u} dyut^{u}nas dād
'tsĕy nishĕ yōt^{u} chuh na kĕh pāy tas' ta. lāgas etc.
756.

748. Husband and wife entered Dvārakā unhindered, but by the mothers naught was understood, that Rati was present together with the welfare (i.e. the son) of Kṛṣṇa.

749. Then all the task on Nārada's shoulder fell. He told them all the wondrous tale and went his way. Then Rukmiṇī her son did recognize, and so rejoiced.

750. Happy became the mothers in the daughter-in-law and in the son. All of them came and him did they embrace, and so did all the daughter-in-law embrace.

751. But ten days had Pradyumna been born when from Rukmiṇī him Śambara carried off. To him, illustrious hero, may there be victory!

752. In Dvāraka there began high festival, and all the Yādavas held jubilee, and in his daughter-in-law and son rejoiceth Kṛṣṇa.

753. He who ever dedicateth himself to Kṛṣṇa, to him will Kṛṣṇa every favour render. In this world glory will he win and thereafter the world of Viṣṇu will he reach. To him posy and posy do I offer lotuses.

XXXVI. THE WAR WITH BHAUMA. THE RAPE OF THE PĀRIJĀTA.
(Bhāg. Pu. X,lix.)

754. Of an Island in the Ocean was Bhauma, the Demon Asura, the ruler, and gods and men did he oppress.

755. When the austerities of the demon to an end had come, he then arose, and upon Indra fell, and of (Aditi), Indra's mother, the earrings did he carry off.

756. To Kṛṣṇa Indra came, and against Bhauma did he make complaint. 'Except with thee, for me against him there is no resource.'

Krushna-jyuv^{i} sath kür^{u} Yindra-rāzas ta
Garuḍas khasith ta gatshith pyōs
shīshĕ-kōṭha māyāyĕ-hȧnd^{i} ös^{i} tas ta
lāgas bŏh dasta dasta pampōsh. 757.

shĕyimis Murāsŏr rôch^{u} kōṭhas ta
Krushna-jyuv shĕshĕway phuṭarith gōs
Murāsŏr tati drāv manza zalas ta. lāgas etc. 758.

gŏḍañ suy log^{u} mōra Krushnas ta
Krushna-jyuv^{i} raṭith ta kala tsoṭ^{u}nas
tawa pata gŏbur ta lūkh mör^{i}nas ta. lāgas etc. 759.

Baumāsŏr drāv pāna laḍanas ta
anīkh rākhĕsa-sīnā hĕth
Shrī-Krushnas sūty log^{u} laḍanas ta. lāgas etc. 760.

Krushna-jyuv^{i} sŏriy lūkh mŏr^{i}nas ta
kĕ̄h tsȧl^{i} kĕ̄h gȧl^{i} chŏkalad kĕ̄h
kunuy rūzith ta log^{u} laḍanas ta. lāgas etc. 761.

raṭith ta Krushna-jyuv^{i} kala tsoṭ^{u}nas ta
hāhākār wŏ̄th^{u} tath nagaras
dŏkh pyōs söris pariwāras ta. lāgas etc. 762.

Baumāsŏrüñ^{u} möj^{u} āyĕ Krushnas ta
putur^{u} sūty hĕth pĕyĕ pādan
'shĕran zi on^{u}may tsĕ pazi rachanas' ta. lāgas etc.
763.

dayā mani āyĕ Shrī-Krushnas ta
möl^{i}-sond^{u} rājy tȧs^{i} biyĕ dyut^{u}nas
santh suh ti zāmot^{u} tas Asŏras ta. lāgas etc. 764.

Krushna-jyuv^{i} zay lob^{u} tsāv nagaras ta
shurāh sās kañĕka mŏkalāvĕn
sārĕy ḍĕka-bajĕ āsa Krushnas ta. lāgas etc. 765.

---

1 This was a wondrous bird, which served as Kṛṣṇa's vehicle.

2 The text says the ramparts were built by Māyā, or Illusion, but the word is probably a mistake for Maya, who was the great artificer and architect of the

757. Kṛṣṇa to Indra gave encouragement. On Garuḍa [1] mounted he and on Bhauma fell. (Of Bhauma's fortress) were the surrounding ramparts of glass by Māyā [2] built.

758. Of the sixth rampart the demon Mura was the guardian, and the six ramparts did Kṛṣṇa shatter. Then from amid the water issued Mura.

759. First of all Kṛṣṇa did he confront, but Kṛṣṇa seized him and cut off his head, and then his son and all his horde he slew.

760. Then to the combat Bhauma did himself come forth, many arrays of demons bringing with him, and against Kṛṣṇa he began to fight.

761. But Kṛṣṇa vanquished Bhauma's people all. Some took to flight, others were slain, and others wounded lay. Bhauma alone remained and he stood up to fight.

762. So Kṛṣṇa seized him and his head cut off. Then in the city a great cry arose and on his household sorrow fell.

763. To Kṛṣṇa Bhauma's mother came, and with her grandson at his feet she fell. 'To thee as sanctuary have I brought him, and for protection do I crave.'

764. Into the heart of Kṛṣṇa mercy came, and to the lad gave he his father's kingdom, for, though of that demon born, a godly man was he.

765. Kṛṣṇa, the victory having gained, the city entered. Sixteen thousand damsels from their bonds did he release, and all became the luck-blessed (wives) of Kṛṣṇa.

Daityas, or demons. Some authorities believe his name to be a corruption of (Ahura-)mazda.

sŏndar kōrĕ yima trailōkĕs ta
tima āsa aňĕmatsa Baumāsŏr^{i}
warihĕkh wuh sās yĕli samanas ta
lāgas bŏh dasta dasta pampōsh. 766.

Krushna-jyuv ḍyūṭhukh ta mana lajĕ tas ta
Bagawānas gayĕ shĕran sārĕy
Krushn^{ü}y bartā lajĕ manganas ta. lāgas etc. 767.

kāmanā chĕh pūrüň^{u} Bagawānas ta
kaňĕkan kāmanā pūrith gav
Dwārakāyĕ sōzan tima waranas ta. lāgas etc. 768.

hást^{i} gur^{i} dana ratha yīt^{i} ös^{i} tas ta
sôruy sŏmbarith sūty dyut^{u}nakh
Dwārakāyĕ yĕli wātsa gayĕ harshĕs. lāgas etc. 769

pāna gav Sŏrga-lūkh Yindra-rāzas ta
kana-wöl^{i} phīrith ta nith dit^{i}nas
Yindra-rāza vĕdi-vĕz^{u} log^{u} pūzanas ta. lāgas etc. 770.

dēwatā sör^{i} lág^{i} pōshĕ-warshĕnas ta
Sŏrgā-pŏras wŏtsav bọw^{u}
vĕṭhān chih Baumāsŏr gālanas ta. lāgas etc. 771.

Satĕbāmā ös^{ü} sūty Krushnas ta
biyĕ ôs^{u} Anirudd sūty nyūmot^{u}
Satĕbāmi pārizāth dyun^{u} ôs^{u} tas ta. lāgas etc. 772.

kaḍith pārizāth Sŏrga-lūkas ta
Aniruddas kun push^{e}rith ta gav
'yih zi gatshi Satĕbāmi dyun^{u} āganas' ta. lāgas etc. 773.

kyāh dáp^{i}zi Vishnu-māyi Bagawānas ta
tatiy Yindra-rāza pūzani ôs^{u}
tatiy Krushnas āv laḍanas ta. lāgas etc. 774.

---

1 Some came from the world of gods, some from the world of demons, and some from the world of men.

2 For Satyabhāmā, see verse 687. She was Kṛṣṇa's favourite and spoilt wife.

766. These were fair damsels of the threefold worlds[1], who thither by the demon Bhauma had been brought. When twenty thousand he should collect, it had his purpose been to wed them all.

767. On Kṛṣṇa fell their gaze, and his became their hearts. To Bhagavān went they, and in him refuge took; and they began each to pray that Kṛṣṇa, and he alone, might be her lord.

768. To fulfil longings is Bhagavān's delight, and thus the desires of the maidens he fulfilled. To Dvārakā he sent them, that he might wed them there.

769. All the elephants and horses, and wealth and chariots that Bhauma had possessed, all that did he collect and give to them, and full of joy at Dvārakā did they arrive.

770. He himself to Indra's heaven set forth. Thither brought he and restored the plundered earrings, and ritely to him did Indra proffer worship.

771. The gods all flowers began to rain and in heaven's city arose high festival, as at the demon's downfall they exulted.

772. Along with Kṛṣṇa Satyabhāmā was, and with him also had he taken Aniruddha. To Satyabhāmā had to be given the Pārijāta tree.[2]

773. In the heavenly region the Pārijāta tree did he pull up. To Aniruddha he entrusted it. 'In Satyabhāma's courtyard plant thou it'.

774. What can be said of Bhagavān's illusive power of delusion? To that same spot where to Kṛṣṇa Indra had proffered worship, did Indra come to wage a war with him.

Aniruddha was Pradyumna's son, and Kṛṣṇa's and Rukmiṇī's grandson. The Pārijāta, or coral tree, was one of the five trees of Paradise produced at the churning of the ocean. It was a valued possession of Indra.

pārizāta-kuli putshy drāv yŏddas ta
Bagawānas nishĕ kyāh pāy tas
mandachun[u] phal drāv tami Yindras ta
lāgas bŏh dasta dasta pampōsh. 775.

Krushn āv Sŏrga-lūka bū-manḍalas ta
Dwārakā-nagaras wŏtsav bọw[u]
wŏtsav sampon[u] prath nagaras ta. lāgas etc. 776.

pārizāth Satĕbāmi wŏt[u] āganas ta
mushkån[i] dār wŏt[i] prath dwāras
Waikunṭh prạkh[o]ṭ[u] ôs[u] kō-na āsihas ta. lāgas etc. 777.

yikawaṭa kañĕka log[u] waranas ta
shurāh sās ta akh hath āsa sārĕy
akiy kshĕna āyĕ pāni-grahanas ta. lāgas etc. 778

yīt[i] rūph kañĕkan tīt[i] Krushnas ta
sārĕn[ü]y okuy lạg[a]n ôs[u]
dēwatā sör[i] ös[i] dẹwa-pūzanas ta. lāgas etc. 779.

sārĕn[ü]y byon[u] byon[u] gara pānas ta
sārĕn[ü]y byon[u] byon[u] Krushna-jyuv sūty
sārĕy sīwā karanas tas ta. lāgas etc. 780.

shurāh sās kañĕka āyĕ waranas ta
tō-ti chuh bāla-brahmatsöriy Brahm
brahmatsör[i]-bāwas pör[i] lagahös ta. lāgas etc. 781.

prabāta-kāla pĕṭha tāñ sāyĕmas ta
prabāta-kāla pāli prath sīwā
āshtsar yiyi na kĕh ti wananas ta. lāgas etc. 782.

sŏndaran-hond[u] kyāh yiyi wananas ta
bāgĕ zi tihond[u] kaitwāh ôs[u]
Mahādīv[i] ḍĕchĕn ta gav muhas ta. lāgas etc. 783.

namaskār brahmatsöris Krushnas ta
namaskār Krushnañĕn ḍĕka-bajĕn
namaskār Krushnanis pariwāras ta. lāgas etc. 784.

775. For the Pārijāta tree to fight he issued forth, but against Bhagavān what resource had he? And so disgrace was all the fruit that came from this to Indra.

776. From heaven's region Kṛṣṇa to the earth descended, and in the city of Dvārakā high festival arose, so thus in each city came high festival.

777. To Satyabhāmā's courtyard came the Pārijāta. Its floods of fragrance reached to every door. Thus did Vaikuṇṭha, Viṣṇu's heaven, there became manifest, and wherefore should that not be so?

778. All at one time the damsels did he wed. Thousands sixteen and eke a hundred were they, and at the same instant came they all to be espoused.

779. As many as the damsels were, so many forms took Kṛṣṇa, and at one wedding did he espouse them all. At the worship of the gods did all the gods present themselves.

780. Each damsel had for herself a house apart, each had a Kṛṣṇa separate to herself, and all engagèd were in doing to him service.

781. Though thus to him were sixteen thousand damsels wedded, yet was he also Brahma the Supreme, in the form of a youth bound celibate by perpetual vows; and to his nature as a celibate do I offer myself in sacrifice.

782. From dawn to eve (is each one lovingly employed), from dawn doth each herself devote to her especial service. At aught that can be said need no one marvel.

783. About these lovely damsels how can all be told! How great was the happy fortune that they found! Even when Mahādēva[1] saw them, with desire was he filled.

784. To Kṛṣṇa's chaste celibacy be reverence. To his spouses of high fortune be there reverence. To all his household reverence be paid.

[1] Mahādēva is represented as impervious to sexual desire.

prath rōnī yĕli lüj^{u} prasanas ta
kūr^{ü} akh ta gŏbar dah prath kaīsi zāy
shurāh sās ta akh hath kōrĕ zāyĕ tas ta
lāgas bŏh dasta dasta pampōsh. 785.

akh lach ta akahaiṭh sās gŏbar tas ta
sārĕn^{ü}y shur^{i}-mur^{i} kaityāh zāy
grand gayĕ na Krushnanis pariwāras ta. lāgas etc. 786.

yus lagi Krushna-jyuwanis nāwas ta
tas kari Krushna-jyuv sarŏ wŏpakār
yiti yĕsh nith ta wāti Vishnu-bawanas ta. lāgas etc. 787.

pör^{i} pör^{i} Krushna-jyuwanis nāwas ta
pör^{i} pör^{i} tasandis autāras
pör^{i} pör^{i} tasandis shŏba tsarĕtas ta. lāgas etc. 788.

XXXVII.

Anirudd gŏbur ôs^{u} Pradyumnas ta
tam^{i} kor^{u} Bānāsŏras ḍās
Bānāsŏran kūr^{ü} dits^{ü}nas ta
lāgas bŏh dasta dasta pampōsh. 789.

Bānāsŏr bọw^{u} bokt^{u} Rudras ta
Shōnitapŏra ôs^{u} rājy karanas
boḍ^{u} ôs^{u} baktĕn manz Dēwas ta. lāgas etc. 790.

sās narĕ āsas boḍ^{u} bal tas ta
Krushna-jyuv^{i} sārĕy narĕ tsacĕnas
bāḍi ahankāra ôs^{u} rājy karanas ta. lāgas etc. 791.

Shiwa-bakth büḍ^{ü} ös^{ü} Bānāsŏras ta
Shiwa-jī tōṭhyōs mong^{u}nas war
'kūṭapāl āstam ts^{a}y nagaras' ta. lāgas etc. 792

bükts^{ü} sūty āyot^{u} gav Shiv tas ta
nagaras kūṭapāl sōpanith rūd^{u}
Bānāsŏr nĕth pūz karihēs ta. lāgas etc. 793.

785. (Bhāg. Pu. X, lxi.) As to each queen there came the time to bear, one daughter and ten sons did each bring forth. Thousands sixteen and eke a hundred daughters did they bear to him.

786. Sons thousands a hundred three score and one had he, and these again had offspring numberless. Thus Kṛṣṇa's household was beyond all count.

787. He who beareth in his heart the name of Kṛṣṇa, to him will Kṛṣṇa every favour render. In this world glory will he win, and thereafter the abode of Viṣṇu will he reach. To him posy and posy do I offer lotuses.

788. Ever dedicating myself to Kṛṣṇa's name, ever dedicating myself to his incarnation, ever dedicating myself to his auspicious deeds, to him posy and posy do I offer lotuses.

XXXVII. ANIRUDDHA AND UṢĀ. (Bhāg. Pu. X, lxii-iii.)

789. Pradyumna's son was Aniruddha, and he the demon Bāṇa did o'ercome, and to him Bāṇa did his daughter give.

790. Bāṇa a devotee of Mahādēva was. Śōṇitapura did he rule as king. Among the devotees of Mahādēva he was great.

791. A thousand arms had he; great was his might. Kṛṣṇa his arms did one and all cut off. Great was the pride with which he held his sway.

792. To Śiva-Mahādēva great devotion did he show. Śiva showed grace to him, and from the god a boon he craved. 'For my city be thou alone the guardian of my fort.'

793. Loyal to his devotion Śiva became and stayed the guardian of the city's fort, while Bāṇa worshipped him without surcease.

yüts^{u}-kāl Mahādēv ôs^{u} nagaras ta
  Bānāsŏrañĕ kāmĕ karawun^{u}
Bānāsŏr ôs^{u} rājy karanas ta.
  lāgas bŏh dasta dasta pampōsh. 794.

dŏha aki pānay war mong^{u}nas ta
  'mĕ hyuh^{u} zi kũh chuh na trĕn bŏwanan
kãtshāh āsihēm som^{u} yŏddas' ta. lāgas etc. 795.

krūd khot^{u} Yīshŏras ta war dyut^{u}nas ta
  zônun zi 'rākhĕsas wŏñ nāsh wôt^{u}'
yiy war tam^{i} mong^{u} tiy dyut^{u}nas ta. lāgas etc. 796.

dop^{u}nas zi 'dŏz cyôn^{u} pĕyi ãganas ta
  kariy vīrāh mānas hān
yĕli pĕyi tot^{u}-tāñ prār samayĕs ta. lāgas etc. 797.

asŏras tas bŏd bākhanēyĕs ta
  dŏzuk^{u} wasith pyon^{u} kãchani log^{u}
yutshun vīrāh tsor^{u} pānas ta. lāgas etc. 798.

samay wôt^{u} yĕli tas asŏras ta
  kĕtha pŏṭh^{i} pānay samponus ḍās
kami pör^{i} Krushna-jyuv yith pyōs tas ta. lāgas etc.
799.

Wushā kūr^{ü} ös^{ü} tas asŏras ta
  Anirudd dŏha aki sŏp^{a}n^{i} ās
Aniruddas pĕṭh man log^{u} tas ta. lāgas etc. 800.

praböt^{i} wŏts^{ü} ta lüj^{ü} wadanas ta
  'hā myôn^{u} bartā kōr-kun gav?'
mandachun^{u} dop^{u}has ta kẽh log^{u} na tas ta. lāgas etc.
801.

sŏp^{a}n rātaki lüj^{ü} wananas ta
  'man nyūnam ta kẽh chum na pāy'
rātas ta dŏhas lüj^{ü} wadanas ta. lāgas etc. 802.

Tsitralēkhā ös^{ü} ṭŏṭh^{ü} vĕs tas ta
  murüts^{ü} tami sārĕn^{ü}y-hanza karĕnas
dēwatā ta manŏsh sör^{i} höv^{i}nas ta. lāgas etc. 803.

794. Long in that city did Mahādēva dwell, doing all Bāṇa's works, while Bāṇa ruled as king.

795. Once on a day from the god he craved (another) boon, 'In the three worlds there is no soul my match. Let someone now my peer in combat be.'

796. Anger in Īśvara[1] arose, and a boon he granted. Well knew he 'Now hath destruction to the demon come.' And so to him he gave the boon he craved.

797. Quoth he 'In thy courtyard shall fall the flag, and a hero shall lower thy haughty pride. Wait thou until the time thy flag shall fall.'

798. Dulled became the demon's understanding. For the falling of the flag did he begin to long, that he might meet a hero mightier than himself.

799. When to the demon came his time, how did destruction hap of itself on him? From what direction did Kṛṣṇa on him fall?

800. The demon had a daughter Uṣā hight, and one day came to her Aniruddha in a dream. Smitten with love for him did she become.

801. At dawn uprose she, and weeping did she cry, 'Alas, my Lord, Ah whither hast thou gone?' 'Shame' to her did they cry, but no whit heeded she.

802. Of her dream of the night did she begin to tell, 'My soul hath he carried off, and I have no resource.' Thus, ever night and day she wept.

803. Citralēkhā was her crony well-beloved. Of all the gods and of all men did she draw picture portraits, and to her them she showed.

[1] I.e. Mahādēva.

wuchān ta wöts^{ü} yĕli Aniruddas ta
dop^{u}nas 'ȧmiy man myôn^{u} nyūnam
wātĕmay ta rōza zinda, na-ta maras ta
lāgas bŏh dasta dasta pampōsh. 804.

Tsitralēkhā gayĕ Aniruddas ta
ākösh^{i} gatshith ta Dwārakāyĕ wöts^{ü}
wötith nishĕ pĕyĕ Aniruddas ta. lāgas etc. 805.

sọp^{a}n^{i} sa ti ös^{ü} āmüts^{ü} tas ta
Anirudd^{i} won^{u}mot^{u} ôs^{u} Nāradas
Nāradüñ^{ü} shĕch^{i} ös^{ü} Aniruddas ta. lāgas etc. 806.

Tsitralēkhā yĕli nishĕ wöts^{ü} tas ta
wuḍith dŏnaway ākösh^{i} gay
Anirudd Wushāyĕ wôt^{u} waranas ta. lāgas etc. 807.

gandarwa-viwāh tati kor^{u}nas ta
bāra-böts^{ü} pānavüñ^{ü} khēlani lȧg^{i}
kĕ̃h rĕth pānavüñ^{ü} lȧg^{i} sŏkhas ta. lāgas etc. 808.

Bānāsŏras āy wananas ta
'Wushā zi pŏrushā̃h sũty hĕth ḍīṭh^{ü}'
Asŏran būzun ta gav kūpas ta. lāgas etc. 809.

dŏha aki bihith ös^{ü} pĕṭh mandiras ta
pānavüñ^{ü} bāra-böts^{ü} khēlān ös^{i}
rākhĕsan ḍīshith ta log^{u} zāganas ta. lāgas etc. 810.

tarwār hĕth āv pĕṭh mandiras ta
lŏti-pöṭh^{i} wötith ta shĕ̃kani rūd^{u}
wuchun ta gindān tim cōpaṭas ta. lāgas etc. 811.

Anirudd^{i} Krushnüñ^{ü} driy höv^{ü}nas ta
'söriy zi zēnay thaway na kā̃h'
Wushāyi Bānüñ^{u} driy höv^{ü}nas ta. lāgas etc. 812.

---

1 A "Gandharva marriage" is a perfectly legal form of marriage among persons of the military caste, i.e., *kṣatriyas*. It is a marriage proceeding entirely from mutual attraction, and is performed without ceremonies and without consulting relatives. In fact it closely corresponds to the 'Scotch marriage' of English

804. And when she came to seeing Aniruddha's portrait, 'Tis he', she cried, 'who hath carried off my soul. If he come to me, I live; if not, I die.'

805. To Aniruddha Citralēkhā hied. Through the welkin did she fly, and Dvārakā she reached; and, as she arrived, near Aniruddha did she alight.

806. In a dream also had Uṣā come to him, and he to Nārada had told the tale. Thus Nārada had tidings of (where) Aniruddha (went).

807. When Citralēkhā thus accosted him, together through the welkin flew they off, and to Uṣā did Aniruddha come, and so espoused her.

808. There a Gandharva spousal [1] with her did he make, and in each other's arms the consorts sported. Thus for a space of months did they in bliss abide.

809. Bāṇa's retainers to their master came and told him how in a man's company Uṣā had been seen. Then, when the demon heard it, he was filled with wrath.

810. Once on a day within her palace was she seated, and with each other were the spouses sporting, when the demon chanced to see them, and on the watch did he remain.

811. Sword in hand the palace did he enter. Stealthily approaching in mistrust he stood, and his gaze fell on them as caupār [2] they played.

812. To Uṣā Aniruddha swore by Kṛṣṇa's name, 'All thy men will I capture, and leave none to thee,' while Uṣā taking Bāṇa's name made oath (that she would capture Aniruddha's men).

---

novelists. The Bhāgavata Purāṇa is not so tender for the morality of the young couple, and makes no mention of any wedding ceremony.

[2] A kind of backgammon.

Krushnani nāwa sūty gav harshēs ta
‘baḍiy kŏḷuk^{u} zi zāmatur^{u} ām’
kĕtshāh lazi gav ta gav kūpas ta
lāgas bŏh dasta dasta pampōsh. 813.

påt^{i}-khūr^{i} wŏthith ta log^{u} kūpas ta
rākhĕsan āgyā log^{u} karanē
gånḍ karanas tas Aniruddas ta. lāgas etc. 814.

ganḍani yĕli låg^{i} Aniruddas ta
tot^{u}-tāñ Anirudd nĕshūk^{u} ôs^{u}
wŏthith ta sīnā sör^{ü} mör^{ü}nas ta. lāgas etc. 815.

Bān ās pānay ta ganḍ phyur^{u}nas ta
Anirudd zāmatur^{u} karihēs kyāh
tsönith thowun bönd^{i}-wānas ta. lāgas etc. 816.

Nārada-ryosh^{u} gav Krushna-zīwas ta
Aniruddüñ^{ü} shĕch^{i} sör^{ü} wüñ^{ü}nas
Krushna-jyuv pŏtra-dādi drāv laḍanas ta. lāgas etc. 817.

bāh akshauhiniyĕ sūty Krushnas ta
Shōnitapŏr āv Krushna-Bagawān
Bānāsŏr drāv yōra yŏddas ta. lāgas etc. 818.

gŏḍañ kūṭapāl brōṭh dyut^{u}nas ta
Mahādēv yoddas Krushnas āv
wazīr z^{a}h mŏkha āy Balabadras ta. lāgas etc. 819.

Kārtikiy mŏkha āv Pradyumnas ta
Sātĕkis mŏkha āv Bānāsŏr
yŏdduk^{u} awasar låg^{i} ganḍanas ta. lāgas etc. 820.

Krushna-jyuv ta Mahādēv låg^{i} yŏddas ta
dŏnaway kuniy ta wån^{i}zĕkh kyāh
kôtwāh tshala bala låg^{i} laḍanas ta. lāgas etc. 821.

Mahādīv^{i} sīnāyĕ taph tshun^{u}nas ta
Krushna-jyuv^{i} phīrith zāla tshuñ^{ü}nas
tana-shut^{u} taph zāla lajĕ zanas ta. lāgas etc. 822.

---

1 Their names were Kumbhâṇḍa and Kūpakarṇa.

2 The god of war and son of Mahādēva. 3 Kṛṣṇa's charioteer.

4 According to one legend Śōṇitapura was near the present Tezpur in Assam.

813. Bāṇa rejoiced on hearing Kṛṣṇa's name, 'Verily of lineage high hath come to me a son-in-law.' Then somewhat of shame he felt and waxed wroth.

814. Hastily in sudden rage rose he, and to his demon henchmen gave command that Aniruddha straight they place in bonds.

815. Till they attempted Aniruddha so to bind, fearless he sat awaiting them. Then he arose and the whole army slew.

816. But Bāṇa came himself, and with knots surrounded him. How could Aniruddha, the son-in-law, oppose him? So into prison him did Bāṇa thrust.

817. Then went the holy Nārada to Kṛṣṇa, and Aniruddha's tidings told he all. Then, in the love he bare his son, did Kṛṣṇa sally forth to war.

818. Twelve mighty armies Kṛṣṇa with him took. To Śōṇitapura straight came Bhagavān, and to the combat Bāṇa issued forth.

819. First, in the van, set he (Mahādēva) the guardian of his fort, and Mahādēva against Kṛṣṇa came, while to oppose Balabhadra there came two viziers.[1]

820. To oppose Pradyumna Kārttikēya[2] came, and against Sātyaki[3] Bāṇa came himself. And so in battle they began to join.

821. Kṛṣṇa and Mahādēva joined in fight. In single combat each encountered other, nor can words tell the tale. With endless wile and endless might did they contend.

822. Then over Kṛṣṇa's army Mahādēva burning fever flung,[4] and Kṛṣṇa in retort flung chilling ague. E'er since that day hath burning fever and hath chill ague been amidst mankind.

Assam is a very feverish country. The present legend is therefore interesting, and seems to rest on a tradition of some epidemic of fever entering India proper from Assam

bajĕr thawun^{u} ôs^{u} Krushna-nāwas ta
Rudras gan tsál^{i} ta zēnana āv
wazīr pĕy mārán^{i} Balabadras ta
lāgas bŏh dasta dasta pampōsh. 823.

Bānāsŏr pāna āv Shrī-Krushnas ta
pönts hath āyŏd dörith kĕth
akiy kāna tim phuṭ^{a}rövinas ta. lāgas etc. 824.

rathawôl^{u} mörith ta ratha phuṭ^{o}runas ta
paikaiy tsalanas trôwun rav
wŏḍanüñ^{ü} drāyĕs möj^{ü} Krushnas ta. lāgas etc. 825.

Mahādēv bákt^{i}-sándi gav krūdas ta
biyĕ Krushnas sūty log^{u} laḍanē
pūsh^{u} na ta shĕran āv Shrī-Krushnas ta. lāgas etc.
826.

Bānāsŏr āv biyĕ yŏddas ta
Krushna-jyuv^{i} sārĕy narĕ tsacyĕnas
Shiwa-sandi zāra-pāra tsōr thavĕnas ta. lāgas etc. 827.

Krushna-jyuv chuh dapān Mahādēwas ta
'mĕ ti buḍ^{i}-baba-sond^{u} pālun^{u} chum
Prahlād kun^{u} ḅokt^{u} bọw^{u} Vishnas ta. lāgas etc. 828.

'mĕ zi zĕv dits^{ü}müts^{ü} chĕh Prahlādas ta
"bŏh zi cyôn^{u} wamsh gāla na zāh"
bŏz^{ü}y tsáṭ^{i}mas ta mad wôl^{u}mas' ta. lāgas etc. 829.

Mahādīv^{i} pôw^{u}nas Bān pādas ta
Bān Aniruddas sūty hĕth ta āv
viwāh karith ta kūr^{ü} dits^{ü}nas ta. lāgas etc. 830.

sŏn mŏkta raṭ^{a}n kūt^{u} dāj dyut^{u}nas ta
akshauhĕn sīnā sūty dits^{ü}nas
Krushna-jyuv hĕth āv nŏshi gŏbaras ta. lāgas etc.
831.

---

1 A name of Mahādēva.

823. High praise be offered unto Kṛṣṇa's name. The troops of Rudra [1] fled and were discomfited The viziers twain fell to be slain by Balabhadra.

824. Then against Kṛṣṇa Bāṇa came himself, holding five hundred weapons in his thousand arms, and with a single arrow Kṛṣṇa broke them all.

825. The charioteer he slew and the chariot shattered, and with all speed Bāṇa did running flee afoot. Then forth came Bāṇa's mother with bared head to Kṛṣṇa.

826. Then for his devotee waxed Mahādēva wroth, and again with Kṛṣṇa did he the issue join. But naught could he prevail, and (in the end) on Kṛṣṇa's mercy did he cast himself.

827. Bāṇa once more the combat to renew came forth, but Kṛṣṇa cut off all his thousand arms, save that, at Mahādēva's prayer, he left him four.

828. And now to Mahādēva Kṛṣṇa saith, 'My promise to his grandsire [2] must I keep, for (in his day) Prahlāda was the only devotee of Viṣṇu.

829. 'With my own tongue to Prahlāda a promise did I give that I his family should ne'er destroy. This Bāṇa's arms alone have I cut off, and his pride have I brought low.'

830. Mahādēva made Bāṇa fall at Kṛṣṇa's feet, and Bāṇa bringing Aniruddha to him came. Then all the wedding rites did he perform and duly to him did his daughter give.

831. Vast dower of gold and pearls and jewels gave he him, and with him sent an army all complete, when Kṛṣṇa his daughter-in law and grandson homeward led.

---

[2] Bāṇa was really great grandson of Prahlāda. The line of descent was Prahlāda, Virōcana, Bali, Bāṇa.

Dwārakāyĕ yĕli wöt^{i} gay harshĕs ta
tsōri rĕti Anirudd wötith pĕv
Rukminiyĕ put^{a}r^{i}-nŏsh wöts^{ü} garas ta
lāgas bŏh dasta dasta pampōsh. 832

Dwārakāyĕ wŏtsav log^{u} sapanas ta
Yādav söriy wadạvĕn tsāy
namaskār Krushna-jyuwanis nāwas ta. lāgas etc. 833

yus lagi pör^{i} pör^{i} Krushna-nāwas ta
tas kari Krushna-jyuv sarŏ wŏpakār
yiti yĕsh nith ta wāti Vishnu-bŏwanas ta. lāgas etc. 834

XXXVIII.

aki dŏha yĕli shur^{i} drāy gindanas ta
samith Krushnån^{i} ta Yādawan-hånd^{i}
tati trēsh lüj^{ü}kh ta gay tshāḍanas ta
lāgas bŏh dasta dasta pampōsh. 835.

krīris akis pĕṭh gay zalas ta
ḍīṭh^{ü}kh kĕ̄kalüṭ^{ü} krīris manz
khārani lajyēy krēri manza tas ta. lāgas etc. 836.

büḍ^{ü} ös^{ü} kĕ̄kalüṭ^{ü} ta boḍ^{u} mān tas ta
khāranas kaīsi-hond^{u} bal log^{u} na tas
āshtsaras gatshith ta phīr^{i} pānas ta. lāgas etc. 837.

wonukh yith ta Krushna-Bagawānas ta
Krushna-jyuv krīris pĕṭh pāna āv
pōsh zan tulith nyūn wāma-hasta. lāgas etc. 838.

krĕri nīrith ta āv rāza-rūpas ta
Krushna-Bagawānas pādan pĕv
zānawån^{i} sör^{u}y shĕch^{i} pritsh^{u}nas ta. lāgas etc. 839.

rāza āv kartūth sôr^{u} wananas ta
dop^{u}nas 'Nruga-rāza ôsum nāv
log^{u}mot^{u} ôsum dān karanas ta. lāgas etc. 840.

832. At Dvārakā when they arrived, they all rejoiced, that Aniruddha after four months had thus returned, and into the home of Rukmiṇī entered her grandson's bride.

833. In Dvārakā began high festival, and all the Yādavas their gratulations made. Reverence offer ye to Kṛṣṇa's name.

834. He who beareth in his heart the name of Kṛṣṇa, to him will Kṛṣṇa every favour render. In this world glory will he win, and thereafter the abode of Viṣṇu will he reach. To him posy and posy do I offer lotuses.

XXXVIII. THE STORY OF NṚGA. (Bhāg. Pu. X, lxiv.)

835. Once on a day when the lads went out to play,—the boys of Kṛṣṇa and of the Yādavas together,—thirsty did they become, and water to seek went they.

836. For water went they to a certain well, and in that well a lizard they descried. Then from the well tried they to lift it out.

837. Huge was that lizard, and of pond'rous weight, and none of them had strength to lift it out. Astonied were they and returnèd home.

838. To Kṛṣṇa Bhagavān came they and told the tale, and he himself went straightway to the well, and with his left hand, as though it were but some flower, the lizard did uplift.

839. When from the well the lizard thus emerged, a king's form took he and at Kṛṣṇa's feet he fell. Kṛṣṇa then asked him for his tale, although he knew it all.

840. To tell his former deeds thus did the king begin. Quoth he, 'King Nṛga was I hight, and all my time I spent in gifts of charity.

'grand kår^{i}zi dĕwa waharöts^{ü} rūdas ta
myānĕn dānan ös^{ü} na kĕ̄h grand
tamiy phala wôtus az darshĕnas' ta
lāgas bŏh dasta dasta pampōsh. 841

'yim dāta ös^{i} yith samsāras ta
timan pĕṭh^{i}-kin^{i} nāv myôn^{u} drāv
myôn^{u} yesh gĕwahön Vaikunṭhas' ta. lāgas etc. 842

'grünz^{ü}-ratsha gōv^{ü} ditsa mahādānas ta
sŏna mŏkta wastrav pūrith kĕth
brāhman anahö r^{a}t^{i} pūzanas' ta. lāgas etc. 843

'dŏha aki logus yĕli dānas ta
brāhmanas åk^{i}-sünz^{ü} kāmadīnāh
gōv^{ü}n manz āyĕ dina dānas' ta. lāgas etc. 844

'brôhmun tshāḍān wôt^{u} brāhmanas ta
panañĕ kāmadīni thaph kür^{ü}nas
brāhmån^{i} dop^{u} "mĕ zi mīj^{ü} dānas"' ta. lāgas etc.
845

'dŏnaway mīlith āy dādas ta
aki kani lach gōv^{ü} dini log^{u}sakh
dŏnaway môn^{u} na ta kara kyāh kas' ta. lāgas etc.
846

'brāhmana-tsakh na zi yiyi wananas ta
kāmadīni-hond^{u} nyāy andyōv na kĕ̄h
tithay samay wôt^{u} mĕ ti maranas' ta. lāgas etc. 847

'Darma-rāza brŏ̄ṭh drāv mān karanas ta
dānan-hond^{u} pŏñ asankhy ôs^{u}
kāmadīni-hond^{u} ti pāph āv lĕkhanas' ta. lāgas etc.
848

'dop^{u}nam zi "tshĕn chuy na zāh pŏñĕs
pāpa-hani-hond^{u} phal kar būgakh."
gōḍañiy būgun^{u} pāna mong^{u}mas' ta. lāgas etc. 849

'Darma-āgyāyĕ pyōs bū-manḍalas ta
yimi dīha būj^{ü}m say pāpa-han
cyāni darshĕna gōm pāph antas' ta. lāgas etc. 850

841. ‘In the season of rains forsooth the rain-drops one may count, but none could count the number of my gifts. Lo, as the fruit of that hast thou to me revealed thyself this day.

842. ‘Mid all who in this world were known as generous, high o'er them all went forth abroad my name. In heaven itself my glory they extolled.

843. ‘In mighty largess gave I countless cows, with gold and pearls and housings all adorned, and to my worship holy Brāhmaṇas did I call.

844. ‘Once on a day as largess I bestowed, amongst my own kine that I gave away, the milch-cow of a certain Brāhmaṇa unwittingly was by me in gift bestowed.

845. ‘To the Brāhmaṇa to whom I gave it came its owner seeking it, and seized the milch-cow saying ’twas his own. Then quoth the other, —he to whom I gave it, “As largess from the king received I it.”

846. ‘Both came before me, each ’gainst each his claim, and for the one cow sought I a hundred thousand kine to give; but assent neither yielded. What could I do for whom?

847. ‘A Brāhmaṇa's wrath can never be explained. In no way could the quarrel o'er the cow be settled, and in the meantime came my time to die.

848. ‘To weigh my deeds Yama came forth to meet me. Unnumbered merits gained I for my gifts, but against them was written the sin of the milch-cow.

849. ‘Quoth he to me, “Ne'er can be cut from thee the happy fruit of all thy pious deeds. When wouldst thou reap the fruit of this small sin?” I asked that I might reap it first of all.

850. ‘By Yama's just decree to earth I fell, and in this body the fruit of that little sin I reaped. Now, by beholding thee, my sin away hath passed.’

wanith pādan pĕv Krushnas ta
vĕmān wothus ta khasith ɠav
pör^{i} pör^{i} Krushna-jyuwanis nāwas ta
lāɠas bŏh ɗasta ɗasta pampōsh. 851.

Krushna-jyuv dapān prath Yāɗawas ta
‘ Brāhmanas sūty zāh kȧr^{i}zi na mān
lāɠ zāh kȧr^{i}zi na brahma-amshĕs ’ ta. lāɠas etc.
852.

yus lagi Krushna-jyuwanis nāwas ta
tas kari Krushna-jyuv sarŏ wŏpakār
yiyi yĕsh nith ta wāti Vishnu-bawanas ta. lāɠas etc.
853

pör^{i} pör^{i} Krushna-jyuwanis nāwas ta
pör^{i} pör^{i} tasandis autārās
pör^{i} pör^{i} tasandis shŏba tsarĕtas ta. lāɠas etc. 854.

XXXIX.

dŏha aki mani āv Krushna-zīwas ta
‘ shĕchāh anahö Nanda-gōrün^{ü}
tim sör^{i} āsan tati shūkas ’ ta
lāɠas bŏh ɗasta ɗasta pampōsh. 855.

sūzun Haladar Rām Gōkulas ta
dŏda-mālinĕn sath ɠav karanē
pādan pĕv mājĕ dŏda-babas ta. lāɠas etc. 856.

dŏshĕw^{ü}y nālamȧt^{i} mīṭh^{i} kȧr^{i}has ta
lōl ākh mutsarana wadanas lȧg^{i}
Rāmani darshĕna lȧg^{i} vĕṭhanas ta. lāɠas etc. 857.

Krushna-Bagawānun^{u} lȧg^{i} pritshanas ta
‘ asĕ ti mani chwā anān zāh
yiticĕ khēla mā chĕs tsētas ’ ta. lāɠas etc. 858.

ɠūpiyĕ khĕli khĕli sārĕ āyĕs ta
wadān ta lajĕs pān wandanē
sārĕn^{i} chuh Haladar dam dinas ta. lāɠas etc. 859.

851. With these words at Kṛṣṇa's feet he fell. From heaven a chariot did descend, and dedicating himself to Kṛṣṇa's name he mounted it.

852. To each Yādava quoth Kṛṣṇa, 'Against a Brāhmaṇa ne'er display ye pride, nor ever even touch a Brāhmaṇa's goods.'

853. He who beareth in his heart the name of Kṛṣṇa, to him will Kṛṣṇa every favour render. In this world glory will he win, and thereafter the abode of Viṣṇu will he reach. To him posy and posy do I offer lotuses.

854. Ever dedicating myself to Kṛṣṇa's name, ever dedicating myself to his incarnation, ever dedicating myself to his auspicious deeds, to him posy and posy do I offer lotuses.

XXXIX. BALARĀMA VISITS GŌKULA (Bhāg. Pu. X, lxv.)

855. Once on a day it entered Kṛṣṇa's heart, 'Fain would I news of Nanda hear, and learn if there they still in sorrow dwell.

856. So Haladhara-Rāma to Gōkula he sent, and to give solace to them of his foster-father's house did he set forth. So at the mother's and the foster-father's feet himself did he prostrate.

857. Him did the twain embrace and fondly kiss. Their pent up love was loosèd and they wept, while at the sight of Rāma they rejoiced.

858. Of Kṛṣṇa Bhagavān they tidings asked, 'Us does he ever call into his mind? His boyish sports of here doth he remember?'

859. Came the herd-damsels all in troops and troops. Weeping, themselves to him they dedicated, as Haladhara comforted them all.

Krushna-Bagawānun^{u} lajĕ wananas ta
‘ tȧm^{i} kẹtha soh^{u} zi ȧs^{i} trāvĕn
kaṭhūr man drāv Krushna-zīwas ta
lāgas bŏh dasta dasta pampōsh. 860.

tȧm^{i} trāvĕ asĕ kĕtha yiyi trāwanas ta
asĕ chuh brinzi brinzi pānas sūty
Krushna-dyān kĕtha yiyi mash^{e}rāwanas’ ta. lāgas etc.
861.

Haladar Rām chukh sath karanas ta
‘ Krushna-jyuv prath jāyĕ wötith chuh
sārĕn^{u}y nishĕ chuwa prath samayĕs ’ ta. lāgas etc.
862.

yih yih lŏkacāra ös^{i} khēla karanas ta
tithay timan sūty khēlani log^{u}
prath khēlan-shāyĕ lȧg^{i} phēranas ta. lāgas etc. 863.

Jamunāyĕ bȧṭh^{i} bȧṭh^{i} rūd^{u} khēlanas ta
khēlāh karith ta phīrith gav
dŏyi rĕti biyĕ wôt^{u} Krushna-darshĕnas ta. lāgas etc.
864.

yus lagi Krushna-jyuwanis nāwas ta
tas kari Krushna-jyuv sarŏ wŏpakār
yiti yĕsh nith ta wāti Vishnu-bawanas ta. lāgas etc.
865.

pör^{i} pör^{i} Krushna-jyuwanis nāwas ta
pör^{i} pör^{i} tasandis autāras
pör^{i} pör^{i} tasandis shŏba tsarĕtas ta. lāgas etc. 866.

XL.

Punḍarīka-nôm^{u} ôs^{u} tath samayĕs ta
Krushna-Bagawānun^{u} vih dörith
rākhĕsas tūr^{i}-kun bŏd āyĕs ta
lāgas bŏh dasta dasta pampōsh. 867.

lüz^{ü}n shĕch^{i} tȧm^{i} Krushna-zīwas ta
‘ bŏh zi chus Krushn ta ts^{a}h kus gōkh
bŏy chus āmot^{u} autāras ’ ta. lāgas etc. 868.

860. Of Kṛṣṇa Bhagavān they 'gan to speak, 'How could he bear thus to abandon us? Ah, Kṛṣṇa's heart hath turned out hard indeed.

861. 'Us he abandoned. Him can we not abandon. At every moment is he with us (in our hearts). To meditate on Kṛṣṇa how can we e'er forget'?

862. To them doth Haladhara-Rāma solace give. 'Kṛṣṇa, the God, pervadeth every spot; at all times is he present with ye all.'

863. In all the sportive games of early childhood, with them he sported, each with each and all, and each spot where they'd played he visited.

864. He halted sporting all along the Yamunā's bank. Then, having sported, he returned home, and after two months showed himself to Kṛṣṇa.

865. He who beareth in his heart the name of Kṛṣṇa, to him will Kṛṣṇa every favour render. In this world glory will he win, and thereafter the abode of Viṣṇu will he reach. To him posy and posy do I offer lotuses.

866. Ever dedicating myself to Kṛṣṇa's name, ever dedicating myself to his incarnation, ever dedicating myself to his auspicious deeds, to him posy and posy do I offer lotuses.

XL. PUṆḌARĪKA THE ANTI-KṚṢṆA. THE WAR WITH KĀŚĪ. (Bhāg. Pu. X, lxvi.)

867. In those days was there a king hight Puṇḍarīka[1], who took the form of Kṛṣṇa Bhagavān, and in that very case the instincts of a demon came to him.

868. A message thus to Kṛṣṇa did he send, 'Lo, I am Kṛṣṇa. Who, I ask, art thou? 'Tis I alone who have become incarnate.

[1] The Bhāgavata Purāṇa gives his name as Pauṇḍraka.

'yā-tay Krushna-nāv trāv pānas ta
na-tay wālay ahankār.'
Krushna-jyuv ta Yādav ṭsāy asanas ta
lāgas bọh dasta dasta pampōsh. 869.

wŏthith ta Krushna-jyuv khot^{u} rathas ta
tat-kshĕn nagaras wŏtith pyōs
Punḍarīk^{i} būzun ta drāv yŏddas ta. lāgas etc. 870.

Kāshi-rāza mẹth^{a}r ôs^{u} Punḍarīkas ta
sīnā sūty hĕth ta sŏr^{ü}y āv
sanmŏkha mŏkha āy Shrī-Krushnas ta. lāgas etc.
871.

Krushna-jyuv^{i} ṭsakra sūty sŏr^{i} mŏr^{i}nas ta
Punḍarīkas gŏḍa kala ṭsoṭ^{u}nas
sīnāyĕ tawa pata nāsh kor^{u}nas ta. lāgas etc. 872.

tami pata ṭsoṭun kala Kāshi-rāzas ta
wŏthith kala tas Kŏshiyĕ pĕv
ḍīshith ta dŏkh pyōs pariwāras ta. lāgas etc. 873.

Krushna-jyuv Dwārakāyĕ āv pānas ta
dēv lág^{i} pōshĕ-warshun^{u} karanē
pŏr^{i} pŏr^{i} Krushna-jyuwanis balas ta. lāgas etc. 874.

Sudakshĕn gŏbur ôs^{u} Kāshi-rāzas ta
mŏl^{i}-sandi mārana gav kūpas
wŏpāy ṭshāḍani log^{u} Krushnas ta. lāgas etc. 875.

shĕran sampon^{u} Mahādēwas ta
Vishvēshŏras tapa ārādani log^{u}
war dyun^{u} gŏn ôs^{u} Paramēshĕs ta. lāgas etc. 876.

Yīshŏr tōṭhyōs war dyut^{u}nas ta
manth^{a}r dyut^{u}nas zapun^{u} kyut^{u}
haṭha sān manth^{a}r log^{u} zapanas ta. lāgas etc. 877.

yihay sĕd ŏs^{ü} tath mantras ta
murathāh wŏpüz^{ü}s ạgnas hish^{ü}
pratimāyĕ diṭs^{ü}n āgyā tạs ta. lāgas etc. 878.

869. 'Either do thou give up the name of Kṛṣṇa, or else thy pride of self will I bring down.' At this did Kṛṣṇa and the Yādavas outright laugh.

870. Kṛṣṇa arose and on his chariot mounted. Straightway he came and on his city fell. This Puṇḍarīka heard and issued forth to fight.

871. The Kāśī king was Puṇḍarīka's friend. Thither did he his army bring complete, and face to face come Kṛṣṇa to oppose.

872. Then with his discus Kṛṣṇa slew them all, and first he cut off Puṇḍarīka's head. Thereafter all his troops did he destroy

873. Then cut he off the head of Kāśī's king. Up in the air it shot and down in Kāśī dropped. Grief seized his household when they saw it fall.

874. Kṛṣṇa returnèd home to Dvārakā. On him the gods a rain of flowers poured. To Kṛṣṇa's might I dedicate myself.

875. The king of Kāśī's son, Sudakṣiṇa, become infuriate at his father's death, sought for a plan to compass Kṛṣṇa's fall.

876. On Mahādēva's mercy did he throw himself, and with austerities began he to do homage to the Lord of the Universe, for to grant boons is of the essence of the Lord.

877. To him did the Lord become gracious, and to be used with muttered prayer a spell he taught him. Then he with singleness of purpose to mutter it began.

878. Now of the spell this verily the harvest was, a Form like fire into being came, and to that image thus he gave command:—

'gatshun[u] Dwārakāyĕ kun' dop[u]nas ta
'Dwārakā zālun lūkav sān'
tatiy Dwārakāyĕ lüj[ü] lāranas ta
lāgas bŏh dasta dasta pampōsh. 879.

gīr[ü]n Dwārakā ta tsāy kōpanas, ta
Shrī-Bagawānas shĕranē āy
Yādav 'trāhi trāhi' lag[i] karanas ta. lāgas etc. 880.

āgyā kür[ü]n Sŏdarshĕnas ta
kŏrōra-sūrĕ-hyuh[u] suh phērani log[u]
pratimā gērani āyĕ tsakras ta. lāgas etc. 881.

Sŏdarshĕna-tsakra nishĕ kyāh pāy tas ta
agnüc[ü] pratimā lüj[ü] dazanē
tsalith ta phīr[ü] tas[i] Sudakshĕnas ta. lāgas etc. 882.

phīrith gayĕs ta kala tsoṭ[u]nas ta
pratimā pānas[ü]y phür[ü] kĕtha tas
tas kyuth[u] pazihē yuth[u] karanas ta. lāgas etc. 883.

tsak[a]r pata lörith rāza-dwāras ta
jalāv dyut[u]nas nagaras sān
Kōshī sör[ü]y gayĕ ḍāsas ta. lāgas etc. 884.

yus lagi Krushna-jyuwanis nāwas ta
tas kari Krushna-jyuv sarŏ wŏpakār
yiti yĕsh nith ṭa wāti Vishnu-bawanas ta. lāgas etc.
885.

pör[i] pör[i] Krushna-jyuwanis nāwas ta
pör[i] pör[i] tasandis autāras
pör[i] pör[i] tasandis shŏba tsarĕtas ta. lāgas etc. 886

XLI.

dŏha aki Haladar ôs[u] phēranas ta
Raiwata-nömis parbatas pĕṭh
panan[i] kĕh zan[i] sūty pānas ta
lāgas bŏh dasta dasta pampōsh. 887.

879. Quoth he, 'To Dvārakā make thou thy way, and with its people Dvārakā consume.' Straightway to Dvārakā it speeded forth.

880. Dvārakā did it beleaguer, and, aquake, the Yādavas with Kṛṣṇa refuge sought, and 'save us, save us' piteously they cried.

881. To Sudarśana, his discus, did he give command, and, like a hundred thousand suns, it took its course. Then came the Image the discus to besiege.

882. But what avail had he against Sudarśana? The Image of fire itself began to be consumed, and, fleeing, to Sudakṣiṇa returned.

883. On its return Sudakṣiṇa's head did it cut off. Why did the Image thus lay low its own creator? How was it meet that thus it should have acted?

884. (And for this cause), the discus to the palace gate did it pursue, and with the whole city did the gate with fire consume. Kāśī became thus utterly destroyed.

885. He who beareth in his heart the name of Kṛṣṇa, to him will Kṛṣṇa every favour render. In this world glory will he win, and thereafter the abode of Viṣṇu will he reach. To him posy and posy do I offer lotuses.

886. Ever dedicating myself to Kṛṣṇa's name, ever dedicating myself to his incarnation, ever dedicating myself to his auspicious deeds, to him posy and posy do I offer lotuses.

XLI. THE FIGHT WITH DVIVIDA. (Bhāg. Pu. X, lxvii.)

887. Once on a day did Haladhara wander forth upon the mountain famed as Raivata, and certain of his folk bare company.

totuy wôtus wā̃durāh tas ta
  Baumāsŏrun^{u} mĕṭh^{a}rāh akh
Dwivid nāv ôs^{u} tas wā̃daras ta
  lāgas bŏh dasta dasta pampōsh. 888.

Baumāsŏrani hīta vĕh tas ta
  mada sū̃ty vĕh kūt^{u} hārani log^{u}
Haladara-rāmas log^{u} lāranas ta. lāgas etc. 889.

anith kañĕ kul^{i} pĕṭha löy^{i}nas ta
  tāñ Balabadr nishĕ tas gav
wŏthith atha-mūri prān koḍ^{u}nas ta. lāgas etc. 890.

yus lagi Krushna-jyuwanis nāwas ta
  tas kari Krushna-jyuv sarŏ wŏpakār
yiti yĕsh nith ta wāti Vishnu-bawanas ta. lāgas etc.
891.

pör^{i} pör^{i} Krushna-jyuwanis nāwas ta
  pör^{i} pör^{i} tasandis autāras
pör^{i} pör^{i} tasandis shŏba tsarĕtas ta. lāgas etc. 892.

XLII.

Duryōdanas Kuru-rāzas ta
  baḍēyĕs kūr^{ü} ta lag^{i} sanzas
sŏyĕmwar kōrĕ-hond^{u} log^{u} karanas ta
  lāgas bŏh dasta dasta pampōsh. 893.

yitsh ös^{ü} Sāmbas Krushna-pŏtras ta
  lörith sŏyĕmwara-sabāyĕ gav
manza-bāga kōrĕ gav nith pānas ta. lāgas etc. 894.

Kaurav söriy gay kūpas ta
  wŏthith söriy pata lāryēs
kun^{u} ôs^{u} tawa pāy na zi Sāmbas ta. lāgas etc. 895.

raṭith ta tsônukh bönd^{i}wānas ta
  awamān kar^{i}has ta karihē kyāh
Nārad^{i} shĕch^{i} üñ^{ü} Krushna-zīwas ta. lāgas etc. 896.

---

1 Bhauma was defeated by Kṛṣṇa. See Chapter xxxvi (pp. 160 ff.).

2 I.e. Haladhara.

888. There did a certain monkey him approach, an ally of the demon Bhauma,[1] Dvivida hight.

889. For Bhauma's sake a poisoned hate he had stored up, and in his madness forth the poison did he pour. At Haladhara charging did he run.

890. Rocks did he bring and trees he hurled at him, but Balabhadra[2] close to him advanced. Then up he rose and with a hand-twist his life-breath wrenched he out.

891. He who beareth in his heart the name of Kṛṣṇa, to him will Kṛṣṇa every favour render. In this world glory will he win, and thereafter the abode of Viṣṇu will he reach. To him posy and posy do I offer lotuses.

892. Ever dedicating myself to Kṛṣṇa's name, ever dedicating myself to his incarnation, ever dedicating myself to his auspicious deeds, to him posy and posy do I offer lotuses.

XLII. THE RAPE OF LAKṢMAṆĀ. (Bhāg. Pu. X, lxviii.)

893. Duryōdhana, the Kuru's king, a daughter had.[3] She became marriage-ripe, and they prepared the rites of a *svayaṁvara*[4] to hold.

894. Sāmba, Kṛṣṇa's son, desired her. Into the *svayaṁvara* gathering he rushed, and from the midst the damsel carried off.

895. Then all the Kauravas with wrath were filled, up they arose and hotly they pursued. Sāmba, alone, could not prevail against them.

896. Him did they seize and into prison cast. Helpless he was. Despitefully they used him. So Nārada the news to Kṛṣṇa brought.

---

[3] Her name is not mentioned here, but according to the Bhāgavata Purāṇa it was Lakṣmaṇā. [4] For a *svayaṁvara*, see note to verse 709.

wŏth^{i} sör^{i} Yādav Kuru-yŏddas ta
Haladara-rāman tim pot^{u} råṭ^{i}
'waira-köm^{u} kĕtha kår^{i}zi böy^{i}cāras' ta
lāgas bŏh dasta dasta pampōsh. 897.

Haladara-rām drāv hĕth Wuddawas ta
'yiman zi Sāmb bŏy mŏkalövith'
Krushna-jyuv^{i} ti böy^{i}cāra tïy môn^{u}nas ta. lāgas etc.
898.

Dili āv Haladar wôt^{u} nagaras ta
nĕb^{a}ray Wuddav shĕch^{i} sūzun
Kaurawau ḍīshith ta gay harshĕs ta. lāgas etc. 899.

söriy brō̃ṭh drāy Balabadras ta
zônukh zi pānay āv manganē
tsönith ādar ta mān kor^{u}has ta. lāgas etc. 900.

Haladara-rām āv shĕch^{i} wananas ta
'āgyā kür^{u}nawa rāza Wugrasīn^{i}
"viwŏh^{i} kanyā diyiv Sāmbas"' ta. lāgas etc. 901.

yithay tsāmåt^{i} ös^{i} vĕṭhanas ta
'Haladar kĕtha pāna manganē āv'
tithay būzith gay shūkas ta. lāgas etc. 902.

Wugrasēnani dapi gay krūdas ta
'Yādawan rāza-nāv kåm^{i} thow^{u}mot^{u}
Yādav asĕ wötiha kụr^{u} manganas ta. lāgas etc. 903.

'Kaurav zi tshatradör^{i} prath samayĕs ta
rāzan pĕṭh^{i}-kin^{i} ziṭh^{i} Kaurav
Yādawan kĕtha sami mān karanas' ta. lāgas etc.
904.

Haladara-rām log^{u} bōzanāwanas ta
'Krushna-jyuv zi sārĕn^{i} dēwan pĕṭh
suh ti mānān rāza-Wugrasēnas' ta. lāgas etc. 905.

'tas khŏta rāza kus ath samayĕs ta
yĕs kari mānatā pāna Bagawān
yūt^{u} mata låg^{i}tav ahankāras' ta. lāgas etc. 906

897. Uprose the Yādavas for a Kuru war, but Haladhara Rāma held them back. 'With kith and kin how can we hostile be?'

898. With Uddhava then set he forth. 'Sāmba will I release, and then return'. As he too felt the claims of brotherhood, Kṛṣṇa to this with heart and soul agreed.

899. To Delhi city hastened Haladhara, and from without by Uddhava a message sent. When him they saw, the Kauravas rejoiced.

900. All to meet Balabhadra issued forth. Then, when they learned that he himself had come to make his supplication (for the damsel), with all due courtesy they led him in.

901. Then came Haladhara Rāma his tidings to deliver. 'Thus hath King Ugrasēna given command, "give ye the maid to Sāmba as his spouse"'.

902. As they with exultation had been filled that Haladhara's self had come to supplicate, so, when they heard his message, were they grieved.

903. At mention of Ugrasēna waxed they wroth, 'Who to the Yādavas hath given the title "king"? Yādavas is it that to ask the maid presume?

904. 'At all times have the Kauravas monarchs been. O'er kings the Kauravas precedence take. How dare the Yādavas with us their pride to match?'

905. With them did Haladhara Rāma seek to reason. 'Above all gods doth Kṛṣṇa reign supreme, yet doth he to Ugrasēna homage pay.'

906. 'In these times than he what king can greater be, to whom Bhagavān himself doth homage pay; and therefore, prithee, show not such self-conceit.'

Wugrasēnani nāwa låg^{i} wōranas ta
‘ tas kĕtha āgyā pazi karanas
söñ^{u}y āgyā shūbihē tas ’ ta
lāgas bŏh dasta dasta pampōsh. 907.

amôb^{u} krūd khot^{u} Balabadras ta
tsakhi sān sabāyĕ nīrith gav
panüñ^{ü} gath tati pĕv hāwanas ta. lāgas etc. 908.

hala dith wul^{a}ṭani log^{u} nagaras ta
söris pralay zan sampanani log^{u}
söriy chā̆g^{a}ri lågi gatshanas ta. lāgas etc. 909.

wuchukh zi Haladara-rām kūpas ta
brunzāh tāmath wul^{a}ṭavihēkh
nīrith söriy pēs pādas ta. lāgas etc. 910.

‘ agyāna asĕ āv na zi zānanas ta
boḍ^{u} chukh ta khĕmā pazi karanas ’
kūr^{ü} üñ^{u}has ta Sāmb on^{u}has ta. lāgas etc. 911.

lågis söriy zāra-pāras ta
viwāh karith ta dits^{ü}has kūr^{ü}
grünz^{ü}-rüts$h^{ü}$ lŏkaran sūty dits^{u}has ta. lāgas etc. 912.

bāh sās mad-håst^{i} sūty dit^{i}has ta
shĕh sās ratha ta wuh sās gur^{i}
pūrith sāsa-baza tsŏnza ditsahas ta. lāgas etc. 913.

hīra-raṭ^{a}n na zi yin kĕh ti wananas ta
sŏna-rŏpa-bör^{ü}n-hånd^{i} ös^{i} bör^{ü}
Haladar nŏsh hĕth āv Krushnas ta. lāgas etc. 914.

namaskār Haladara-rāma-zīwas ta
namaskār tasandis zay karanas
namaskār tĕlikis tath zanas ta. lāgas etc. 915

yus lagi Krushna-jyuwanis nāwas ta
tas kari Krushna-jyuv sarŏ wŏpakār
yiti yĕsh nith ta wāti Vishnu-bawanas ta. lāgas etc.
916

907. At Ugrasēna's name to howl did they begin. 'What right hath he to issue thus commands? 'Tis our command he would do well to follow'

908. Then Balabhadra waxed exceeding worth. Raging from the assembly went he forth, and his own ways began to them to show.

909. Grasping his plough, the city to upturn did he begin, as though destruction utter menaced it, and all in terror's turmoil fell dismayed.

910. When Haladhara Rāma's wrath they saw, how in the twinkling of an eye he would upturn them, then came they forth and at his feet they fell.

911. 'Through ignorance it was not known to us. Mighty art thou, we pray for thy forgiveness.' The maid and Sāmba then they brought to him.

912. Humbly of him did they entreaty make. Espousals made they, and the maid they gave, adornments with her gave they out of count.

913. Fierce elephants bestowed they thousands twelve, chariots six thousand, twenty thousand horses, thousand of handmaids all adorned they gave.

914. Diamonds gave they, nor can the tale be told; loads gave they,—loads of gold and silver. So Kṛṣṇa's daughter-in-law did Haladhara bring.

915. To Haladhara Rāma reverence! And to his victory reverence be paid. To the men of those days be reverence paid!

916. He who beareth in his heart the name of Kṛṣṇa, to him will Kṛṣṇa every favour render. In this world glory will he win, and thereafter the abode of Viṣṇu will he reach. To him posy and posy do I offer lotuses.

pör^{i} pöri Krushna-jyuwanis nāwas ta
pör^{i} pör^{i} tasandis autāras
pör^{i} pör^{i} tasandis shŏba tsarĕtas ta
lāgas bŏh dasta dasta pampōsh. 917

XLIII.

aki phiri manas zi gav Nāradas ta
'Krushna-jyuv wuchahön Dwārakāyĕ manz
shurāh sās triyĕ kĕtha akis waranas ta
lāgas bŏh dasta dasta pampōsh. 918

kŏsa tsür^{u} priy āsi Shrī-Krushnas ta
kŏsa sana rönī ẓiṭh^{u} āsĕs
kyāh sana tsarĕth āsi Bagawānas ta. lāgas etc. 919

gŏḍa tsāv Rukminiyĕ-hond^{u} tsartsanas ta
tami garüc^{u} warnan kyāh wȧn^{i}zĕs
sŏna-sond^{u} gara ôs^{u} tas cĕmakanas ta. lāgas etc. 920

sŏṭh^{a}kȧk^{i} dārĕ bar prath dwāras ta
hīrau ta raṭnau sūty jȧr^{i}mȧt^{i}
raṭnan-hȧnd^{i} tsŏg^{i} prath tāras ta. lāgas etc. 921

zamrūd nīlam wasa-tālawas ta
chatan wuphawȧn^{i} zan kōtar
mōr natsawȧn^{i} zan prath bāmas ta. lāgas etc. 922.

caundani-hond^{u} kyāh yiyi wananas ta
hīrau ta zamrūda sör^{u} bür^{u}müts^{u}
alönd^{i} mŏkta-grūph^{i} hih^{i} tsandramas ta. lāgas etc. 923.

sŏgand pārizātuk^{u} ḍalanas ta
prath shāyĕ phērān mushkȧn^{i}dār
prang kyuth^{u} pazihē Bagawānas ta. lāgas etc. 924.

swörgī watharun^{u} ta kyāh wȧn^{i}zĕs ta
tȧth^{i} pĕṭh shūbān pāna Bagawān
mŏkuṭa shūbān shēri Krushnas ta. lāgas etc. 925.

917. Ever dedicating myself to Kṛṣṇa's name, ever dedicating myself to his incarnation, ever dedicating myself to his auspicious deeds, to him posy and posy do I offer lotuses.

XLIII. NĀRADA'S VISIT. (Bhāg. Pu. X, lxix.)

918. Once to the thought of Nārada it came, 'In Dvārakā fain would I Kṛṣṇa see; how hath he, being one, wedded sixteen thousand wives?

919. 'Which wife of them his best beloved is? Which among all takes place as chiefest queen, and what may be the deeds of Bhagavān?'

920. First set he himself Rukmiṇī to observe. Who can rehearse the glory of her home, a radiant palace was it all of gold.

921. Windows and doors of crystal in each doorway, with diamonds and with jewels all inlaid, while on each lampstand stood a jewelled lamp.

922. Rubies and sapphires on the painted ceiling, as though upon the thatch were flying doves, and on each roof were peacocks dancing.

923. Of the home-altar what can I set forth? With diamonds and with rubies was it incrusted, and from it hung in bunches pearls like moons.

924. Here was diffused the Pārijāta's[1] scent, from place to place there wafted odours sweet. What kind of couch for Bhagavān was meet!

925. The couch's coverlet celestial how can I describe! On it doth Bhagavān in beauty sit, with a tiara beauteous on his head.

---

[1] See note to verse 772.

tsandana-ṭyok^{u} ḍĕki shōla dinas ta
kana-wöl^{i} kana-wājĕ z^{a}tsa trāwān
pampōshĕ-paṭra hih^{i} nith^{a}r zīṭh^{i} tas ta
lāgas bŏh dasta dasta pampōsh. 926.

mŏkta-hār shūbān nöl^{i} kanṭhas ta
shūbawun^{u} asawun^{u} mŏkha-pampōsh
bŏh ta pāda-kamalan muñč wandahas ta. lāgas etc. 927.

brō̃ṭha-kani Rukminī pakha-wāyĕnas ta
ȧnd^{i} ȧnd^{i} hata-bŏza tsŏnza pūrith
Rukminī yĕs pāna sīwā karanas ta. lāgas etc. 928.

Rukminī shūbān hish^{ü} tsandramas ta
Mōhinī pānay kyāh wȧn^{i}zĕs
Lȧkh^{i}mī kitsh^{ü} hish^{ü} Bagawānas ta. lāgas etc. 929.

Nārod^{u} wuch^{i} wuch^{i} gav muhas ta
Krushna-jyuv^{i} yāñ ḍyūṭh^{u} wŏthith ta gōs
brāhmana-bāwa sūty pād rȧṭ^{i}nas ta. lāgas etc. 930.

cōki pĕṭh khŏrith ta pād chȧl^{i}nas ta
brāhmana-pādĕ-zal shēri dôrun
namaskār dörith shĕch^{i} pritsh^{u}nas ta. lāgas etc. 931.

myūṭh^{u} myūṭh^{u} khyon^{u} cyon^{u} nishĕ on^{u}nas ta
tsāmar pānay karān chus
dop^{u}nas zi 'shŏba drashṭa mĕ pazi karanas' ta. lāgas etc. 932.

'tŏh^{i} chiwa gyānawān brahma-bāwas ta
krutārth kor^{u}was darshun^{u} dith
ŏh^{i}yāh kȧr^{i}tōm yith kuṭumbas' ta. lāgas etc. 933.

Nārod^{u} tŏtān Krushna-zīwas ta
'sŏstĕstu' dapith drāv pānas
pata pata Krushna-jyuv drāv Nāradas ta. lāgas etc. 934.

biyis garas tsāv wuchanas ta
tami khŏta r^{o}t^{u} ta kyāh wȧn^{i}zĕs
Satĕbāmā tati sūty Krushnas ta. lāgas etc. 935.

---

1 Rukmiṇī herself was an incarnation of the goddess Lakṣmī. Mōhinī is the name of a superlatively beautiful female form taken by Viṣṇu (i.e. Kṛṣṇa) for the delusion of the demons at the famous churning of the ocean.

2 Nārada was the minstrel of the gods.

926. On his brow there blazeth forth a sacred mark of sandal, and his earrings, large and small, pour forth sheen as of the moon. Long are his eyes, and shaped like lotus leaves.

927. All glorious from his neck there pendent hangeth a string of pearls, and on his lotus-face there is a beauteous smile. Before his lotus-feet as offerings the pupils of mine eyes I humbly lay.

928. All around stand hundreds of maid-servants all adorned, and before him doth Rukmiṇī wave a fan. Lo, he it is to whom Rukmiṇī[1] herself doth service tender.

929. Like unto the moon glorious is Rukmiṇī, Mōhinī[1] herself is she, and her fairness how may I rehearse! To what may I compare Lakṣmī the energic power of Bhagavān!

930. Nārada, as he gazed, enraptured stood, but Kṛṣṇa, when he saw him rose and as was fitting grasped the Brāhmaṇa's feet with reverence due.

931. Upon a chair he seated him, and washed his feet. Then on his own head placed he the water hallowed by a Brāhmaṇ's sole, and with all reverence news of welfare asked.

932. Sweet food and drink of varied kinds he laid before him, the while himself he served him with the fly-whisk, and, with kindly words, invited him to cast a gracious glance on him.

933. 'Through thy Brāhmaṇa-hood with knowledge art thou filled, By this thy visit hast thou fulfilled all desires of mine. Thy blessing give, I pray thee, to this house and all that dwell therein.

934. To Kṛṣṇa did Nārada sing[2] a hymn of praise. Then, after a blessing, alone did he depart, but Kṛṣṇa followed after him.

935. Another house did Nārada enter that he might see it. The first did it exceed in excellence, how may I rehearse its marvels. There found he Satyabhāmā, and with her Kṛṣṇa.[3]

---

[3] The point is that Kṛṣṇa multiplied himself, so that each of his sixteen thousand wives thought that she had him to herself. In the meantime, Kṛṣṇa was also following Nārada on his visit of inspection, and amusing himself with his amazement

z^{a}tsa trāwān kūtsa pĕṭh prangas ta
bāra-böts^{ū} cōpaṭas gindān ös^{i}
mot^{u} gōmot^{u} ôs^{u} tȧth^{i} tsarĕtas ta
lāgas bŏh dasta dasta pampōsh. 936.

ḍyūṭhun Nārod^{u} ta pādi nom^{u}nas ta
'khĕmā mĕ kȧr^{i}zĕm grahasthas
kar öwȧ az kĕtha mani on^{u}was ta. lāgas etc. 937.

rumāh rūz^{i}tōm sūty cōpaṭas ta
yi-na Satĕbāmā niyĕm böz^{i}
tawa pata katha paīshĕ karahöv asta'. lāgas etc. 938.

Nārod^{u} kaḍith ṭ^{a}kh drāv pānas ta
prath rāza-dwāras phērani log^{u}
prath gari rönī sūty Krushnas ta. lāgas etc. 939.

prath shāyẹ Krushna-jyuv byon^{u} tsarĕtas ta
prath gara Waikunṭh hyuh^{u} zan ôs^{u}
prath gari shur^{i} böts^{ū} pariwār tas ta. lāgas etc. 940.

akis gari nĕcivĕn sūty gindanas ta
pȧt^{i} pȧt^{i} brūṭh^{i} brūṭh^{i} laḍa karanas
shurĕn-handi khēlana pray chĕy tas ta. lāgas etc. 941.

akis gari Krushna-jyuv pĕṭh āsanas ta
akis gari shurĕn karawun^{u} shrān
akis gari rönī pād malanas ta. lāgas etc. 942.

akis gari Krushna-jyuv zapa-dyānas ta
akis gari Krushna-jyuv karawun^{u} hūm
biyis gari Krushna-jyuv brahma-būzanas ta. lāgas etc. 943.

akis gari kāmadīna dini dānas ta
biyis gari pŏrāna-katha bōzān
biyis gari pȧnḍ^{i}tan samwādas ta. lāgas etc. 944.

akis shāyi diwān dana darmas ta
biyis shāyi danas likha bōzān
biyis shāyi dyāran gạnz^{a}rāwanas ta. lāgas etc. 945.

936. Who can count the moon-rays that poured forth from her as she reclined upon the couch? Playing *caupār* [a kind of backgammon] sat the happy spouses. Impassioned became he as he gazed upon the scene.

937. Kṛṣṇa saw Nārada, and at his feet he bowed. Cried he, 'But a poor rustic householder am I. Thy forgiveness would I crave [for any lack of courtesy.] When didst thou come? How didst thou bring me to thy memory?

638. 'Stay, prithee, but a moment, and join me in this game, for, verily, thy help I need, lest Satyabhāmā conquer me; and after that let us gently hold a discourse brief[1].'

939. Nārada hasted on his way with speed, and from palace door to palace door he wandered. Lo, in each abode there was a queen with Kṛṣṇa.

940. In each venue was Kṛṣṇa occupied in some different matter; each room was like Vaikuṇṭha, Viṣṇu's heaven; in each were Kṛṣṇa's children, wife, and retinue.

941. In one abode he found him playing with the children, sportively battling with them, now behind and now before; for dearly doth he love a frolic with the bairns.

942. In another was he seated on a throne, in another the urchins was he bathing, in yet another did a queen massage his feet.

943. Here was Kṛṣṇa rapt in meditation and uttering muttered prayers; there was he offering a burnt sacrifice; and elsewhere was he busy feeding Brāhmaṇas.

944. Here of milch-kine was he making gifts to holy men; there was he listening to tales of olden time; and elsewhere was he holding deep discussion with the learned.

945. Here was he largess in charity dispensing; there was he listening to the budget of his wealth; and elsewhere was he his coinèd money counting.

---

[1] Lit. Let us make but five words

akis gari kōrĕn shĕch[i] pritshanas ta
akis gari khēlān triyĕn sūty
akis gari tshāṭa-tshāṭh manz zalas ta
lāgas bŏh dasta dasta pampōsh. 946.

akis shāyi phulaṭa-böz[i] karanas ta
akis shāyi kōtar wuḍanāwān
akis shāyi pöz[ü]n wuḍanāwanas ta. lāgas etc. 947.

akis shāyi gurĕn phiranāwanas ta
biyis shāyi rathan cāl wuchawun[u]
biyis shāyi mad-hȧst[i] khēlanāwanas ta. lāgas etc. 948.

akis shāyi hȧth[i]yār athi Krushnas ta
shurĕn astra-vidyā hĕchanāwān
tihond[u] wuch[i] wuch[i] chuh zi vĕṭhanas ta. lāgas etc. 949.

kuni shāyi wŏtsav gŏbar zĕnas ta
akis shāyi viwāh kōrĕn-hond[u]
akis shāyi khādaruk[u] sanz karanas ta. lāgas etc. 950.

akis shāyi banḍāra karanāwanas ta
akis gari bihith gīth bōzān
akis gari mōran natsanāwanas ta. lāgas etc. 951.

akis shāyi log[u]mot[u] bōpāras ta
bōpārĕn sūty likha bōzān
dara-dar karān prath wastas ta. lāgas etc. 952.

akis shāyi bahiyĕn phyur[u] dinas ta
akis shāyi dyāran ṭhēli ganḍān
akis shāyi mŏharan parkhāwanas ta. lāgas etc. 953.

akis shāyi rạtnan mŏl karanas ta
akis shāyi mŏkta-hār wurạnāwān
akis shāyi mŏkuṭa shēranāwanas ta. lāgas etc. 954.

akis gari pōthĕn lēkhanāwanas ta
akis gari pön[i]-pāna pōthĕ lĕkhān
akis gari bihith pūth[i] paranas ta. lāgas etc. 955.

946. Here was he asking anent the welfare of his daughters; there was he sporting amidst his women; and elsewhere in water did he throw forth his arms a-swimming.

947. Here was he swinging athlete's clubs; there pigeons was he flying; and elsewhere was he flying hawks.

948. Here horses was he exercising; there was he watching the motions of his chariots; and elsewhere was he making maddened elephants show off in the arena.

949. Here were warlike weapons in the hand of Kṛṣṇa; there was he teaching children the lore of arms, and, as he watched them, exulted Nārada in joy.

950. Here, for a new-born son high festival they held; there solemnized he the marriage of his daughters; and elsewhere a wedding party was he a-preparing.

951. Here was he having a feast given to the mendicants; there, seated at his ease, to songs he hearkened; and elsewhere was he setting peacocks at their dance.

952. Here, behold, was he engaged in trade, and with the merchants busy trafficking, as for each article he bargained on the price.

953. Here, of account books the pages turned he over; there money was he tying in a bag; and elsewhere was he having tested coins of gold.

954. Here, of jewels the value he was fixing; there, of pearls a necklet was he stringing; and elsewhere a tiara was he having formed.

955. Here, was he having books a-written; there, a book was he himself a-writing; and elsewhere, seated at his ease, over a book he pored.

akis gari brŏ̄ṭha-kani Wasudēwas ta
akis jāyi Dēwakiyĕ pād malanas
pritshān zi 'kĕ̄h mā chuwa manas' ta
lāgas bŏh dasta dasta pampōsh. 956.

akis shāyi pöth^{a}r karanāwanas ta
akis shāyi natsiñĕn natsanāwān
akis shāyi bå̄ḍan gĕwanāwanas ta. lāgas etc. 957.

akis shāyi böyis bōzanāwanas ta
'sön^{i} åth^{i} zi söriy sŏkha bår^{i}tan.'
Kashmīra-dīshuk^{u} ār yiyihēs ta. lāgas etc. 958.

Kashīri ti āsihē zay darmas ta
brāhmanan zi baḍihēkh darmuk^{u} tīz
sŏkhith ta lagahön Krushna-nāwas ta. lāgas etc. 959.

ḍēchan shurāh sās khēla Krushnas ta
shurāhwån^{i} sāsan garan phyūr^{u}
Vishnu-māyā sör^{ü} log^{u} wuchanas ta. lāgas etc. 960.

phērān phērān prath garas ta
Nārada-mŏnīshŏr thakith ta āv
pādan pĕṭh pĕv Krushna-zīwas ta. lāgas etc. 961.

shēr dörith ta rūd^{u} pāda-kamalas ta
nānā-rång^{i} tŏtā log^{u} karanē
'Krushna-Bagawānas pör^{i} lagahös' ta. lāgas etc. 962.

'pör^{i} pör^{i} lagahös prath rūpas ta
pör^{i} pör^{i} lagahös prath nāwas
kuni kuni tōshihē mĕ ti abalas' ta. lāgas etc. 963.

Nāradan yüts^{ü} yüts^{ü} bakth kür^{ü}nas ta
yitshi sān vīnā log^{u} wāyĕnē
vĕṭhān chuh wuch^{i} wuch^{i} Krushna-zīwas ta. lāgas etc.
964.

Shrī-Krushna-Bagawān log^{u} asanas ta
prasan gōs ta dyut^{u}nas war
āgyā hĕth gav Vishnu-bawanas ta. lāgas etc. 965.

956. Here was he (standing in attendance) before (his father) Vasudēva; there the feet of (his mother) Dēvakī did he massage; and asking them was he if aught they had upon their minds.

957. Here, a drama for the theatre was he arranging; there was he setting dancing girls a-dance; and elsewhere was he making buffoons sing their songs.

958. Elsewhere his brother (Balabhadra) was he instructing; 'At our hand may all be filled with bliss,' and may his mercy come thus to the land of Kashmīr!

959. In Kashmīr, too, may there be victory for virtue; of the Brāhmaṇas may the puissance of their virtue be enhanced, and, full of bliss, devoted to Kṛṣṇa's name may they become!

960. Thus were the sixteen thousand sports of Kṛṣṇa seen by Nārada as through the sixteen thousand palaces he roamed, and so the whole of Viṣṇu's magic power began he to perceive.

961. Wandering and wandering from hall to hall, Nārada, at length became a-wearied. Before the feet of Kṛṣṇa in homage did he cast himself.

962. On Kṛṣṇa's lotus foot he laid his head, and so remained, and, crying 'To Kṛṣṇa Bhagavān myself I dedicate,' hymns in varied measures did he begin to sing.

963. 'To each of his many forms myself I dedicate; to each of his many names myself I dedicate. May he, perchance, at some time on poor weak me his grace bestow'.

964. Loving devotion of many kinds did Nārada display. With desire began he his lute to strike, rejoicing as he gazed and gazed on Kṛṣṇa.

965. Kṛṣṇa, the Mighty God, then cast on him a smile. Pleased at his words, he granted him the boon. So, taking his leave to Viṣṇu's heaven did Nārada return.

yas lagi Krushna-jyuwanis nāwas ta
tas kari Krushna-jyuv sarŏ wŏpakār
yiti yĕsh nith ta wāti Vishnu-bawanas ta
lāgas bŏh dasta dasta pampōsh. 966.

pör^{i} pör^{i} Krushna-jyuwanis nāwas ta
pör^{i} pör^{i} tasandis autāras
pör^{i} pör^{i} tasandis shŏba tsarĕtas ta. lāgas etc. 967.

XLIV.

Krushna-jyuv log^{u}mot^{u} nitĕ-karmas ta
pahara hĕth āsān zāgi phērān
prath gari Krushna-jyuv wŏthi karmas ta
lāgas bŏh dasta dasta pampōsh. 968.

āsān bihith lagi dyānas ta
yōguk^{u} sār pāna yōgīshŏr
samād rōzi dith patim-paharas ta. lāgas etc. 969.

brŏhmī-muhūrtas shŏba-samayĕs ta
pankhī bōlān mŏd^{ü}r^{ü}y būl^{i}
pārizāta-kuli yiyi wāv karanas ta. lāgas etc. 970.

Krushna-jyuv wŏthith wasi tīrthas ta
snān kari yāra-bala vĕdi pūrwakh
sandyā ta tarpan yitha pazihēs ta. lāgas etc. 971.

dŏhali Bagawān manz ā̆ganas ta
cōkĕ pĕṭh bĕhān zanga trövith
aina hĕth nöyid yiyi hāwanas ta. lāgas etc. 972.

tawa pata tīla-mardan kor^{u}has ta
aushada-zala sū̆ty nāwanas tan
dōtyāh lögith sŏgand malanas ta. lāgas etc. 973.

atsith ta ṭhôkur log^{u} pūzanas ta
gāyĕtrī-zaph kari biyĕ havĕ-kavy
brāhmanan kāmadīna diyi dānas ta. lāgas etc. 974.

---

1 I.e. with his legs hanging down in front, not tucked cross-legged, as Indians

966. He who beareth in his heart the name of Kṛṣṇa, to him will Kṛṣṇa every favour render. In this world glory will he win, and thereafter the abode of Viṣṇu will he reach. To him posy and posy do I offer lotuses.

967. Ever dedicating myself to Kṛṣṇa's name, ever dedicating myself to his incarnation, ever dedicating myself to his auspicious deeds, to him posy and posy do I offer lotuses.

XLIV. A DAY IN KṚṢṆA'S LIFE. (Bhāg. Pu. X, lxx.)

968. Ever in his daily rites engrossed is Kṛṣṇa. Taking his guards he goeth on his rounds inspecting. In each house doth he rise up early for his duty.

969. (First) seateth he himself in meditation, for Yōgêśvara is he, —himself the essence of all Yōga,—and for the last watch of the night abideth he in deepest contemplation wrapt.

970. At the propitious moment on the nick of dawn, as their sweet voices carol forth the birds, and from the Pārijāta tree the Wind his breezes wafts.

971. Kṛṣṇa ariseth, to the river-bank descendeth, and at the bathing *Ghāṭ* with hallowed rite his body doth he lave, as duly the morning prayer and libation he doth make.

972. By daytime Kṛṣṇa Bhagavān the courtyard entereth. Upon a chair himself he seateth with his legs at ease [1], and the barber cometh to show to him the mirror.

973. His body then with oil did they anoint, with water of fragrant herbs did they wash him, and with a scented towel wiped they him.

974. (His chapel) next he entereth, and to the idol doth he worship pay. The holy Gāyatrī he muttereth and maketh his oblations, then to the Brāhmaṇas giveth he milch-kine in benefaction.

---

[1] usually sit

būzan ta dakhĕnā prath brāhmanas ta
öhiyĕ mangĕkh atha dörith
dapanas 'āy boḍ^{u} ösin tas' ta
lāgas bŏh dasta dasta pampōsh. 975.

tsandun^{u} ta aguru-kāṭh nishĕ ananas ta
gŏḍa mali brāhmanan aḍa pānas
tawa pata dupaṭāh wali pānas ta. lāgas etc. 976.

pāna-bīr biyĕ diyi prath brāhmanas ta
pān hĕth ta brāhman sŏst dapanas
sŏst būzith ta atsi mahala-khānas ta. lāgas etc. 977.

garȧk^{i} böts^{ü} nishĕ aina ananas ta
Kāma-dēv pānay ta kō-na wuchihē
wuchān ainas ras lagi tas ta. lāgas etc. 978.

nānā-ranga būzan nishĕ ananas ta
nānā-ranga phal mūl mŏd^{a}r^{i} ta tsŏk^{i}
tsŏnza sārĕ āsān sīwā karanas ta. lāgas etc. 979.

rönï wŏthadañĕ pakha wāyĕnas ta
Krushna-Bagawānas ranzanāwān
rūzith pananis sör^{i} pāyĕs ta. lāgas etc. 980.

bāṭh prath dwāras yĕsh gĕwanas ta
Krushna-tsarĕtan-hond^{u} tulān wād
timan dyār kūt^{i} lȧg^{i} ladanas ta. lāgas etc. 981.

khĕtriy yim yin rāza-dwāras ta
pāna-bīr sārĕn^{i} sōzanāvĕkh
vaishy ta shūd^{a}r sör^{i} tsāph karanas ta. lāgas etc.
982.

tawa pata prath gari nēri phēranas ta
nĕb^{a}rĕmi bara āsi okuy zon^{u}
sūrĕ zan ta dayā kari nagaras ta. lāgas etc. 983.

ratha-wôl^{u} pūrith ratha anĕs ta
raṭnau sūtin sôr^{u} jor^{u}mot^{u}
shūbawȧn^{i} gur^{i} jān shōla trāwanas ta. lāgas etc
984.

975. To each Brāhmaṇa giveth he food and maketh largess. Then folding his hands from them a blessing doth he crave, and to him do they say, 'May thy life be long and prosperous'.

976. Sandal and aloe-wood they bring to him, first to the Brāhmaṇas and afterward to himself doth he apply them, and then his outer cloak he doeth on.

977. To each Brāhmaṇa offereth he a roll of betel-leaf. This take the Brāhmaṇas and give to him their blessings, and with these blessings in his ears he entereth the palace.

978. The ladies of his household bring to him a mirror. 'Why,' say they, 'should not the god of love gaze on himself alone (and not on us)? Relish will he gain as he looketh in the mirror.'

979. Food of divers kinds they bring him,—sweet and acid, fruits and roots of divers kinds. All the maidservants are busy in his service.

980. His queen stands up and fans him, bringing content to Kṛṣṇa Bhagavān. In her own duty standeth each one (ready).

981. Bards proclaim his glory at each gate. Discourse of Kṛṣṇa's deeds do they set up. Countless is the wealth he sendeth them (in reward).

982. To all the knights who come to the palace gate, he sendeth betel-rolls; to the commonalty and to them of lowly caste he sendeth salutations.

983. Thereafter, from each house he goeth forth to stroll. At the outer gate he may be but a man alone, yet still, like the sun, he showeth mercy on the city.

984. The charioteer bringeth up his chariot caparisoned and studded all with jewels. Handsome and well-trained horses display their fiery natures.

ratha-wôl^{u} atha raṭi khasi rathas ta
ratha pěṭha Krushna-jyuv z^{a}tsa trāwān
pata-kani Wuddav tsāmar karanas ta
lāgas bŏh dasta dasta pampōsh. 985.

lŏti lŏti rathas pakanāwanas ta
prath triy prath chata nēri wuchanê
věṭhān ta söriy zuv wandanas ta. lāgas etc. 986.

brõṭh brõṭh āsān bāṭh gěwanas ta
sabāyě wātān trāwān tīz
tīzas ta wūzas kala wandahös ta. lāgas etc. 987.

sabāyě yěli běhi simhāsanas ta
prath kãh chuh pāyěs tal Yādav
bąḍ^{i} rāza yith ta sör^{i} tati namanas ta. lāgas etc.
988.

gěwan-wöl^{i} söriy gěwanāwanas ta
maskhara sör^{i} yith asanāwanas
ṭhaṭha-mot^{u} yitha lagi ṭhaṭha karanas ta. lāgas etc.
989.

tawa pata pąnḍithāh běhi āsanas ta
pŏstakas zi pūzā karanāvěs
Vyāsa-sünz^{ü} pūzā kari pāna tas ta. lāgas etc. 990.

pąnḍith pŏrān lagi wananas ta
Krushna-jyuv bōzān kan dörith
baktěn-hünz^{ü} pray tas Krushnas ta. lāgas etc. 991.

yus yus mangawun^{u} yiyi manganas ta
tas tas dana ratha gur^{i} diwawun^{u}
kuni nēri sailas kuni shikāras ta. lāgas etc. 992.

yus lagi Krushna-jyuwanis nāwas ta
tas kari Krushna-jyuv sarŏ wŏpakār
yiti yěsh nith ta wāti Vishnu-bawanas ta. lāgas etc.
993.

pör^{i} pör^{i} Krushna-jyuwanis nāwas ta
pör^{i} pör^{i} tasandis autāras
pör^{i} pör^{i} tasandis shŏba tsarětas ta. lāgas etc. 994.

985. The charioteer graspeth his hand and the chariot doth he mount; and from it Kṛṣṇa poureth, as it were, rays of moonlight, while behind him, wielding his fly-whisk standeth Uddhava.

986. Gently gently doth he drive the chariot, as on each roof-top every woman cometh forth to see him. In ravished exultation do all offer their lives as a sacrifice to him.

987. Before him, as he goeth on, the bards are singing. As he reacheth the hall of audience majesty and prowess from him stream. To his prowess and his glory mine own head do in sacrifice I offer.

988. As on the throne he sitteth in the hall of audience, each Yādava prostrates himself before his feet. Great kings come and bow all in reverence.

989. With each other vying, chaunteth the whole choir of singers. The buffoons with their merry antics come to raise his laughter, that he who is ever full of quips may join in quips.

990. Thereafter cometh a learned man and sitteth on a seat of honour. A bulky tome doth he produce, and ordereth them to worship it, while he himself to Vyāsa [1] offereth homage.

991. The learned man beginneth to read aloud the Purāṇas, while Kṛṣṇa lendeth an attentive ear,—[not that he doth not know all knowledge, but] because to those devoted to him beareth he tenderest love.

992. To each suppliant that cometh to him with a petition, granteth he wealth, chariots, and horses. Sometime goeth he forth to stroll, and sometime to the hunt.

993. He who beareth in his heart the name of Kṛṣṇa, to him will Kṛṣṇa every favour render. In this world glory will he win, and thereafter the abode of Viṣṇu will he reach. To him posy and posy do I offer lotuses.

994. Ever dedicating myself to Kṛṣṇa's name, ever dedicating myself to his incarnation, ever dedicating myself to his auspicious deeds, to him posy and posy do I offer lotuses.

[1] The supposed compiler of the Vēdas and author of the Mahābhārata.

XLV.

dŏha aki sabāyĕ ôs[u] harshĕs ta
won[u]has zi 'āmot[u] chuh lūka-sāsāh
bar pĕṭh bihith chih ḍāb trāwanas' ta
lāgas bŏh dasta dasta pampōsh. 995.

akhāh mongun nishĕ pānas ta
pritshagör[ü] kür[ü]nas ādara sān
'kawa putshy āmàt[i] chiwa dād wananas' ta. lāgas etc. 996.

dop[u]has zi 'rāza sör[i] chih bŏnd[i]wānas ta
Zarāsandan ràṭ[i]màṭ[i] chih'
sabāyĕ sān log[u] 'trāhi' karanas ta. lāgas etc. 997.

wuh sās aiṭh hath kūd[i] wàn[i]has ta
byon[u] byon[u] prath kāh wananē āv
Krushna-jyuv būz[i] būz[i] wŏsh trāwanas ta. lāgas etc. 998.

dop[u]has zi 'rākhyus chuh ahankāras ta
"mĕ zi tsalanôwum Krushna-Bagawān"
sadāhi phiri tsalun[u] tsĕtas na tas' ta. lāgas etc. 999.

Nārod[u] wôtus tàth[i] samayĕs ta
Krushna-jyuv Nāradas wŏthith gav
brāhmanas tsaranan atha lŏg[i]nas ta. lāgas etc. 1000.

dop[u]nas zi 'Pānḍav làg[i] jagas ta
rāzasūyĕ-jaguk[u] sanz karanē
tana mana wata cyāñĕ sör[i] wuchanas' ta. lāgas etc. 1001.

'tihünz[ü] yĕtsh patsh pazi pūranas ta
timan zi cyöñ[ü] büḍ[ü] āshā chĕkh
bajĕ āshi sūz[u]has shĕch[i] karanas' ta. lāgas etc. 1002.

Krushna-jyuv sabāyĕ log[u] pritshanas ta
'dŏyi kāmi pazi kŏsa gŏḍa karanas'
Wuddawan nīth dits[ü] gŏḍa jagas ta. lāgas etc. 1003.

---

[1] For the account of Jarāsandha's combat with Kṛṣṇa, see verses 550ff.

[2] A *Rājasūya* is a coronation sacrifice performed by a universal monarch, and attended by tributary princes in token of his admitted sovereignty. The five Pāṇḍava princes were Yudhiṣṭhira, Bhīma(sēna), Arjuna, Nakula, and Sahadēva.

XLV. THE DEATH OF JARĀSANDHA. (Bhāg. Pu. X, lxx–lxxiii.)

995. Once on a day was Kṛṣṇa joyfully seated in the hall of audience, when announced they to him that at the gate were a thousand people, lying as though fainting in their woe.

996. One of them called he to him, and courteously made question. 'Wherefore hast thou come to tell a tale of woe?'

997. Then to him they said, 'Bound fast in prison are all our kings. By Jarāsandha have they all been seized'; and with the assembled courtiers cried they for protection.

998. Quoth they, 'Twenty thousand and eight hundred hath he imprisoned; each one of us hath separately come to tell the tale.' And Kṛṣṇa as he heard them heaved a sigh.

999. Quoth they, 'a demon is he, and of self-pride full. Saith he "Kṛṣṇa Bhagavān put I once to flight." Forsooth, forgetteth he that before thee seventeen times he fled.' [1]

1000. Just at that moment Nārada arrived, and to meet him Kṛṣṇa rose and with his hands the Brāhmaṇa's feet he clasped.

1001. Quoth Nārada 'Upon a sacrifice are the Pāṇḍavas engaged and preparations make they for a *Rājasūya*.[2] Body and soul (with longing eyes), watch they all the way by which thou mayest come.

1002. 'Their longing and their trust in thee shouldst thou fulfil, for great is the hope in thee in which they live, and in this mighty hope this message have they sent by me.'

1003. (Bhāg. Pu. X, lxxi.) Then of the assembled courtiers Kṛṣṇa asked, 'Twain be the cases to the which I now am called. To which of these first should I set myself?' Then Uddhava straightway counsel gave, 'First to the sacrifice.'

They lived at Indraprastha, near the modern Delhi, and were first cousins (Kuntī, their mother, being his father's sister) and close friends of Kṛṣṇa. Their chief enemy was their cousin Duryōdhana. It was Yudhiṣṭhira, the eldest of the Pāṇḍavas who claimed universal monarchy.

rāzan dilāsa log^{u} ladanas ta
　　'gŏḍa Dili wātun^{u} chĕh yiwān nīth
tamiy hīta wāta Maga-dīshĕs' ta
　　lāgas bŏh dasta dasta pampŏsh. 1004.

sŏriy rāza rūd^{i} wata wuchanas ta
　　bŏnd^{i}wān zŏnith sŏrgāh zan
'Krushna-Bagawān chuh asĕ ḍakhas' ta. lāgas etc.
1005.

Krushna-jyuv^{i} sanz kor^{u} pariwāras ta
　　sŏruy hĕth drāv rāza-sālas
Dwārakā push^{u}r^{u}n Balabadras ta. lāgas etc. 1006.

sŏna-sanza ḍōlĕ āsa shōla dinas ta
　　pata brŏṭha chērĕ-wŏl^{i} jōrĕ jōrĕ drāy
ḍĕka-bajĕ sārĕy drāyĕ sālas ta. lāgas etc. 1007.

lacha-bâd^{i} ashŏwār jil^{i}bi pakanas ta
　　sāsa-bâd^{i} ratha hâst^{i} tas brŏṭh brŏṭh
Krushna-jyuv ratha pĕṭha dyār chakanas ta. lāgas etc.
1008.

damām ta sŏrnayĕ ḍōl wazanas ta
　　karnayĕ shĕnkh ta shĕbd karawân^{i}
shur^{i} bŏts^{ü} sūty hĕth gav jagas ta. lāgas etc. 1009.

nērān wati wati sŏr^{i} darshĕnas ta
　　sārĕn^{i} kāmanā sapūñ^{u} sĕd
namaskār tihandis tath bāgĕs ta. lāgas etc. 1010.

Dili wŏt^{u} Krushna-jyuv rāza-nagaras ta
　　brŏṭha drāy nanawŏr^{i} pŏnts Pānḍav
padi padi wati lâg^{i} ḍĕka g^{o}h^{u}nas ta. lāgas etc. 1011.

Krushna-jyuv ziṭhĕn khŏr raṭanas ta
　　nālamati roṭun Arzŏna-dēv
Nakul ta Sahadēv pyēs pādas ta. lāgas etc. 1012.

nagarâk^{i} lūkh sŏr^{i} pata rāzas ta
　　Krushnañi lōlari āy lārān
sārĕn^{i} Krushna-jyuv sāntwanāwanas ta. lāgas etc.
1013.

1004. A message of solace sent he to the imprisoned kings. 'First must I haste to Delhi—such be the counsel given,—and taking that as my excuse, to Magadha will I wend my way.'

1005. So all the imprisoned kings watched the roads (waiting in patience for his promised help), and to them now their dungeons seemed like heaven. 'Kṛṣṇa Bhagavān,' they cried, 'is now our certain prop.'

1006. So Kṛṣṇa then his retinue equipped, and with his whole train set forth in answer to the invitation of the king, leaving his brother Balabhadra in charge of Dvārakā.

1007. (Of the ladies of the court) resplendent shone the golden palankeens. In front and eke in rear marched out the wand-bearers two and two. Good luck indeed had all these wedded ladies who to the festival set forth.

1008. Cavalry, hundreds of thousands, curveted and pranced, chariots and elephants in thousands passed in front, and from his own chariot Kṛṣṇa scattered money as he went.

1009. Double-drums, hautboys, kettledrums sounding, clarions and conches blaring, with his children and his wives, Kṛṣṇa to the sacrifice marched out.

1010. Along the road all men hastened out to watch. At the mere vision every wish of their hearts was as it were fulfilled. Let reverence meet be paid to their good fortune.

1011. At the royal city Kṛṣṇa in due course arrived, and barefoot came out the five Pāṇḍavas to meet him, rubbing their foreheads on each of his footprints on the road.

1012. Of his elders did he grasp the feet, but Arjuna, he grasped in an embrace, while at his feet fell Nakula and Sahadēva.

1013. After Yudhiṣṭhira came all the citizens, running in their great love for Kṛṣṇa, and he in graciousness gave solace to them all.

wātān yāñ wōt^{i} rāza-dwāras ta
padi padi nĕwāzun kôtwāh ôs^{u}
lacha-bȧd^{i} ālüts^{ü} lȧg^{i} chakanas ta
lāgas bŏh dasta dasta pampōsh. 1014.

pŏphi nishĕ gŏḍa tsāv rāza-manḍapas ta
mātā Kuntiyĕ nālamati roṭ^{u}
Krushna-jyuv^{i} gŏḍañiy pād rȧṭ^{i}nas ta. lāgas etc.
1015.

bābath^{a}r-nŏshĕ āyĕ sārĕ mēlanas ta
pŏpha-hashĕ sārĕy pĕyĕ pādan
wuchun ta mana bŏz^{ü} āyĕ phŏlanas ta. lāgas etc.
1016.

Draupadī pādan pĕyĕ Krushnas ta
Sŏbadrā ti böyis kākañĕn sān
Pānḍav ti pūzi lȧg^{i} Krushna-zīwas ta. lāgas etc.
1017.

nīts^{ü} lȧg^{i} jagakis sanz karanas ta
tsōr böy^{i} cyukūṭh^{i} vizayĕs drāy
rāza ta dana hĕth phīr^{i} garas ta. lāgas etc. 1018.

söriy rāza āy tas zēnanas ta
kȧh rāza pōshĕhē na Zarāsandas
pānavüñ^{ü} wŏpāy lȧg^{i} tshāḍanas ta. lāgas etc. 1019.

Wuddavüñ^{ü} nīth āyĕ tshal^{a}rāwanas ta
Krushna-jyuv Bīmasēn ta Arzŏn drāy
brāhman lögith gös tshalas ta. lāgas etc. 1020.

Zarāsȧnd^{i} ḍīṭhin brahma-bāwas ta
mān kor^{u}nakh ta mong^{u}has dān
ŏts^{ü}-kār hyot^{u}has ta syod^{u} won^{u}has ta. lāgas etc.
1021.

'daba-dab karüñ^{ü}' dān mong^{u}has ta
'trayĕ manza yĕs sūty mani yiyi tsĕ
Krushnas Arzŏnas Bīmasēnas' ta. lāgas etc. 1022.

---

1 The word *ālath* means a certain ceremony of adoration, in which a platter, containing a five-wicked lamp, flour, water and incense, is waved round the head of an idol or honoured guest.

2 Kuntī, the mother of the Pāṇḍavas, was a sister of Kṛṣṇa's father, Vasudēva.

1014. As, in their progress, to the palace gate they came, at every step uncounted gifts were offered to him and myriads of people censered him.[1]

1015. He entered the royal palace, and first approached his father's sister. Mother Kuntī[2] him embraced, but he first reverently grasped her feet.

1016. Then to greet her advanced her brother's daughters-in-law.[3] They all fell at the feet of their father-in-law's sister,[4] and as she saw them, heart and soul she blossomed out.

1017. Draupadī[5] fell at Kṛṣṇa's feet, and eke Subhadrā[6] at the feet of her brother and of her brother's wives. Then all the Pāṇḍavas did him reverence.

1018. (Bhāg. Pu. X, lxxii.) Then, according to due rule, began they to make the preparations for the sacrifice. Yudhiṣṭhira's four brothers to the four quarters of the earth went forth to seek for victory, and home returned with kings and plundered wealth.

1019. In confession of Yudhiṣṭhira's victories all the kings attended, —(all except one)—for against Jarāsandha should no king prevail; and so between themselves against him for a device they sought.

1020. (Bhāg. Pu. X, lxxii.) To Uddhava came there counsel to outwit him, and Kṛṣṇa, Bhīmasēna and Arjuna put on Brāhmaṇa dress, and forth went they for his ensnaring.

1021. In Brāhmaṇa guise did Jarāsandha see them. He paid them reverence, and they asked of him a gift. They took the promise them a boon to grant, and only then plainly did they speak.

1022. The boon they asked was this, that he with one of three, whom he might choose, with Kṛṣṇa, Arjuna, or with Bhīmasēna, should in a bout of wrestling strive.

---

[3] I.e. Kṛṣṇa's wives.

[4] I.e. Kuntī, who was sister of Vasudēva, their father-in-law, and Kṛṣṇa's father.

[5] Draupadī was the joint wife of the five Pāṇḍavas.

[6] Subhadrā was Kṛṣṇa's sister. She was married to Arjuna.

dop^{u}nakh zi ' ṭhahari na Arzŏn yŏddas ta
Krushn chum Dwārakāyĕ tsạl^{a}rôw^{u}mot^{u}
athāh ginda wŏñ sūty Bīmas ' ta
lāgas bŏh dasta dasta pampōsh 1023.

dŏnaway bala-vīr drāy yŏddas ta
satōwuh dŏh tāñ dŏha laḍahön
rāth-kyut^{u} asanas ta biyĕ gindanas ta. lāgas etc.
1024.

bal sūr^{u} Bīmas ta wani Krushnas ta
nālamati roṭun ta tsari tas bal
daba-dabi-samayĕ ti tshal hôw^{u}nas ta. lāgas etc.
1025.

Bīmasīn^{i} zangi tal zang rüṭ^{u}nas ta
Zarāsand zangi-ts^{a}sa nirbal gav
z^{a}h aḍ karith ta prān kạḍ^{i}nas ta. lāgas etc. 1026.

Zarasand yĕmi vizi āv māraṇas ta
Sahadēv gŏbur pĕv Krushna-pādan
möl^{i}-sond^{u} sôr^{u} rājy tāñ dyutun tas ta. lāgas etc.
1027

Krushna-jyuv gŏḍa gav bŏnd^{i}wānas ta
rāza yĕti wuh sās ta aiṭh hath ös^{i}
bŏnd^{i}wāna kạḍin ta pēs pādas ta. lāgas etc. 1028.

pādan pĕth pĕth war mong^{u}has ta
' bakth cyöñ^{u} karahöv rājy trövith '
drĕshṭi sūty wạrin ta lạg^{i} tŏtanas ta. lāgas etc. 1029.

sör^{i} rāza sūty āy tath jagas ta
tana mana lạg^{i}mạt^{i} Krushna-dyānas
jai-kār tihandis tath bāgēs ta. lāgas etc. 1030.

rāza sūty hĕth ta āv wôt^{u} nagaras ta
trashĕway shĕnkhan lạg^{i} wāyĕnē
Yudishṭhir brōṭha drāv pata sör^{i} tas ta. lāgas etc.
1031.

---

[1] Kṛṣṇa tore the branch of a tree in twain. Bhīma took the hint, and did the same to Jarāsandha.

1023. Quoth he, 'Arjuna in battle will not stand. Kṛṣṇa have I made to flee to Dvārakā. Now will I play a hand with Bhīmasēna.'

1024. To the combat went forth the heroes twain; for seven and twenty days by day they fought, while anight they spent the time in laugh and sport.

1025. As Bhīma's strength began to flag, Kṛṣṇa did he apprize; so Kṛṣṇa seized him in his (divine) embrace, and his strength waxed great again; then, as he wrestled, Kṛṣṇa to him pointed out a trick.[1]

1026. Under his own leg did Bhīmasēna hold his leg, and through that leg-wrench became Jarāsandha powerless. Then in two halves did Bhīmasēna rend him, and so tore out his life.

1027. When Jarāsandha thus was slain, his son, Sahadēva[2] hight, at Kṛṣṇa's feet did fall, and to him all his father's kingdom gave.

1028. (Bhāg. Pu. X, lxxiii.) First went Kṛṣṇa to the prison-house, where were confined the twenty thousand and eight hundred kings. Forth from the prison-house he set them free, and at his feet they fell.

1029. And fallen so, from him a boon they begged. 'Grant thou that we our kingdoms may renounce, and henceforth do thee service in devotion.' With a glance their boon he granted, and forthwith began they with hymns of praise to laud him.

1030. Then to the sacrifice with him came all the kings, body and soul in Kṛṣṇa-contemplation wrapt. Utter ye cries of glory for their happy lot.

1031. When with the kings at the city he arrived, the three conch blasts did they sound, and, followed by the others, Yudhiṣṭhira came forth to meet him.

---

[2] He is of course not the same as the Pāṇḍava of the same name.

yus lagi pör^{i} pör^{i} Krushna-nāwas ta
tas kari Krushna-jyuv sarŏ wŏpakār
yiti yĕsh nith ta wāti Vishnu-bŏwanas ta
lāgas bŏh dasta dasta pampōsh. 1032

XLVI.

Yudishṭhir rāza log^{u} jaga-sanzas ta
zagi-hånd^{i} rāza sör^{i} sŏmb^{a}rith kĕth
Krushna-Bagawānas nīth pritshanas ta
lāgas bŏh dasta dasta pampōsh. 1033.

brāhman sör^{i} låg^{i} manganāwanas ta
sārĕn^{i} kāmĕ log^{u} maṭi karanē
böy^{i} sör^{i} āgyāyĕ kun wuchanas ta. lāgas etc. 1034.

Drĕtarāshṭr āv ta gŏbar pata tas ta
sūty Bīshma-pitāmah ta Vidur hĕth
biyĕ yim Kaurawan båḍ^{i} dwāras ta. lāgas etc. 1035.

yim rāza cyukūṭh^{i} ös^{i} rājĕs ta
tim sör^{i} yĕtsh patsh låg^{i} baranē
maṭi rūz^{ü} prath köm^{ü} prath rāzas ta. lāgas etc.
1036.

låg^{i} jaga-pĕnḍav sambālanas ta
sŏmb^{ü}r^{ü}kh sŏna-sanza liwañau sūty
sumuhūrth wuchith ta låg^{i} jagas ta. lāgas etc. 1037.

sŏstibadr sata-rĕsh^{i} låg^{i} paranas ta
Kashĕpa-mŏnīshŏr ta Parāshĕr
Shrī-Vyāsa-mŏnīshŏr baḍi ōjas ta. lāgas etc. 1038.

Vishwāmitras Vāmadēwas ta
Gautama-rĕshis ta biy^{ä} Daumĕs
sārĕn^{i} ras log^{u} vēd paranas ta. lāgas etc. 1039.

---

1 Dhṛtarāṣṭra, the blind king of Hastināpura, was paternal uncle of the Pāṇḍavas. He had many sons, of whom the eldest was Duryōdhana, the implacable enemy of Yudhiṣṭhira and his brothers. Bhīṣma, famous for his wisdom and unflinching devotion to God, had been the guardian of the Pāṇḍavas and of the Kauravas (the sons of Dhṛtarāṣṭra). In the Great War between the two sets of cousins he sided with the latter. He was not actually their grandfather, but his old age and wisdom entitled him to the appellation. Vidura was the younger

1032. He who beareth in his heart the name of Kṛṣṇa, to him will Kṛṣṇa every favour render. In this world glory will he win, and thereafter the abode of Viṣṇu will he reach. To him posy and posy do I offer lotuses.

XLVI. THE CORONATION RITES. (Bhāg. Pu. X, lxxiv, lxxv.)

1033. Yudhiṣṭhira the preparations for the sacrifice began, for now had he all kings of earth assembled. So now, from Kṛṣṇa Bhagavān he counsel asked.

1034. All the Brāhmaṇas he summoned, to each his own apportioned duty giving, while all his brothers watched for his commands.

1035. Thither came Dhṛtarāṣṭra followed by his sons, and bringing with him grandfather Bhīsma and Vidura,[1] and other great men of the Kauravas at the gate.

1036. All kings who reigned on each of the four sides of the kingdom were there. All they were filled with longing and with trust. On each one's shoulder was laid the burden of a special duty.

1037. The sacrificial altar began they to prepare, and with golden spades they levelled it. Then observing an auspicious moment did they the sacrifice begin.

1038. The seven sages[2] began to recite the Svastibhadra hymn,—Kaśyapa, the lord of saints, Parāśara, Vyāsa, the lord of saints, of majesty sublime.

1039. Joy was (in the hearts) of all,—of Viśvāmitra, of Vāmadēva, of Gautama the Sage, and of Dhaumya (the family priest),—as they the Vēda did recite.

---

brother of Pāṇḍu, and therefore uncle of the Pāṇḍavas.

[2] The seven ṛṣis, or sages, are usually said to be Marīci, Atri, Aṅgiras, Pulastya, Pulaha, Kratu, and Vasiṣṭha. Here the author apparently means Kaśyapa, Parāśara, Vyāsa, Viśvāmitra, Vāmadēva, Gautama, and Dhaumya, all of whom were also famous sages. Perhaps, however, he means to include both sets of seven. The Bhāgavata Purāṇa gives a much longer list. The Svastibhadra hymn is the name of an auspicious text.

sārĕn^{i} kun log^{u} rāza pritshanas ta
‘gŏḍa kus pūz^{i}zĕn sampani sĕd
sārĕn^{ü}y wŏttam gŏḍa shūbi kus’ ta
lāgas bŏh dasta dasta pampōsh. 1040.

ṭ^{a}kān Sahadēv wọth^{u} rāzas ta
‘gŏḍañ pūzun^{u} Krushna-Bagawān
Purushōttam suy tribuwanas’ ta. lāgas etc. 1041.

pūzā karani låg^{i} Bagawānas ta
söriy rĕsh^{i} dēv pūzana āy
sör^{ü}y pūzā āyĕ pālanas ta. lāgas etc. 1042.

söriy båḍ^{i} låg^{i} tiy mānanas ta
dēv rĕsh^{i} pitar ta rāza yim ös^{i}
‘gŏḍañiy pūzā pazi Krushnas’ ta. lāgas etc. 1043.

rāzā Yudishṭhir gav harshĕs ta
yiy ôs^{u} yitshawun^{u} tiy dop^{u}has
baji yĕtshi patshi log^{u} pūzāyĕ tas. lāgas etc. 1044.

Yudishṭhir^{i} khōr chål^{i} Shrī-Krushnas ta
pādĕ-zal gŏḍañ shēri dôrun
tawa pata chokun rāza-mandiras ta. lāgas etc. 1045.

pūzā kür^{ü}nas vĕdi-vĕz^{ü} tas ta
arga-pōshĕ-d^{a}pa-dīpa-navīda sūty
swörgī wastrau ti yitha pazihēs ta. lāgas etc. 1046.

Krushna-jyuv praṅga pĕṭha shōla trāwanas ta
kana-wājĕ kana-wöl^{i} z^{a}tsa trāwān
shūbā zi sör^{ü} āyĕ yĕgñĕ-manḍalas ta. lāgas etc. 1047.

söriy chih vĕṭhān tath darshĕnas ta
Yudishṭhira-rāzas tŏth karawån^{i}
asandiy hīta āy zi bāgĕ wŏdayĕs ta. lāgas etc. 1048.

Brahmā Mahēshŏr āy darshĕnas ta
söriy dēwatā lūka-pāl hĕth
biyĕ yim båḍ^{i} ös^{i} dēwa-lūkas ta. lāgas etc. 1049.

1040. Then of the whole assembly asked the king (Yudhiṣṭhira), 'Whom should we worship first, to bring success? Who first will rightly seem unparagoned of all?'

1041. At once stood up Sahadēva, and thus addressed the king, 'First to be worshipped is Kṛṣṇa Bhagavān; of the three worlds is he the Being Supreme.'

1042. So with worship to Bhagavān did they begin, next were worshipped all the sages and the gods, and thus was all the worship ritely done.

1043. All the great people there approved,—gods, sages, Manes of ancestors, and kings, all these approved that Kṛṣṇa should receive the worship first.

1044. Rājā Yudhiṣṭhira at this was with joy full filled, for that was said to him which he himself desired. So, filled with a longing great and loving trust, to worship Kṛṣṇa he began.

1045. Śrī Kṛṣṇa's feet did Yudhiṣṭhira wash. Then first the laving water on his head he placed, and next about the assembly-hall he sprinkled it.

1046. With all befitting rites performed they the worship; offerings of fruit, of flowers, of incense, and of lights made they to him; and, as was meet, with heaven-splendid garments (clothed they him).

1047. From on the throne Kṛṣṇa sent forth a blazing light. His smaller earrings on his ear-pendants moonlight poured, so that all glory filled the hall of sacrifice.

1048. At such a glorious sight were all filled with exultation; loud sang they praises of Yudhiṣṭhira, in that through him alone had such consummate fortune come to them.

1049. Brahmā and Śiva came down to see the spectacle, with all the gods and regents of the quarters, and the great people of the region of the gods.

pör^{i} pör^{i} Krushna-jyuwanis darshěnas ta
namaskār rāzan ḍěka-bajěras
namaskār tihandis bakth karanas ta
lāgas bŏh dasta dasta pampōsh. 1050.

rāza-Shishupālas dŏrbŏdis ta
Rukminī nina shut^{u} ôsus wair
hyokun na z^{a}ravith log^{u} wōranas ta. lāgas etc. 1051.

boḍ^{u} ôs^{u} rāzāh tath samayěs ta
ahankāra tsari ôs^{u} mad phũkān
Shrī-Krushnun^{u} věh něth ôs^{u} tas ta. lāgas etc. 1052.

Krushnun^{u} nāv log^{u} yüts^{ü} wananas ta
sabāyě santan něndani log^{u}
'kětha mön^{i}zi gūr^{i}-shur^{u} gŏra-pūzanas ta. lāgas etc.
1053.

Brahmāděkh sör^{i} yith yěgñěs ta
wŏttam rěsh^{i} ta mŏnīshŏr
tim sör^{i} trövith pūzā kas' ta. lāgas etc. 1054.

yih na kĕh pazihē zěvi hěnas ta
tiy tiy wani Krushna-nāwas pěṭh
bōzān sabā gayě krūdas ta. lāgas etc. 1055.

wŏthis söriy tas māranas ta
Krushna-jyuv^{i} söriy råṭin path
dop^{u}nakh zi 'diyūs sôr^{u} wananas' ta. lāgas etc. 1056.

'wån^{i}tan yih kĕh chus manas ta
sôruy poz^{u} poz^{u} wanān chum'
path rūd^{i} tim ta man rōzi kas ta. lāgas etc. 1057.

yot^{u}-tām hath apamān wån^{i}nas ta
tot^{u}-tām Krushna-jyuv wanēs na kĕh
suy hath ôsus tas manas ta. lāgas etc. 1058.

Sŏdarshěna-tsakra sūty kala tsoṭ^{u}nas ta
tasandi dīha nishě tīzāh drāv
khasith ta gav syod^{u} Vishnu-bŏwanas ta. lāgas etc.
1059.

1050. Ever dedicating myself to that manifestation of Kṛṣṇa, reverence do I pay to the happy fortune of those kings, and reverence eke to the devotion shown by them.

1051. But, ever since the rape of Rukmiṇī,[1] the evil-hearted Śiśupāla had borne hate to Kṛṣṇa; nor these doings could he endure, and loud did he begin to howl.

1052. In those days a mighty king was he. Full of exceeding haughtiness was he, and arrogance was he ever breathing forth. Against Kṛṣṇa bore he an unending poisonous hate.

1053. Vehemently cried he out Kṛṣṇa's name, and on the righteous members of the assembly blame he cast. 'How is this cow-boy to be worshipped as a holy teacher?

1054. 'To this sacrifice Brahmā and all the other gods are come, and with them sages supreme and lords among the saints. To whom, except such, is worship to be done?'

1055. Whatever is not seemly on the tongue, that and that saith he anent the name of Kṛṣṇa, and wroth went the assembly as they heard his words.

1056. Against him all arose to kill him, but Kṛṣṇa held them back and said to them, 'Let him say everything.'

1057. 'Whatever be in his mind, that let him say. All that he saith concerning me is in each item true.' So they refrained, but whose heart was not in tumult tossed?

1058. Up to a hundred abuses against him did Śiśupāla utter, and up to that hundred no word uttered Kṛṣṇa, but that same hundred was (the limit) in his mind.

1059. Then (when the hundred was completed), with his discus named Sudarśana, Kṛṣṇa cut off his head, and, lo, from Śiśupāla's body there issued forth a flame of brightness, and upwards, straight unto Viṣṇu's abode did it ascend.

---

[1] The story of the Rape of Rukmiṇī, and of how Kṛṣṇa carried her off from Śiśupāla, is told above in verses 638ff.

tati āv phīrith nishĕ Krushnas ta
Krushna-jyuwanis mŏkha-kamalas tsāv
sabā zi sör^{u}y gayĕ āshtsaras ta
lāgas bŏh dasta dasta pampōsh. 1060.

Brahmā chuh dapān prath pŏrashĕs ta
'wuch^{i}tav Krushnani wairuk^{u} phal
bükts^{ü}-hond^{u} phal kyāh yiyi wananas ta. lāgas etc.
1061.

suh ti ôs^{u} Krushnas waīsi sŏranas ta
yĕna Rukmini-hünz^{ü} pĕyĕs laz
waira ti sŏranuk^{u} phal dyut^{u}nas ta. lāgas etc. 1062.

yih phal chuh waira Krushna-jyuv sŏranas ta
baktimānan pāna zānakh phal
namaskār baktĕn bakth karanas' ta. lāgas etc. 1063.

vĕgnāh kösith ta lȧg^{i} yĕgñĕs ta
prath kaīsi prath kā̃h köm^{ü} maṭi ös^{ü}
prath kā̃h mani dörith Krushnas ta. lāgas etc. 1064.

rāza log^{u} jagas ta jaga-sangas ta
yĕgñüc^{ü} sāmagrī sör^{ü} sŏmb^{a}rith
yĕgñuk^{u} wŏtsav log^{u} baḍanas ta. lāgas etc. 1065.

prath böyis log^{u} kāmi lāganas ta
Arzŏna-dĕwas ta Bīma-sēnas
biyĕ Nakulas ta Sahadēwas ta. lāgas etc. 1066.

Draupadiyĕ-handis prath pŏtras ta
yus yus yĕth yĕth kāmi lagihē
prath rāza rūzith dāsa-bāwas ta. lāgas etc. 1067.

rasöy^{i} maṭi ös^{ü} Bīmasēnas ta
Duryōdanas banḍāra-köm^{ü}
Nakul ta Sahadēv pūz karanas ta. lāgas etc. 1068.

---

[1] The flame of brightness was Śiśupāla's soul, which thus attained salvation by becoming absorbed into Kṛṣṇa in his character of the Supreme Deity. The point is that continued meditation on Kṛṣṇa ensures salvation. Śiśupāla had been perpetually thinking of Kṛṣṇa, and the fact that this meditation was born of hate

1060. Thence came it back to Kṛṣṇa, and into his lotus-mouth it entered, and with amazement was the assembly filled.[1]

1061. To each man present Brahmā saith, 'Behold ye the fruit of hating Kṛṣṇa. (If that be so great), of devoted love how great must be the fruit!

1062. 'He, also, all his life, since on the score of Rukmiṇī he had been put to shame, the memory of Kṛṣṇa had been keeping; and the fruit of remembering, even though 'twas rankling, hath to him been given.

1063. 'Such was the fruit of keeping him in memory with hatred. Hence shalt thou thyself know the fruit by those devoted to him gained. Reverence be to the devotion of his devotees!'

1064. With all impediments removed, to the sacrifice themselves did they apply. To each one was assigned a several duty, while each one carried Kṛṣṇa in his heart.

1065. The king began his preparations for the sacrifice; for it all the materials were collected, and the great festival began to reach its height.

1066. (Bhāg. Pu. X, lxxv.) A share of duty was given to each brother,—to Arjuna, to Bhīmasēna, to Nakula, and to Sahadēva;

1067. To each son of Draupadī, to each king who acted as a servant,—to each was given his allotted task.

1068. The cooking of the food was Bhīma's charge; Duryōdhana's the treasure-house control; of rites of worship had Nakula and Sahadēva charge.

---

and entirely that of an enemy, but was still meditation of a sort on Kṛṣṇa, thus produced salvation. In the next verse Brahmā points this out, and argues that if this be the result of enmity, how great must be the bliss of salvation resulting from meditation in love.

Krushna-jyuv pūzāyĕ prath brāhmanas ta
pād chalanas ta bāna ananas
sārĕn^{u}y bāwa sūty sīwā karanas ta
lāgas bŏh dasta dasta pampōsh. 1069.

rāzasūy yĕg^{a}ñ āv sôr^{u} karanas ta
dana dyār kaityāh dān dina āy
grand gayĕ na dānas darma-karmas ta. lāgas etc.
1070.

rāza-nīti sārĕn^{i} pazi yuth^{u} yĕs ta
timan ti byon^{u} byon^{u} samponukh mān
söriy santushṭ gay harshĕs ta. lāgas etc. 1071.

namaskār Yudishṭhiranis bāgĕs ta
namaskār tasandis tath wŏdayĕs
namaskār tasandis bakth karanas ta. lāgas etc. 1072.

yus lagi Krushna-jyuwanis nāwas ta
tas kari Krushna-jyuv sarŏ wŏpakār
yiyi yĕsh nith ta wāti Vishnu-bawanas ta. lāgas etc.
1073.

pör^{i} pör^{i} Krushna-jyuwanis nāwas ta
pör^{i} pör^{i} tasandis autāras
pör^{i} pör^{i} tasandis shŏba tsarĕtas ta. lāgas etc. 1074.

XLVII.

namaskār Sŏdāmas Krushna-baktas ta
mātā Sŏshīlāyĕ namaskār
namaskār tihandis bakti-bāwas
lāgas bŏh dasta dasta pampōsh. 1075.

Sŏdām boḍ^{u} bokt^{u} bọw^{u} Krushnas ta
yāra-layĕ tas sūty gindān ôs^{u}
tsāṭa-hāla shut^{u} tas yār zānihĕs ta. lāgas etc. 1076.

gŏḍañiy wātsāv yĕli Kansas ta
Sŏdām pōshĕ-māla hĕth āyās
Krushna-jyuv^{i} bŏkth mŏkth ditsöyĕ tas ta. lāgas etc.
1077.

1069. To Kṛṣṇa was the worshipping of each Brāhmaṇa allotted, to lave their feet and bring to them the dishes. Thus each one with all courtesy did service.

1070. So was the coronation sacrifice all performed. The tale of gifts, wealth and coinèd money, who can tell; for no counting was there of the alms and other pious works.

1071. Just as to each by courtly punctilio was proper deemed, so to each one was proper honour shown, and all were satisfied and filled with joy.

1072. Reverence be to Yudhiṣṭhira's great good fortune; reverence be to his high exultation; and reverence be to the devotion shown by him to Kṛṣṇa.

1073. He who beareth in his heart the name of Kṛṣṇa, to him will Kṛṣṇa every favour render. In this world glory will he win, and thereafter the abode of Viṣṇu will he reach. To him posy and posy do I offer lotuses.

1074. Ever dedicating myself to Kṛṣṇa's name, ever dedicating myself to his incarnation, ever dedicating myself to his auspicious deeds, posy and posy do I offer lotuses.

XLVII. THE STORY OF SUDĀMAN. (Bhāg. Pu. X. lxxx, lxxxi.)

1075. Reverence be to Sudāman, the faithful devotee of Kṛṣṇa; to Mother Suśīlā, his wife be reverence; reverence be to their adoring faith.

1076. Greatly devoted to Kṛṣṇa became Sudāman. (In boyhood) Kṛṣṇa was wont to play with him in bosom friendship, and from his schooldays knew him as his friend.

1077. When first Kṛṣṇa before Kaṁsa's court arrived, to him with flower-garlands Sudāman[1] came, and to him Kṛṣṇa gave the boons of worldly bliss and ultimate salvation.

---

[1] See verse 423.

tawa pata tsāṭa-hāla sũty ôs^{u} tas ta
Krushna-jyuv tas rost^{u} barihē na sŏkh
pānavüñ^{ü} shur^{i}-bāwa ös^{i} gindanas ta
lāgas bŏh dasta dasta pampōsh. 1078.

Nanda-gōrini bŏv^{i} gūr^{i}-shur^{i} tas ta
ati ôs^{u} Sŏdām gindan-bôj^{u}
yot^{u}-tāñ Dwārakāyĕ gav basanas ta. lāgas etc. 1079.

nēth^{a}r yĕli ôs^{u} Sŏdāmas ta
Sŏshīlā pativrath bāgĕ āyĕs
sa ti lüj^{ü} Krushna-bakth tsür^{ü} karanas ta. lāgas etc. 1080.

pānavüñ^{ü} āsān pānañāras ta
rāth dŏh pānavüñ^{ü} yĕtsh barawàn^{i}
bāra-bātsan bakth lüj^{ü} baḍanas ta. lāgas etc. 1081.

gŏras nishĕ gav yĕli paranas ta
pūth^{i} dūj^{ü} athi tàs^{i} Sŏdāmas
Krushna-jyuv ti bālukh zan gindanas ta. lāgas etc. 1082.

dŏha aki gŏran sūz^{i} wanas ta
söriy tsāṭa-shur^{i} zyun^{u} ananē
Sŏdām sũty gav Krushna-zīwas ta. lāgas etc. 1083.

gōr-māji kẽtshāh sũty dyut^{u}nas ta
byon^{u} byon^{u} ti sārĕn^{i} tsāṭa-bājĕn
Shrī-Krushnun^{u} athi tàs^{i} Sŏdāmas ta. lāgas etc. 1084.

wöt^{i} yĕli wanas ta làg^{i} phēranas ta
söriy zin^{i}-hür^{ü} sŏmb^{a}rani làg^{i}
Sŏdām Krushnani kani ananas ta. lāgas etc. 1085.

Sŏdām zin^{i}-hür^{ü} log^{u} sŏmb^{a}ranas ta
Krushnüñ^{ü} ta panüñ^{ü} yīts^{ü} hĕkihē
söriy tsāṭa-böj^{i} làg^{i} gindanas ta. lāgas etc. 1086.

hanga ta manga āyĕ ōd^{i} wanas ta
waharöts^{ü} rūd log^{u} wālani tsor^{u}
wāwuk^{u} kẽh na zi yiyi wananas ta. lāgas etc. 1087.

1078. Thereafter, in the school was he ever his companion, nor was Kṛṣṇa happy when apart from him, and in their childish ways they played together.

1079. In Nanda the cowherd's home were his herdboy children, and there was wont Sudāman to be his playmate until he went to dwell in Dvārakā.

1080. In course of time Sudāman married, and so Suśīlā his faithful wife became. She too a mighty adoring faith in Kṛṣṇa began to hold.

1081. Mutually were they united in each other's longing. Night and day were they with but one desire mutually full filled, and thus of the spouses the adoring faith ever went on in increase.

1082. When Kṛṣṇa for his lessons to his teacher went, it was only in Sudāman's hand that books and writing tablet were conveyed, while the boy Kṛṣṇa playing ran along.

1083. Once on a day, to fetch kindling firewood were the schoolboys to the forest by their teacher sent, and with Sudāman did Kṛṣṇa also go.

1084. The teacher's wife gave them some (food to take) with them, a separate portion for each schoolfellow's meal, and into Sudāman's hand she Kṛṣṇa's portion gave.

1085. Arrived at the forest wandered about they all, and to collect kindling-wood and sticks began; and Sudāman also for Kṛṣṇa brought a share.

1086. So far as he was able did Sudāman his own and Kṛṣṇa's share of kindling-wood collect, and when this was done the schoolfellows their play began.

1087. Suddenly, in the forest rose a storm. Monsoonlike rain it caused to fall in floods; as for the wind, who can its tale unfold!

rāth lüjᵘ tsāṭan manz wanas ta
sārĕnⁱ phal dāna pānas sūty
Shrī-Krushnunᵘ athi tȧsⁱ Sŏdāmas ta
lāgas bŏh dasta dasta pampōsh. 1088.

rāth kyutᵘ yĕli sörⁱ lȧgⁱ khĕnas ta
Krushna-jyuv Sŏdāmas mangani logᵘ
khĕna ôsᵘ āmotᵘ tih Sŏdāmas ta. lāgas etc. 1089.

dopᵘnas 'drölida! khyōth pānas ta
mĕ rostᵘ khĕnas kĕtha pazihē'
drölⁱdözᵘ prāpath ösᵘ baktis ta. lāgas etc. 1090.

büḍᵘ chĕh āsān yĕḍ brāhmanas ta
Krushnaṣ ti shāph tas kāsunᵘ ôsᵘ
yi-na kĕh rōzĕs push būganas ta. lāgas etc. 1091.

hīta aki wākh dith ta shāph kôsᵘnas ta
yuthᵘ pāpa-karm sörⁱ gatshi būgith
na-ta kŏsa bŏcha trēsh Bagawānas ta. lāgas etc. 1092.

tana shutᵘ Sŏdām bakti-bāwas ta
Sŏshīlāyĕ sān ôsᵘ bakth karawunᵘ
Krushna-jyuv Dwārakāyĕ sŏkh baranas ta. lāgas etc. 1093.

rāth dŏh Vishnu-bakth ôsᵘ karanas ta
drölⁱdözᵘ zōnith sampadā zan
Sŏshīlā sīwāyĕ bartāhas ta. lāgas etc. 1094.

bikshā kȧrⁱ kȧrⁱ nishĕ anihēs ta
manza bükts ᵘ nishĕ ḍalihēs na man
Shrī-Krushna-Bagawān mani dāranas ta. lāgas etc. 1095.

yotᵘ-tāñ anth gōkh pāpa-karmas ta
sāwadān būgukh pāpukᵘ phal
samay ākh ākh bāgĕ wŏdayĕs ta. lāgas etc. 1096.

---

[1] The idea is that all Sudāman's sins in former births had necessarily to be expiated. Till this was completed, salvation was impossible to him. Kṛṣṇa, in order to secure the expiation as speedily and as completely as possible, condemned him to undergo poverty for a certain period. This would be the 'fruit' of sins in

1088. While still within the forest on the boys fell night, each had his fruit and grain for food with him, but Kṛṣṇa's was in care of that Sudāman.

1089. When at nightfall they all began to eat, Kṛṣṇa for his share Sudāman asked, but it had all been eaten by Sudāman.

1090. Cried Kṛṣṇa, 'Eaten it all thyself has thou, thou beggarly knave! What right had thou to eat it in my absence!' (And by this speech) of this devoted friend a beggar's lot the fate became.

1091. But great is the belly of a Brāhmaṇa (and much food doth it demand). So Kṛṣṇa determined that such a curse must be removed, that to him there be no shortcoming of the means of life.

1092. 'Twas but as a pretext that these words he uttered, and then removed the curse. His object real was that all the fruits of his sins in former lives might be (at once) experienced (and so exhaust the evil that was in them). Otherwise, how could hunger and thirst be felt by Bhagavān[1]?

1093. From that time, while Kṛṣṇa dwelt happily in Dvārakā, did Sudāman and Suśīlā live in faith and loving adoration.

1094. Night and day devotion did they to Viṣṇu offer, looking upon their poverty as wealth, while Suśīlā did wifely service to her spouse.

1095. Begging here and there and never ceasing, would she to him bring the collected alms; still, (in all their poverty), in his adoring faith he never faltered, but fixed his mind on Kṛṣṇa Bhagavān.

1096. Until the end came of the fruit of their sins in former lives, so long with steadfastness did they experience it. When the full time came to them, then did their good fortune begin to be exalted.

---

former births, and would cause this fruit to be exhausted. He had to have some pretext for uttering the curse, and he took the consumption of his food as such. The poverty was to be only for a period, and after that Sudāman would enjoy worldly prosperity and ultimately gain salvation.

dŏha aki Sŏshīlā wŏtsh^{u} brāhmanas ta
‘Krushna-jyuv chuh Bagawān pāna autār
rachani āv sād santh zanmas ta
lāgas bŏh dasta dasta pampōsh. 1097.

‘būmi-bār kāsani āv zanmas ta
rākhĕs sör^{i} gatshi gölith kĕth
sād chis rachán^{i} yitha titha tas’ ta. lāgas etc. 1098.

‘wuñ-kĕn chih söriy sôr^{u} sŏkhas ta
Krushna-Bagawānani darshĕna sūty
sampadā sūty sūty chĕh Shrī-Krushnas’ ta. lāgas etc.
1099.

‘yĕna āv Krushna-jyuv autāras ta
tana chuh sārĕn^{i} sāryukuy sŏkh
shāph pāph sārĕn^{i} gay antas’ ta. lāgas etc. 1100.

‘māy söñ^{u} kūts^{u} bŏy^{u} Shrī-Krushnas ta
tsĕ rost^{u} ôsus na wasān myonḍ^{u}
kyāh zön^{i}zi kĕtha söñ^{u} māy mūṭh^{u} tas’ ta. lāgas etc.
1101.

‘tih kĕtha māy söñ^{u} tsür^{u} āsi tas ta
sāri khŏta kal söñ^{u} tsür^{u} āsĕs
bakta-watsala-nāv chuh Bagawānas’ ta. lāgas etc.
1102.

‘mani ās zi shāph gav asĕ antas ta
Krushna-jyuv asĕ kari dayā yūts^{u}
kūt^{u} kāl būgav nītsa-bāwas’ ta. lāgas etc. 1103.

‘gatshith ta Dwārakāyĕ pān hāvtas ta
wuchakh zi Krushna-jyuv kūt^{u} tōṭhiy
drĕshṭi aki nĕhāl kari baktis’ ta. lāgas etc. 1104.

Sŏdŏm^{i} phīrith phraṭh kor^{u} tas ta
‘dĕkh-kār bŏy^{i}nay triyĕ-bāwas
ṭhahari na dayĕ-güts^{u} pĕṭh man yĕs’ ta. lāgas etc.
1105.

---

[1] I.e. the burden of sin, which weighed down the earth.
[2] Lit. No morsel descended (his gullet).

1097. Once on a day Suśīlā up and to the Brāhmaṇa, her husband, said, 'Kṛṣṇa is Bhagavān himself incarnate, and himself to human birth hath come, the pious and the virtuous to protect.

1098. 'To human birth came he the burden[1] of the earth to lift, nor will he leave it till all the demons he hath destroyed; for such is his purpose, that the pious be protected.

1099. 'Now are all men in every happiness; for to them hath Kṛṣṇa Bhagavān revealed himself, and welfare is ever in the company of Kṛṣṇa.

1100. 'Since Kṛṣṇa hath become incarnate, all men possess felicity of every kind; curses and sins all to an end have come.

1101. 'How great is the love that to Kṛṣṇa we have borne! When thou wast not present he would eat no food.[2] How can we think that our love by him hath been forgotten?

1102. 'How can that be? Surely his love for us is great. Belike for us his yearning greater is than for others all, for "Compassionate to the Devoted" is a name of Bhagavān.

1103. 'He will have thought that to an end his curse hath come, and on us great compassion will he show. How long must we endure this lowly state?

1104. 'Go thou to Dvārakā and show thyself to him, and thou shalt see how Kṛṣṇa will be pleased. Then, with a single glance on his devoted one, prosperity will he bestow.'

1105. Sudāman in reply to her made violent reproach,[3] 'Shame be upon thy woman's temper, thou, whose soul waiteth not patiently upon fate!

---

[3] Lit. Caused her sudden death,—an idiomatic term for violent abuse.

'asĕ chuh Bagawān sūty pānas ta
sōñ^{u} hish^{u} sampadā kas āsē
Krushna-nāv chuh yiha-lūka-para-lūkas' ta
lāgas bŏh dasta dasta pampōsh. 1106.

'mĕ kĕh gatshĕm na rost^{u} Krushnas ta
ts^{a}h ti nay ṭhaharakh ta mata rōztam
drüḍ^{u} rütsh^{u} triy chĕy ādĕ-antas' ta. lāgas etc. 1107.

Sŏshīlāyĕ bāgĕ āmot^{u} wŏdayĕs ta
ḍyūṭhun zi bartā chuh santōshĕ-dor^{u}
zĕv phir^{u}nas ta biyĕ won^{u}nas ta. lāgas etc. 1108.

dop^{u}nas zi 'pād cyön^{i} dāra shēras ta
cyāniy darshĕna ḍĕka-büḍ^{u} chĕs
Krushna-bükts^{u} sôn^{u} hyuh^{u} ḍĕka āsi kas ta. lāgas etc.
1109.

'bŏh chĕs cyāni khŏta santōshĕs ta
ts^{a}y lastam biyĕ manga na kĕh
Krushna-nāv ös^{i}tan asĕ manas' ta. lāgas etc. 1110.

'yiy ām Krushna-jyuv chuh autāras ta
yüts^{ü} kāl wôtuy wuchanas tas
tasond^{u} darshun^{u} athi yiyi kas' ta. lāgas etc. 1111.

'yōgiyĕn chuh dŏrlab dyāna-sŏranas ta
wuñ-kĕn chuh darshun^{u} prạkh^{o}ṭuy dith
bāgĕwān nĕth yim chih wuchawån^{i} tas' ta. lāgase tc.
1112.

'darshunāh karith ta yita pānas ta
Krushna-jyuwa-darshun^{u} dŏrlab chuy
tsĕ kĕtha rōzān chuh man rost^{u} tas' ta. lāgas etc.
1113.

yitha titha wŏṭi lüj^{u} ananē tas
Sŏdāmas ti lōl ôs^{u} wŏthith ta gav
Krushna-darshĕna-kăchi āv phaṭanas ta. lāgas etc.
1114.

dop^{u}nas zi 'gatshahö kĕtha wāta tas ta
tasond^{u} wās āsi pĕṭh mandaras
bŏh kami shūbi wāta nērinyūr^{u} tas' ta. lāgas etc.
1115.

1106. 'With us even now is ever Bhagavān himself, and thus what wealth can be compared with ours; for our wealth is the Name of Kṛṣṇa, and serveth both for this world and for the world to come.

1107. 'Save Krsna nothing need I. If patiently thou canst not wait, then with me abide no longer. From first to last a woman lacketh steadfastness.'

1108. But Suśīlā's fate had come unto the time of its uprisal; still saw she that her spouse was firm in his content, and so she turned her tongue, and thus addressed him :—

1109. Quoth she, 'Thy feet in humbleness I set upon my head; great is my happy lot in only seeing thee; and in our love for Kṛṣṇa whose fate can be compared with ours!

1110. 'Than thee more full am I of high content. Mayst thou live long for me,—aught else ask I not, and ever in our hearts may Kṛṣṇa's name abide.

1111. 'But this hath come to me,—Kṛṣṇa a human form hath taken; but many days have passed since thou hast seen him, and to what other wight should come the (rapture of) beholding him?

1112. 'That rapture e'en ascetics fail to gain with all their meditation and their calling him to mind, and now, behold, freely and openly to all he giveth it. They who behold him are for ever blessed.

1113. 'To him make thou but one visit and then home return. A vision of Kṛṣṇa is hard for thee to gain; how can thy heart remain at peace without him?'

1114. This way and that led she him to leap (from his inaction); and in Sudāman's heart a passionate love too arose, till in its longing for the sight of Kṛṣṇa it was like to burst.

1115. Quoth he, 'Fain would I go, but how may I approach him, for in a palace is his dwelling place, and what fine apparel have I that near him I may go?'

dop^{u}nas zi 'Krushna-jyuv chuh rāza-bāwas ta
brāhmanan kaīsi chĕh na atsanas raṭh
tsĕ kyāh chuh wuchun^{u} mŏkh wuchanas' ta
lāgas bŏh dasta dasta pampōsh. 1116.

dop^{u}nas 'kami hīta nishĕ gatsha tas ta
bŏcha-hot^{u} wātahŏ yitha titha tot^{u}
tō-ti kĕh āsihēm kyut^{u} Krushnas' ta. lāgas etc. 1117.

wŏthith ta Sŏshīlā drāyĕ manganas ta
kōm^{ü}-sir^{i} mŏchĕ tāra athi ditsanas
raṭith ta rawa-zacĕ log^{u} ganḍanas ta. lāgas etc. 1118.

rawa-zacĕ kuni chĕs na dür^{ü} mŏy tas ta
yitha titha kah^{i}-tām ganḍ kor^{u}nas
Sŏdām Krushna-lōla log^{u} lāranas ta. lāgas etc. 1119.

wati kari bajĕ süts^{ü} mana-rāzas ta
'mĕ kĕtha Sŏshīlāyĕ wŏpakār kor^{u}
sanmŏkha wāra wāta Krushna-darshĕnas ta. lāgas etc.
1120.

'ḍĕlān ti man chum kĕtha wātas ta
kami mŏkha rāzas höv^{i}zē pān
rāzas kas tas mahārāzas' ta. lāgas etc. 1121.

'yātsaka-bāway kĕh mangas ta
kĕtha kĕh mang^{i}zē bakti-bāwas
santōshĕ-bāwa kyāh köm^{ü} baktis' ta. lāgas etc. 1122.

biyĕ biyĕ karān chuh süts^{ü} manas ta
'suh nay ta tasonduy dwār ḍēshĕn
dwāras tasandis muñĕ wandas ta. lāgas etc. 1123.

'ḍĕka g^{a}h^{a} yĕti āsi wath Krushnas ta
tasand^{i} cākar tō-ti ḍēshĕkh
tihandi darshĕna gatsha sŏrgas' ta. lāgas etc. 1124.

kuni pān sŏrith ta khōr ḍĕlanas ta
kuni bŏcha lagān pakanas na kŏṭh^{i}
wāv pata yith ta zōr pakanāvĕs ta. lāgas etc. 1125.

1116. Quoth she to him, 'Kṛṣṇa is of kingly quality, nor is there interdict to any Brāhmaṇa his palace entering. What need for thee is thought how thou shouldst look upon his face?'

1117. Quoth he to her, 'With what excuse can I present myself, when, hunger-stricken, somehow or other there do I arrive? And even so, is there aught of mine that I can offer to him as a present?'

1118. Uprose at this Suśīlā, and went out to beg. (On her return) three fistfuls of broken rice-chaff into his hand she put. These did he take and tied them in the corner of the rag that served to him for blanket.

1119. Hardly anywhere were the rags strong enough to hold themselves together; but natheless somehow did he tie the knot, and full of ardent love for Kṛṣṇa forth Sudāman ran.

1120. On the road his fancy fills him full of hopes. 'Wondrous indeed is the good turn that Suśīlā hath done for me, for now shall I easily attain to seeing Kṛṣṇa face to face!

1121. 'Yet unmanned is my heart within me, for how can I attain my journey's aim? With what face can I before a king present myself,—and before what a king! before a very king of kings!

1122. 'As a suppliant will I come, and of him something beg. (And for what shall I beg?) What greater boon is there beyond adoring faith? Of (worldly) contentment what need hath an adorer?'

1123. Again and again with hopes filleth he his heart. 'If I see not him, as least the gateway of his palace will I see; and there, at his gate, for his sake would I offer in sacrifice the pupils of mine eyes.

1124. 'Wherever be the path that Kṛṣṇa goes, there will I rub my forehead in the dust. There also shall I at least his servants see, and as I behold them will leave this earth for heavenly bliss.'

1125. At one stage on his journey, while his body remembereth and urgeth him on, his legs become aweary; at another, famished by hunger, no progress make his knees; but still behind him bloweth strong the wind and speedeth him up on his way.

yitha titha nyūr^{u} wôt^{u} tath nagaras ta
    Krushna-jyuv gari log^{u} sanz karanē
'mĕ zi āv yārāh ta brō̃ṭha nēras' ta
    lāgas bŏh dasta dasta pampōsh. 1126.

'yuth^{u} yār kăh chum na yith samayĕs ta
    yuth^{u} bokt^{u} chuh na kăh yith bŏwanas
wŏlinjĕ wŏṭa-wŏṭh chĕm kăchi tas' ta. lāgas etc.
1127.

dapān tih wŏthith gav brō̃ṭha tas ta
    lārān chuh nanawāri-pāda-kamalau
mātā Rukminī pata pata tas ta. lāgas etc. 1128.

gatshith ta dūr myūl^{u} nẹb^{a}ray tas ta
    nālamati raṭith ta lōl bor^{u}nas
phīr^{i} phīr^{i} biyĕ biyĕ cīra raṭĕs ta. lāgas etc. 1129.

atha-wāsa tsônun sũty pānas ta
    Rukminiyĕ athi khōr chalanöv^{i}nas
māna bĕhanôwun pẹṭh prangas ta. lāgas etc. 1130.

myūṭh^{u} myūṭh^{u} khyon^{u} cyon^{u} nishĕ on^{u}nas ta
    Krushna-jyuv^{i} pānay atha chāl^{i}nas
kôtwāh ādar ta bāv kor^{u}nas ta. lāgas etc. 1131.

aiṭh paṭa-röniyĕ pakha wāyĕnas ta
    pānay Krushna-jyuv tsāmar hĕth
sāsa-baza tsōnza sārĕ sīwā karanas ta. lāgas etc.
1132.

Krushna-jyuv vĕṭhanas ta biyĕ tōshĕnas ta
    ṭôṭh^{u} bokt^{u} wuch^{i} wuch^{i} gav harshĕs
pritshān zi 'az kĕtha mani on^{u}thas' ta. lāgas etc.
1133.

Sŏdām chuh mandachān nītsa-pānas ta
    dapān chuh 'mani kĕ̃h brō̃t^{u} mā chus
myōñ^{u} kăch kĕtha sana yīts^{u} āsihēs' ta. lāgas etc.
1134.

Krushna-jyuv^{i} zônun ta log^{u} pritshanas ta
    'Sŏdām-juwa, chuyĕ tsĕtas kĕ̃h
lŏkacāra nērahöv kĕtha gindanas' ta. lāgas etc. 1135.

1126. Somehow came he thus the city near, and in his palace Kṛṣṇa began the preparations for receiving him. 'A friend hath come to me. Beforehand go I forth to meet him.

1127. 'In these days is there no friend so dear as he. In this world is there no devotee like him. With throb and throb leapeth forth my heart in my yearning passionate for him.'

1128. Saying thus did he arise, and forth he went to meet him. His lotus feet were bare, yet swift he ran, and along after him ran Mother Rukmiṇī.

1129. A great way far outside the palace met he him and lovingly embraced him. Again and again, and yet again, he pressed him to his heart.

1130. By his hand he took him and home to the palace led him. By Rukmiṇī's own hand his feet in cooling water laved he, and with all courtesy upon a couch he seated him.

1131. Delicious food and drink of varied kinds he brought, and, (after eating), his hands himself did Kṛṣṇa wash. Great was the honouring welcome shown to him.

1132. Eight of the chief queens fanned him, while Kṛṣṇa himself with the whisk the flies kept off, and servant-maids in thousands did him service.

1133. While he was being cherished and all his wants were being satisfied, Kṛṣṇa, as his beloved devotee he watched, in his heart rejoiced. He asks, 'How was I brought into thy mind this day?'

1134. Of his humble self becometh Sudāman full of shame. In himself he saith, 'Perchance he maketh some mistake. How could my wishes in their fulfilment ever soar so high?'

1135. But Kṛṣṇa knew his thoughts, and asked again, 'Sudāman, hast thou no memory, how in our boyhood we were wont to go out and play?

'tsāṭa-hāluk^{u} kẽh chuyĕ manas ta
    tsāṭa-hāl gatshahöv gindān kyāh
gŏra-sond^{u} bayĕ kyuth^{u} ôs^{u} manas ta
    lāgas bŏh dasta dasta pampōsh. 1136.

'gŏran yĕli sōzāy zyun^{u} ananas ta
    wana ȭd^{i} āyēyĕ wājyān rūd
sārĕn^{i} lajyēyĕ rāth wanas ta. lāgas etc. 1137.

'söriy zin^{i}-hür^{ü} sŏmb^{a}rāwanas ta
    myāni kani zin^{i}-hür^{ü} añēyĕth tsĕy
tsĕtas tiy chum wuñĕ manas ta. lāgas etc. 1138.

'cyāni nētruk^{u} chum sôr^{u} tsĕtas ta
    Sŏshīlā myôn^{u} kūt^{u} barihē prīm
tsĕ kĕtha kĕtha mana mashĕhö tas ta. lāgas etc. 1139.

'bŏh zāh wôtus na tot^{u} darshĕnas ta
    tŏhĕ kĕtha samyōwa bāṛa-böts^{ü}n
bŏh kō-na on^{u}was zāh tsĕtas' ta. lāgas etc. 1140.

ạnd^{a}ra chuh phŏlān man brāhmanas ta
    nĕḅ^{a}ra tas mandachi khasān na kẽh
tana mana log^{u}mot^{u} Krushna-pādas ta. lāgas etc. 1141.

asān Krushna-jyuv log^{u} pritshanas ta.
    'mĕ kyut^{u} zi kẽtshāh chuyĕ on^{u}mot^{u}
tūr^{i} kun kal chĕm tsür^{ü} manas' ta. lāgas etc. 1142.

Sŏdām khåṭ^{i} khåṭ^{i} log^{u} thawanas ta
    mandachān chuh 'kŏm^{ü}-phol^{u} yina ḍēshĕm'
Krushna-jyuv^{i} tshöḍith zacĕ koḍ^{u}nas ta. lāgas etc. 1143.

ganḍ mutsarith ta pāna nyūnas ta
    Krushna-jyuv kŏm^{ü}-mŏchĕ khĕnē log^{u}
sir^{i} phål^{i} pạth^{a}ra log^{u} tulanas ta. lāgas etc. 1144.

z^{a}h mŏchĕ lāyĕn mŏkha-kamalas ta
    trayim^{ü} ti yāmath lāyĕni log^{u}
Rukminiyĕ ṭ^{a}kān atha roṭ^{u}nas ta. lāgas etc. 1145.

1136. 'Hast thou forgotten in thy heart the school, and how upon the way to it we played, and in what fear we held the dominie?

1137. 'How, when the master sent us to fetch kindling wood, on the forest came a storm, and how the storm poured the rain; how in the forest on us fell the night?

1138. 'How all the others collected their own sticks, and how thou didst also collect my share. That, even now, is treasured in my heart.

1139. 'Well is the memory of thy nuptials in my heart, and how with love for me was Suśilā filled. How can I have been forgotten by thee and her?

1140. 'Never did opportunity arise that I might thither go to visit thee, to see how ye two spouses lived as one. Was I never to your memory recalled?'

1141. Inwardly blossometh forth the Brāhmaṇa's heart, but outwardly, through his shame, no (sign of joy) ariseth. Still body and heart were laid at Kṛṣṇa's feet.

1142. (Bhāg. Pu. X, lxxxi.) Next with a smile did Kṛṣṇa ask, 'For me hast thou no present brought? In that respect have I great longing in my heart.'

1143. Sudāman privily and secretly began to hide (his gift). Full of shame is he lest Kṛṣṇa should chance to see his grains of chaff, but Kṛṣṇa searched him, and pulled out the blanket-rag.

1144. The knot did he untie, and himself did Kṛṣṇa, taking out from it the fistfuls of rice-chaff, begin to eat. Anon, from the floor began he to pick up the rice-grains (that had fallen and lay scattered there).

1145. Two fistfuls into his own lotus mouth he cast, but, as the third to cast did he begin, with haste did Rukmiṇī his hand restrain.

trayim$^{\ddot{u}}$ kŏm$^{\ddot{u}}$-mŏṭh$^{\ddot{u}}$ atha niyĕnas ta
    ṭ^{a}kān tami ti mŏkhas lŏy$^{\ddot{u}}$
na-ta sör$^{\ddot{u}}$ Vishnu-Shĕk^{a}th wātihē tȧs^{i} ta
    lāǵas bŏh dasta dasta pampōsh. 1146.

dapān chuh Krushna-jyuv Sŏdāmas ta
    'mĕ chum na yuth^{u} kẽh khyōmot^{u} zāh
yuth^{u} swād loǵum na kuni sālas' ta. lāǵas etc. 1147.

dŏha pĕṭha rāth tāñ ös^{i} harshĕs ta
    Krushna-jyuv brāhmanas shĕch^{i} pritshawun^{u}
atha ḍöl^{i} ḍöl^{i} lōla mŏṭh$^{\ddot{u}}$ dits$^{\ddot{u}}$nas ta. lāǵas etc. 1148.

pȧt^{i} kin^{i} ǵatshun^{u} pĕv Vishŏkarmas ta
    pruthiviyĕ Waikunṭh banāwanē
ǵȧr^{i} kin^{i} Vishnu-bawan ladanôw^{u}nas ta. lāǵas etc. 1149.

rātas$^{\ddot{u}}$y sôruy wātanôw^{u}nas ta
    sör$^{\ddot{u}}$ sampadā yitsh$^{\ddot{u}}$ pazihē tath
tsŏnza ta cākar sör^{i} tath ǵaras ta. lāǵas etc. 1150.

Sŏshīlāyĕ söriy tsāmar karanas ta
    kathan söriy atha dārān
sampüz^{u}-hond^{u} kẽh yiyi na wananas ta. lāǵas etc. 1151.

yih yih Waikunṭhas tiy ǵari tas ta
    zĕv hĕki tŏtāh kyāh wananas
Sŏshīlā pör^{i} lüj$^{\ddot{u}}$ Baǵawānas ta. lāǵas etc. 1152.

Sŏshīlāyĕ ānand āshtsar bŏwanas ta
    kus hĕki warnanā karith tath
zinday Waikunṭha-dām zan tas ta. lāǵas etc. 1153.

drölid-bāwa manza zan sŏp^{a}nas ta
    avināshi-sampad prāwana sūty
vikār na kuni mani bakti-bāwa tas ta. lāǵas etc. 1154.

Sŏdām prātas drāv shrānas ta
    āǵyā ti Krushnas loǵ^{u} manganē
Krushna-jyuv^{i} ti môn^{u}nas ta drāv pānas ta. lāǵas etc. 1155.

1146. The third fistful took she from his hand, and hastily into (her own) mouth cast she it; for otherwise the whole of Viṣṇu's Energic Power into Sudāman would have found its way.

1147. Then Kṛṣṇa to Sudāman saith, 'Ne'er have I eaten aught so good as this. Ne'er at the finest banquet such perfect flavour have I tasted.'

1148. Thus, the whole day till nightfall were they in their joy,—Kṛṣṇa of the Brāhmaṇa's doings asking news, patting him with his hand and stroking him in his love.

1149. Unknown to Sudāman had he to go to Viśvakarman,[1] and tell him on the earth to build a second heaven; and so, at Sudāman's residence, a Viṣṇu's palace caused he to be built.

1150. In the one night that palace caused he to be completed, with every luxury that beseemed it, and filled was it with serving maids and men.

1151. Over Suśīlā fly-whisks all were waving; all into their hands her words were humbly taking. Beyond description was the ease and luxury.

1152. Whatever doth in Viṣṇu's heaven exist that also in her house was found. How can my tongue have power to sing its praises! To Bhagavān did Suśīlā offer herself in sacrifice.

1153. Wondrous, beyond telling, became Suśīlā's joy. To her it seemed as though in Viṣṇu's heaven an abode she found while yet alive.

1154. 'Twas like a dream brought out from poverty, caused by attaining everlasting bliss. But still into her heart there came no change of any kind of all her loving faith.

1155. At dawn Sudāman issued forth to bathe, and to ask leave of Kṛṣṇa to depart. Kṛṣṇa too bore him in mind, and himself went forth.

---

[1] Viśvakarman was the artificer of the gods.

kĕtshāh dyut^{u}nas na sūty tati tas ta
wuch^{u}nas zi 'man kyuth^{u} bŏyi baktis
santōshĕ nishĕ mā man ḍalĕs' ta
lāgas bŏh dasta dasta pampōsh. 1156.

māyā na kĕh ti tas sūty dits^{ü}nas ta
bük^{ü}ts^{ü} nishĕ ḍali mā bigarĕs man
sāwadāna mana sūty āgyā dits^{ü}nas ta. lāgas etc. 1157.

vĕṭhān ta Sŏdām log^{u} pakanas ta
drŏlidāzĕ panañĕ tsĕntā na kĕh
Krushna-dyān sŏr^{i} sŏr^{i} ôs^{u} harshĕs ta.' lāgas etc. 1158.

shūkh santāph kyuth^{u} Vishnu-baktis ta
sahaza-baktis chuh sôruy r^{o}t^{u}
bakth^{ü}y āsi ta kyāh mång^{i}zĕs ta. lāgas etc. 1159.

pakān ta Sŏdām wôt^{u} nagaras ta
gāsa-pahŏr^{ü} panüñ^{ü} log^{u} tshāḍanē
rāza-dwār ḍīshith ta gav āshtsaras ta. lāgas etc. 1160.

dapān chuh 'wath mā chĕm na tsĕtas ta
kot^{u} wôtus ta yih kus dwār
yuth^{u} rāza-dwār chuh na kaïsi rāzas' ta. lāgas etc. 1161.

pritshān chuh wati pĕṭh prath zanas ta
'Sŏdāmüñ^{ü} pahŏr^{ü} yiti pazihē'
nēb kuni ās na ta pĕv dōranas ta. lāgas etc. 1162.

Sŏshīlā wŏtsh^{ü}müts^{ü} yĕli prātas ta
Bagawān-tōshĕna tōshān ös^{ü}
thavith mahaniv^{i} wati brāhmanas ta. lāgas etc. 1163.

Sŏdām ḍyūṭhukh pādi nom^{u}has ta
tshaṭajĕ ta wāwajĕ sŏr^{i} karanas
athan pĕṭh wātanôwukh dwāras ta. lāgas etc. 1164.

pra̱kh^{o}ṭuy wôt^{u} yĕli Waikunṭhas ta
Bagawān-tōshun^{u} zānana ās
mani log^{u} pŏr^{i} pŏr^{i} tas Krushnas ta. lāgas etc. 1165.

1156. There gave he to Sudāman nothing to take with him, for he watched him, and fain would see what would become the nature of the heart of his devoted one, and lest peradventure, from content it should shaken be.

1157. No worldly wealth to take with him he gave, for fear his heart should be corrupted, and he be shaken in his faith; and so, in peace of mind he bade farewell.

1158. In rapture exultant Sudāman started on his way, nor gave on his poverty a single thought. Ever and again on Kṛṣṇa meditating was he filled with joy.

1159. What sorrow or what trouble hath the faithful devotee of Viṣṇu? To the devotee innate is good in everything, and if he hath adoring love what be there he need ask?

1160. Along went he, and at his town arrived. There for his straw hut began he to make search, but, filled with amazement, in its place saw he a palace.

1161. To himself saith he, 'Peradventure the way have I forgotten. Whither have I come, and what this doorway? Of some great king must such a palace be.'

1162. He asks each person that upon the road he meets, 'should not here have been Sudāman's hut?' but no one could give him any clue, and, frightened, set he himself to run away.

1163. When at dawn arose Suśīlā, gladdened was she by Bhagavān's gladdening, and on the Brāhmaṇa's way men did she station.

1164. Sudāman did they see, and at his feet they bowed. Cooling of the hot air and fanning did thev all for him, and on their hands led they him to his door.

1165. Manifest was it to him that in Viṣṇu's heaven had he arrived, and the grace of Bhagavān became known in full to him. Then in his heart did he to Kṛṣṇa offer himself in sacrifice.

zinday pāna ôs^{u} Vishnu-bŏwanas ta
Sŏshīlā ti sŏkhith rāja-bāy zan
yih kēh gotshus tiy ôs^{u} tas ta
lāğas bŏh dasta dasta pampōsh. 1166.

Sŏdām log^{u}mot^{u} bakti-bāwas ta
manas ḍal kēh ğayĕs na zāh
Shrī-Krushna-dyān nĕth mani dāranas ta. lāğas etc.
1167.

zanmāntara-sŏr^{i} ös^{i} sŏkhas ta
tsari tsari Krushna-lōla karān bakth
Sŏshīlā pativrath vrath dāranas ta. lāğas etc. 1168.

samay wôtukh ta ğay pānas ta
yith samsāras yĕshāh nith
jai-kār tihandis bakth karanas ta. lāğas etc. 1169.

tihond^{u} ğara bǫw^{u} Waikunṭhas ta
Bağawāna-baktĕn chuh namaskār
namaskār Bağawān-dayā ğatshanas ta. lāğas etc.
1170.

yĕs yitshi Bağawān kus raṭi tas ta
tasandĕn bāğĕn kus kari mān
pör^{i} pör^{i} lág^{i}zi-nā Bağawānas ta. lāğas etc. 1171.

dyūn^{u} ās shĕran Krushna-pādas ta
shĕran ās ta kō-na tōṭhĕm
pör^{i} pör^{i} tasandis pāna tōṭhanas ta. lāğas etc. 1172.

yithay tōṭhyōkh Sŏdāmas ta
shĕk^{a}th tsĕy dits^{ü}thas kür^{ü}n bakth
tithay tōṭhtam mĕ ti abalas ta. lāğas etc. 1173.

yithay tōṭhyōkh prath baktis ta
yithay tōṭhyōkh prath sādas
tithay tōṭhta mĕ ti pāpa-pūrnas ta. lāğas etc. 1174.

namaskār Sŏdāmas ta tath bāğĕs ta
Sŏshīlā-mātāyĕ namaskār
namaskār tihandis bakth karanas ta. lāğas etc. 1175.

1166. Even while yet alive found he himself in the abode of Viṣṇu. Suśīlā, too, in happiness was like a queen. All that he needed, that was there for him.

1167. Sudāman was established in adoring faith; no shaking ever came into his heart, for in it were his thoughts on Kṛṣṇa firmly fixed.

1168. They abode in happiness, (being granted) the memories of their former births. In their love for Kṛṣṇa fervently practised they devotion, the while Suśīlā chastely kept the vow that she had vowed unto her husband.

1169. Their time came and, having won glory in this world, to their (heavenly) home did they depart. All honour be to them who had such loving faith.

1170. Viṣṇu's heaven itself became their home. All reverence to Bhagavān's adorers (such as they); and to the graciousness of Bhagavān be reverence.

1171. Who can hold back him whom Bhagavān desireth? His blessed fortune who can emulate? Hence, shouldst not thou again and again to Bhagavān offer thyself a sacrifice?

1172. I, Dīnanātha, the humble, have to Kṛṣṇa's feet for refuge come. Refuge have I taken, and what other contentment do I need? As a sacrifice myself I offer, and in him is my content.

1173. As to Sudāman favour didst Thou show, and as by Thee alone to him was given strength, and in him devotion was created; so on this strengthless one,—on me,—show Thou Thy grace.

1174. As on each faithful one Thy favour Thou hast shown; as on each pious man Thy favour Thou hast shown; so on this sin-filled one,—on me,—show Thou Thy grace.

1175. To Sudāman and to his happy fate be reverence! and eke to Mother Suśīlā be there reverence! reverence be to the devoted love they showed.

namaskār Vyāsas ta Shukadēwas ta
namaskār sārĕn[i] bakta-lūkan
namaskār tihandis ģyāna-wananas ta
lāgas bŏh dasta dasta pampōsh. 1176.

yus laģi Krushna-jyuwanis pādas ta
tas kari Krushna-jyuv sarŏ wŏpakār
yiti yĕsh nith ta wāti Vishnu-bawanas ta. lāgas etc.
1177.

pör[i] pör[i] Krushna-jyuwanis nāwas ta
pör[i] pör[i] tasandis autāras
pör[i] pör[i] tasandis shŏba tsarĕtas ta.
lāgas bŏh dasta dasta pampōsh. 1178.

---

iti KĀSHMĪRIKA-DĪNANĀTHA-racitaṁ
ŚRĪ-KṚṢṆÂVATĀRA-CARITAṀ
samāptam.

1176. Reverence be to Vyāsa and to Śukadēva; reverence be to all the devotees of Kṛṣṇa; reverence be to the tale of true knowledge that they tell.

1177. He who clingeth to the feet of Kṛṣṇa, to him will Kṛṣṇa every favour render. In this world glory will he win, and thereafter the abode of Viṣṇu will he reach. To him posy and posy do I offer lotuses.

1178. Ever dedicating myself to Kṛṣṇa's name, ever dedicating myself to his incarnation, ever dedicating myself to his auspicious deeds, to him posy and posy do I offer lotuses.

Here ends THE LAY OF THE INCARNATE KṚṢṆA
composed by
DĪNANĀTHA THE KĀSHMĪRĪ.

